CHARIOT OF THE SUN

AN INFORMAL HISTORY OF A SIAMESE FAMILY

CHARIOT OF THE SUN

AN INFORMAL HISTORY OF A SIAMESE FAMILY

Shane Bunnag

RIVER
BOOKS

First published and distributed in 2022 by
River Books Press Co., Ltd.
396/1 Maharaj Road, Phraborommaharajawang,
Bangkok 10200 Thailand
Tel: (66) 2 224-6686, 2 225-0139, 2 622-1900
Fax: (66) 2 225-3861
Email: order@riverbooksbk.com
www.riverbooksbk.com

Editor: Narisa Chakrabongse
Production supervision: Suparat Sudcharoen
Design: Ruetairat Nanta

ISBN 978 616 451 063 0

Printed and bound in Thailand by Parbpim Co., Ltd.

For Dean

Contents

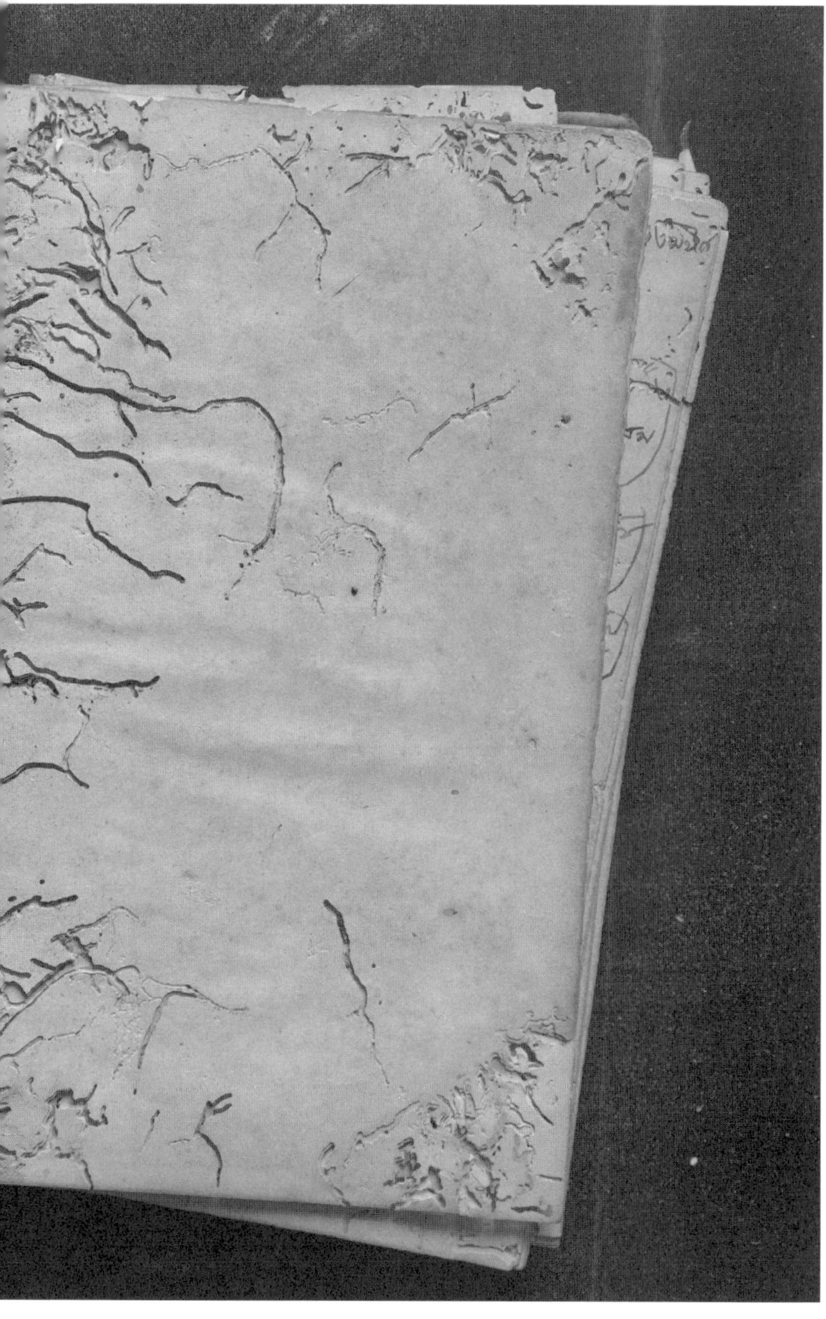

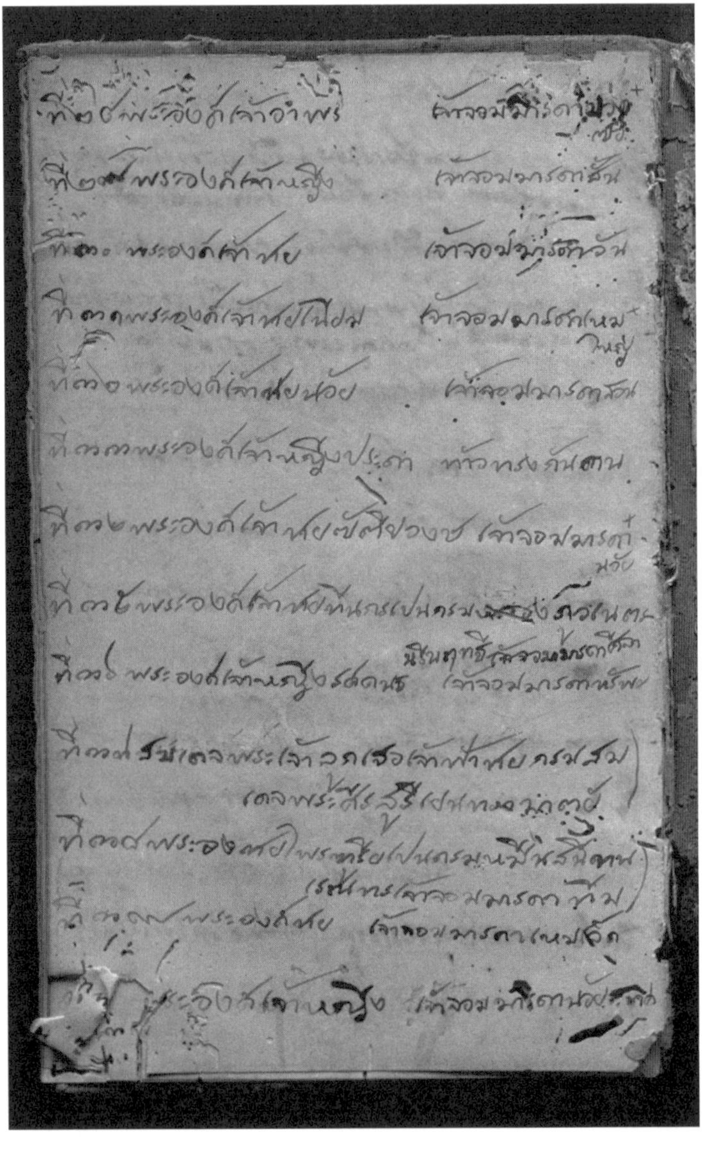

The Great Flood of 2011

A great flood spread across central Thailand. At its peak the flood zone was roughly the size of Denmark. The waters reached the outskirts of Bangkok, but the capital was spared. Even so it felt like the end of something, a pivot in time.

There had been talk of Bangkok's watery doom for decades. The flood resonated with fears and projections about the future. The vague spectre of impending disaster coalesced as shops ran low on supplies, tap water came out gritty, and seemed pungent after boiling.

That year people blamed each other while the flood stretched out across the Siamese heartlands at the centre of the country. Ayutthaya, the ancient capital and crucible of modern Thailand, saw the worst of it. Some said the deluge was holy water sent to cleanse the nation of evil politics, others that it was a clear case of planned negligence, a sabotaging of water management to discredit the incoming government.

The Thai psyche does not turn about the salty freedom of the archipelago, or the expanses of an untouched frontier, it gazes out at rivers, waiting for the waters to rise. A flood is the most Siamese event, pertaining to earth and the heavens, intangible and yet banal, and still unpredictable. The conditions that give rise to the flood speak of Siamese life, culture and history. The flood bringing rain comes on western winds, the draughts that brought Hindu abstractions: mathematics, astronomy, religion.

The rains begin gradually in late May and tail off by November, buttressed by two raucous holidays. Songkran, the Thai New Year, comes in the middle of April, at the hottest and driest time of the year. It features water splashing, drunkenness and road carnage. Loy Krathong is a more placid affair. It celebrates the end of the monsoon at the full moon of November, and is the time when people flock to the rivers to float miniature rafts bearing flowers, incense, and candles. It is also rumoured to be when Thai girls are most likely to lose their virginity.

When the landmass of mainland Southeast Asia is at its hottest, water rises up out of the Bay of Bengal, forming clouds. These are dragged across the sea by pleistocene era laws of thermal distribution, atmospheric pressure, and fluctuations within the Intertropical Convergence Zone. Formal cloud designations – the low flying stratocumuli or the cirrostrati – paraphrase tottering thunderheads, blackened anvils, and raspy ceilings of brutalist grey.

The rains are not the only cause of flooding. It happens that the heaviest rains coincide with the Great Tides of the September Equinox, when the sun is directly over the equator, exerting its greatest attraction over the oceans. High tides slow the drainage of river water into the Gulf of Thailand.

In 2011 Thailand's reservoirs were high before the rains began. By late August they had reached capacity and needed to be eased. The network of canals and tributary rivers were already backed up and as the monsoon continued there was nowhere to divert the water. The rivers running south to the gulf broke their banks by September, in time for the high sea tides of a joint full moon and equinox.

• • •

"This is the place, I know it." He told me. He looked vaguely perplexed, as if disturbed by an uncertain memory, or the effort of attempting to see in poor light.

"This is where they met. It was night, just a handful of them. This is where they made their pact, before heading out. The rivers lead across the country from here."

He told me this later, years after the flood of 2011, in Ayutthaya during the rainy season again. He spoke about the monk who could walk on the river, and of those fighters who vowed to throw out the invaders. In this myth there was no time. The sack of Ayutthaya, the reconquest, the occupation, kings and their court, all were happening simultaneously, endlessly. Our conversations had that quality, subjects opened, continued, and left incomplete, over decades.

Remembrance has its own time, casting dappled light on expansive clearings.

Almost a decade earlier, back in the flood, we had put up at a factory for the night in Ayutthaya. We talked late into the night – floating in the dark of the drowned countryside. It was easy to talk because it was hard to sleep. Outside the water lapped at our little island.

I knew that he believed in past lives. I would listen to him, as he spoke with conviction, with nothing to add. I knew that he had undergone many rites of atonement that had taken him to distant parts of the country. His submerged history was detailed and specific.

That morning we had driven north from Bangkok. He told me he would go to the flood zone to help people. I was still bleary with jetlag. In the week before catching my flight back, I had been following the floods in the news. I was curious. I went along.

We journeyed in silence. The motorway was deserted, the bridges and high ground lined solidly with parked cars. After an hour the road markings disappeared into water. A few people had gathered at the edge of the new sea.

We stared out at the vast, still body of water, before continuing onwards. As the car bonnet was submerged, the engine sputtered, giving out fumes and complaints, but kept going. At a patch of dry ground along our route a family had set up camp. A man was hurling a spear, attached to a rope about his wrist, into the water in angry motions.

People straggled through the flood, which curled and pulled in currents, creating treacherous rapids along the way. Snakes swam through the water, their heads bobbing along, and as the sun went down the air was shrill with birdcalls.

The final stage was by boat. We passed few vehicles on our way through this desolation and arrived after nightfall. The only place we could stay was in the office of an abandoned plastics factory. We washed our grimy legs as best we could before settling down on the concrete floor. In choosing our beds, care was taken that our heads pointed neither west, like the dead, nor at each other's feet.

Everything is equal under the water, the factories and the sacred sites, the battlefields and the orchards. Inundation is timeless. Flooding brings fear of the future, although the deluge is the past too, when it was yearly. Ayutthaya depended on a good flood season for defence, and easy nourishment. The inhabitants of the great city did not need rice paddies, the entire countryside was their rice bowl.

Flooding is fecund, pushing up forests and fruit, from which come cities made of wood – eaten by gnawing insects – returning in humid clumps to the earth, or as ash. Almost everything that speaks of the past is made up of organic matter and so the past is devoured each season, and human endeavour, built structures, books, fabrics, must disintegrate.

Time becomes fluid in these tropics, with water, heat, scent; the senses connected, erased, suspended, in an encroaching obscurity that gives nothing up, that is and is not. Time is not dependable, and materials are short lived. Myths flourish, myths made up of breadcrumb trails.

• • •

A few weeks later my friend picked me up at dawn. There was a faint drizzle, the morning city was flatly grey. We crossed Bangkok with a car-boot full of strange offerings. These were unloaded at the temple, sacks of rice, jerry cans full of uniquely sacred water, along with the standard floral offerings. The water had been collected from the morning washbowl of a holy man. We carried these materials into a scruffy, neon-lit room with a simple altar and dusty looking walls.

I was informed that this was a very rare ceremony, conducted by one of its last great ritual practitioners. We would have our past life actions cleansed, opening the way for lighter futures, unburdened by the sins of previous existences. It was not something I asked for, but I let myself be carried along by a certain momentum, one that rippled out of our experiences in the flood.

The monk was ancient, and receding into his robes. He told us to arrange the sacks of rice in the shape of bodies, and then to lie supine on top, matching our limbs to the beds of rice.

The monk began to chant. I gazed up at the glaring lights as the monk's apprentice spread a sheet fully over my head and body. This was a funeral shroud. It had looked stained but I did not know if it had come from a real funeral. We lay there, my friend and I, as dead. Our death rites were chanted. I felt suffocated beneath the veil, but lay unmoving, my eyes shut. The chanting ended and we were left for a long time. Eventually the shroud was lifted and I opened my eyes. The monk gave us a blessing for our re-entry into this world and splashed us with the holy water. Our past life actions had been taken from us, absorbed by the bed of rice. I felt no sense of change or renewal. Instead, I wondered what would become of the rice, if it would be cooked and eaten.

I do not recall any further conversation later that day and we didn't talk about the ritual afterwards.

Hyrcania

Ahmad. Three motions from four and a half centuries ago. *Ah*, softly guttural, a suspended expiration. Lips close for the primal syllable, *ma*, followed by the final glossal see-saw of *de*. Ahmad is a short name, easy to pronounce but not familiar.

It is the name of a first ancestor and has the quality of something from another life. He was from Persia. That is what is said. "Sheikh Ahmad, the Persian ancestor of the powerful Bunnag family".

Ahmad came from the coastal region of the Caspian Sea. He was born in or around the town of Gorgan, which will be known by many different names, including Astarabad and Gun.

In these parts the lowland soil is saline and alkaline rising to more fertile foothills and high mountain pastures beyond. The weather is cold in the winter and the summers hot and humid. There are large forests in this country, and four main rivers, which rush down from the snow-capped mountains, spill their banks, and cast out boulders. This land looks out to sea, and to the northeast is a salt marsh, beyond which are wastelands and the ranged steppe. It is a seismic zone, and dust comes in from the northern deserts. To the west the littoral is more lush and humid. An early name for this place was Varkana, from Old Persian, via Akkadian. Varkana meant Land of the Wolf, from which the Greeks made Hyrcania.

The tentative, and essential, toponyms must quickly betray selective anachronisms: Hyrcania looks across the Caspian Sea, and to the northeast it opens onto the Central Asian Steppe, where modern Iran meets Turkmenistan.

Herodotus places Hyrcanians among the Persian forces in his wars[1]. He tells of the giant dams of Hyrcania, enabling a fickle king to cause drought and famine at his pleasure[2].

Alexander led his army into Hyrcania in pursuit of Darius' murderers. He installed a Satrap to administer for him and is credited, incorrectly, with building a vast defensive wall, a futile rampart against the wild steppe. The Turkomans called this wall the Red Snake. It was 170 kilometres long, and stretched from the Caspian to the Pishkamar Mountains, shielding the coastal plain and a nearby city named variously Gorgan, Jorgan, and Gunbad-i-Kavas[3].

Over time the jagged names Vrakana-Hyrcania were exchanged for the rounded name Gorgan. For a time it was a county of Khorasan, until it was absorbed by the province of Mazandaran, and finally broken off into modern Golestan, the land of roses.

The names are unruly and confusing. They don't stay put because their currency is different for travellers, traders, and locals. Gorgan, that town of sun-dried bricks, with its bridge of boats and famous silk, was turned back to dust by the Mongols[4].

It can be imagined that its names travelled south with those who had survived the massacre. The new city was named Astarabad, or star city, while retaining the nostalgic, and resilient, monikers Gunbad, Gun and Gorgan. Like its earlier incarnation, it was also known for its silk production and textiles, was a centre of Shia learning and devotion, but was also a place of war, displacement and sectarian strife.

Astarabad fell under the control of one of Timur's sons for a time, was a site of warfare with the Ismailis of the Alborz Mountains, and became a temporary capital in exile for the ruling Prince of Mazandaran. By the late 16th century this region had been integrated into Safavid Persia, which is to say it had seen decades of heavy fighting between the Qizilbash Turkoman militias of the Safavids and the Uzbeks.

This is the war-swept borderland where Ahmad was born in the 1570s[5]. He had a brother called Mohammed Sayyid, who would also become a Thai ancestor figure. Ahmad gained the honorific Sheikh at some point, which along with his brother's Sayyid, suggests a scholastic lineage.

Even under casual scrutiny, the family tradition of Persian ethnicity begins to fall apart. Georgians, Armenians and Circassians migrate into the region. The Turkomans and other non-Persians intrude into the national story and it is known that most of the Sayyids in the Caspian area had been brought there by the Safavids from Lebanon, one of the few places to have a strong Shia intellectual tradition. The Sayyids were part of the Safavid conversion of then majority Sunni Persia.

The family chronicles refer to Ahmad, in typical Thai disregard for foreign specifics, as a Mogul from Guni, from which it is surmised that he spent time in Mogul India and that he came from the town of Gun, which is to say Astarabad, or Gorgan.

• • •

Further support for Ahmad and Mohammed Sayyid's provenance, regardless of race or blood, is offered by the history of Mohammed's son, Agha Mohammed Astarabadi, who was to play a prominent role at the court of King Narai the Great of Ayutthaya. But it is by no means a settled fact that Ahmad was from the town of Gun. American historian David Wyatt, whose work on the family politics of Siam is foundational, wrote that the brothers might have hailed from an Arab-speaking island in the Persian Gulf called Kuni,[6] and many others believe that Ahmad was an émigré from the religious city of Qom.[7]

Ahmad, having existed in relative obscurity for centuries has been fleshed out over the past decades. It is an ongoing, politicised process,[8] whose narrative has been accompanied by small pieces of well-placed evidence:

The first is a portrait of Ahmad which began circulating some years ago. He is depicted as a gaunt man, with slightly puckered lips, a sparse short beard, and uneven arched eyebrows. He wears a neat white turban, and robe that recalls the graduation garments of Thai university students. It is an artist's depiction, with a subtle shadow falling over the left of his face, and a nose that has been botched.

The origins of this image are unclear, it is credited to a book entitled *History of Muslim leaders from Ayutthaya to the Thaksin Era*, 2008.[9]

The second piece of evidence is connected to the Iranian Revolution. A letter was published in a 1978 edition of the Iranian Journal Darsha'i az Maktab-i Islam. It was from the Thai Shia community and stated that they numbered over 2000 in Bangkok and were the descendants of a Sheikh Ahmad. They claim that Ahmad was from the Islamic holy city of Qom and that he founded the Shia faith in Thailand. The letter explains that they use four mosques, but have no religious leader, and only a rudimentary knowledge of the Shia doctrine – it is a plea for support.[10]

The third: in the 1980s archaeological digs in Ayutthaya's Thung Khaek district, unearthed the foundations of a tomb structure. By the 1990s this tomb had been rebuilt, with a plaque certifying that this was the tomb of Sheikh Ahmad. The site has become a minor pilgrimage spot for Southeast Asian Shias and Ahmad is now venerated there every year on the 8th of June.[11]

Bunnags

Bunnag is a tree – Ironwood, or Mesua Ferrea in Latin. It is very hardy and slow growing and is the national tree of Sri Lanka, where it is associated with spiritual practice and can often be found in the grounds of ancient temples.

In Thailand, the Bunnag tree blossoms in late February, when the heat comes in. The flowers have white petals and opulent yellow stamens. They are surprisingly soft and silken for this strong tree that recalls a conifer, or something bearing tough seedpods. The flowers appear high up amidst the green needle-like leaves, and rain down petals on the ground, beckoning the passerby to look up, and investigate the foliage.

Boon Naark, first syllable mid tone, second falling tone. A homophone of Bunnag renders the Thai words for merit and Naga, a mythical serpent of the waters. But the real spelling of Bunnag has an obscure etymology.

In the past, Bunnag could be a given name, seldom used these days. Nowadays it is a surname, and the name of some historical figures, who are not all related. It was the first name of my grandfather's nanny. Her name in usage was shortened from Bunnag to *Nark*, the syllabic suffix. Bunnag was also my grandfather's surname – Tula Bunnag. Born in 1918, Tula was the first of our line to be named Bunnag from birth, since surnames had only been introduced in 1913.

Nark was from an old family, of Mon descent, called the Rattanakul. She entered my great-grandfather's household as a teenager. Tula's mother, "Son", died of tuberculosis when he was two. Subsequently Nark and great-aunt Chua brought him up, and were often blamed for spoiling him. Tula grew up to be a difficult and irascible individual.

After Tula, Nark helped raise Tej, my uncle, and Tew, my father. Nark was a devout Buddhist, who forbade my father killing insects. A mosquito was to be brushed off and she administered painful pinches to transgressors. Nark travelled to England with the family in 1954, when Tula was posted to the Royal Thai Embassy in London. She would ride the buses on her days off, leaving various charming English malapropisms and mispronunciations in her wake. She called the actor Harold Lloyd, "Haloloy" and said that Tula's father Tom was as handsome as matinee idol Douglas Fairbanks, which she transformed into "Sakat Serbang".

The Bunnag family is said to be the largest in Thailand. Naturally it is split up into numerous subdivisions, to simplify matters. But the family describes less a tree than a collection of houses, in a town made of streets that lead back on themselves. It is a place with many fine monuments alongside stretches of dilapidation and tropical overgrowth.

The metaphorical house is apt, because it is expansive. It is a labyrinth of memory, and a flimsy bulwark within and upon shifting space against time – all bound up with images and desire, and the cloying thing called Life-Style.

Tula dreamed of having a Thai house. He was a diplomat's child, who had spent part of his youth in France and America. When he came back from England in 1960, from his own short career as a diplomat, he bought a plot of land, in Phra Khanong, on the outskirts of Bangkok.

The district was famous for a ghost story, a tale about separation. The story tells of a woman called Nak who is expecting a child. Her husband is dragged away to fight in a war, and Nak dies alone in childbirth. He returns years later, oblivious to Nak's fate and thinking she's still alive. She greets him lovingly at their stilted house, where presumably they reunite as man and wife. Afterwards, he realises that all is not well. Nak is cooking for him when a lime falls through the floorboards to the ground below. Impossibly, she reaches down and her arm extends to pick it up. Terrified, at her, and at himself, he makes an excuse to go downstairs, and runs off to take refuge at a temple. The spirit of his deceased wife pursues him, and wails for him outside the temple walls – she has become a Fury, born of injustice, agony, and vengeance. In one of the traditions, her spirit is coaxed by an exorcist into an urn which is dropped into the river. Years later, in the 19th century, the urn will be disturbed and Nak's ghost let loose once again. A famous monk, Somdet Toh (who was said to be an illegitimate child of King Rama II and therefore a second cousin of the Bunnags) is called to pacify the spirit. He captures Nak inside a human bone, which he keeps.

The bone is a powerful talisman, and rumours abound about its current owner.

The ghost of Nak is synonymous with Phra Khanong, and associated with the canals of the district – people say that the female spirit with long black hair can be seen rowing along the waters at night. It was beside one of these waterways that Tula built his residence.

Tula's house would be made up of antique stilted buildings, set in a garden by a canal. He found the four original houses in Ayutthaya province at Bang Bal. They were in the village of one of his best friends at the Foreign Ministry. After Tula bought them, the houses were transported down river and reconstructed by villagers from Bang Bal, according to a design by a friend of the family.

Tula lived there with my grandmother, Chancham, for the rest of his life. The house appeared in numerous coffee-table books and magazines throughout the 1980s and 90s. It was listed several times as The Bunnag House.[1] Several pages were dedicated to the house in a 1980s edition of *Thai Style*, which also featured the home of Patsri, a distant aunt, and her French husband, Jean Michel. Patsri, another diplomat's child, had also favoured traditional Thai architecture over the greater comfort of a modern dwelling.

Her house had been built in the 1970s. Jean Michel recounted that when they had decided to build their place, all of the experts, French and otherwise, thought they were mad. Bangkok was going to fall like Saigon or Phnom Penh, in a maximum of five years.

I was at Tula's house twice while people came to take photos. The first time I was 12, and felt repudiated when Tula introduced me as his nephew, a linguistic slip between Thai and English.[2] I was so shocked that I forgot to shake the photographer's hand, which hovered weakly as I gaped.

The second time was around 1999 or 2000. I was in my mid-twenties and dad was also in Thailand. The photographer, Luca

Invernizzi Tettoni, had already done the house in the past, so he wasted no time. At some point he stopped to tell us that he could see the house was subsiding, "it is no longer straight." Tettoni's team ran around with flowers to decorate, moving furniture, hiding things and cleaning up, all the while trying to keep ahead of the storm that was moving in. The photos appeared in the book *Classic Thai*, with some of these images later rehashed in a book called *Things Thai*[3].

Thai Style is now in its third edition, in which Tula and Patsri's houses live on as they were in the 1980s. Tula's is gone but Patsri's house stands. The last time I visited we had to keep moving seats to avoid the raindrops, as the ceiling of its reception room leaks.

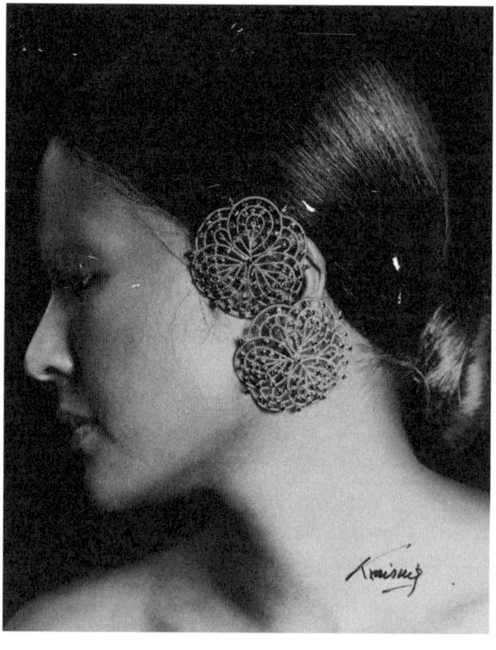

The City of Memory

The two brothers named Ahmad and Mohammed Sayyid travelled east from their home in Persia and arrived in Ayutthaya around 1600. The images we are able to discern of the two brothers are filtered through the dark prism of Ayutthaya, whose fall would not be for another 150 years.

When the Burmese sacked the city in 1767, its inhabitants were dispersed or marched away in captivity, and most of the city's records were destroyed. The lives of Ahmad, and his first descendants, are broken into fragments. Fifteen generations have passed since Ahmad and the reconstitution of these shards is both torturous and precarious – it is not certain what will come out.

The search for what has been lost or misconstrued has its culture and antecedents. Even the origins of glassy Bangkok can be found in games of memory.

• • •

After the fall of Ayutthaya, it took almost a decade for peace to come. War tore through the country, first against the invaders, and later against rival claimants, pretenders, and unruly allies and vassals. With peace, the survivors would set down their memories of Ayutthaya. Their reminiscences came to be known as The Testimony,[1] and out of these works another city was born, which foreigners called Bangkok.

The Testimony was used to plan and build the new city, with

copied canals, temples and palaces – often built from materials salvaged from the former capital. Ayutthaya, an iteration of a mythical Hindu city, was reincarnated as Bangkok.

The new capital was rendered directly out of the minds of survivors, who attempted to recall every detail of the old city. They gave back life indiscriminately: the districts for buying nails and types of fabric, where to buy pleasure, the height of bridges, and the size of boats that could pass beneath them. They inserted sentimental elements, such as the names of the shop owners and guardians of the gates. In the looping present tense of the Testimony, old Ayutthaya lives on.[2]

Bangkok was an exercise in historical consciousness, claiming seamless continuity from the old capital, reinvigorating its traditions, and cleansing its political weaknesses. Bangkok's grand families were the blood continuum of this ancestor capital.

• • •

In the mid 19th century, an eighth generation descendant wrote a chronicle of Ahmad's family in Thailand. He was a nobleman who had run the Ministry of Trade for a time, helped negotiate a treaty with the British, and, before going blind, had written the first histories of the Bangkok Era, as well as a curious tome called *A Book on Various Things*. His name was Kham Bunnag, but he is generally referred to as Chaophraya Thiphakorawong.

Kham's stated objective was to set down the history of this family for the benefit of future generations. He consulted with relatives, who had kept partial records of the Persian ancestors. The scant details that are handed down about the lives of Ahmad and Mohammed, and their offspring, come largely from this legacy. These histories are based on lineage records, memory and oral transmission.

• • •

Ahmad and his brother left Astarabad at some point towards the end of the 16th century travelling to India. They would have journeyed south from Astarabad to join the Great Khorasan Road, connecting to Mashad, and then to Herat, Farah, Kandahar, crossing the mountains through the Bolan Pass, to Sukkur, and finally Hyderabad.[3] It is thought that they lived in Hyderabad for some years, working as traders. The city was in the Persianate state of Golkonda, which had attracted many people from Persia's Caspian area.

There had been contact between Persia and Ayutthaya for hundreds of years. Ayutthaya was a trading state controlling the Chaophraya river basin from its eponymous capital, a large fortified river island. The Persians referred to it as Shahr-I Naw, New City, and although it was a predominantly Buddhist state, Ayutthaya was known as a place of Shia practice even before Ahmad's arrival. The Malay mystic Hamzah Fansuri, who was active in the mid 16th century, some time before Ahmad's birth, is said to have undergone a conversion or awakening of sorts in Ayutthaya.

"Hamzah of Shahr-I Naw is truly effaced,
Like wood, all burnt to cinders;
His origin is the Ocean without currents"[4]

By 1600 the trade route to Ayutthaya had re-opened after years of war. The Thai forces under King Naresuan had recently pushed back the Burmese and now controlled ports on the Indian Ocean side of the peninsula, as well as the portage routes across to their capital Ayutthaya.

The brothers, and their retinue, would have taken a ship from Masulipatham in India to Mergui, on the Andaman Coast. From there travellers either went north to Tavoy and from there through the Three Pagodas Pass towards Ayutthaya, or they crossed the peninsula via Tenasserim and made for the town of Petchburi, from where they could travel by boat back out into the Gulf of Siam and up the Chaophraya River to Ayutthaya.[5]

They are thought to have settled in an area of Ayutthaya called Thung Khaek.[6] The land had been granted by the king to Persian traders. It was on the main island, south of the palace complex, with a nearby landing pier, still called Tha Kayee, The Agha's Pier.

Within a few years the brothers were working for the crown. They are credited with reorganising Ayutthaya's Western Trade Department, dealing with India, Persia, and the Malay states.

Ahmad begins to appear in the histories, in various shadowy forms, around 1612. He is involved in suppressing a Japanese rebellion, and supporting an ambitious nobleman, who was to usurp the throne as King Prasat Thong.[7]

At some point Mohammed returned to Persia, and Ahmad married a lady called Choey. They had two sons, Chuen and Chom, and a daughter, Chi.

Ahmad's career was worldly. He accumulated wealth, he fought, conspired, sired, and yet he was the religious leader of Ayutthaya's Muslims at a time when the city was still a centre of Shia learning, and conversion to the Muslim faith was at its height.[8]

Under Prasat Thong, Ahmad became the Minister of the North, a position that equates roughly with Minister for Civil Affairs. He is believed to have died in 1659 at the age of 88, with the title Chaophraya Sheikh Ahmad Rattana Thibodi.[9]

Facts are fragile, and dates tentative.

The History of Siam, published in 1911 by Thai historian K.S.R Kulap, features an illustration of a Siamese Official with the caption, "dignitaire Siamois en grande uniform; Ocja Chau Phraja Bovora Raja Najok (Xekamat) Le Premier Ministre de Siam et Commandant en chef sous le regne de Phra Chau Songdham Roy de Ayuthdhaja A.D 1603.[10]

The image is a crude depiction of a figure. He stands with his legs apart, as in the ballet second position, one hand suspended as it points to the side. He wears slippers, sports a cone on his head that looks like a dunce's hat, a long open flowing shirt, fabric wrapped into shorts tied up at the waist. He has a prominent nose, and the cross-hatching over his skin makes him swarthy. Kulap does not cite the source of the illustration which seems to be a copy from a French book.[11]

At one point Kulap was sued for historical falsification. He had a mania for books, and access to works that have since been lost but he was also known to alter texts to fit his researches. His book, *Great Official Families*, published in 1905, includes a genealogy of Ahmad's family that has some parallels with a 17th century Persian account of a diplomatic mission to Ayutthaya.[12]

Calling Up The Past

"Well the only gay bar was on Henry Dunant Road, and I got fed up with going there every night so I decided to make my own." Pitya was telling me.

"I opened it in the house my mother left me. It was right in front of the Bangrak Police station, but since I opened it with Prince Kraisingh, who knew the head policeman there, it was OK."

Pitya is an uncle of sorts. He is known for his work identifying and tracing Persian influences in ancient Siamese architecture. The archaeological story has been a counterweight to the paucity of written sources about the pre-modern Persian community.

He also wrote a book specifically about our Persian ancestors, and had owned Bangkok's second gay bar, called "The Green Carnation".

I knew that he had spent time in Iran conducting research for his book, and I wanted to test a sentence I had heard second-hand. "He said Iran was so dusty and desolate, no wonder Ahmad and his brother stayed in Thailand."

When he answered the phone he was lying in bed, sick. It was his fate, he said. He is in his late 70s.

"No, Iran was not dusty." He had visited the Caspian coast and found it beautiful, with the rivers fed by mountains in the distance. He had spent many happy months in Iran with his work. But he did not think Ahmad was a Persian, he was a Georgian captured in war as a child, and brought up as a soldier.

I asked if he had any source material for this, and he said that it had all been such a long time ago, and promised to send me his latest book, *Remembrance of Things Past,*[1] which included some stories on the family.

It was early May in 2020 and the pandemic here in Thailand was still relatively young. I had recently become a father for the first time. I had a sentimental idea. I thought of stories being handed down from one generation to the next, like old heirlooms. The stories were about the family, and of half forgotten events and places. I imagined they were worn and patched up, and well used – precious things that carry no weight. At this point, so tiny and fragile, my son slept a lot, and I found I could sit and type with one hand during the many hours I was immobile. I set about writing down as many stories as I could recall. After a short time I found that the stories were hard to grasp, they were defiant, picking up unwanted dross or too nebulous, changing shape in the seeing.

The impulse stemmed from a curiosity about residue, the familial dust on famous Ahmad and the Bangkok statesmen from centuries later. While collecting the perishable I would fill in narrative gaps. It was an area that had beckoned for some time.

I began to call up relatives, in the hope that they might share the patrimony, or lend a hand in the task. I would put them on speakerphone and record their answers. The voices echoed out: You must speak to someone else. Call again. They would have a look for me. This was not the way to do it.

The spoken past is even more multiple than the written. It is configured around mood, and moment, and shifting contexts and myriad associations. There is no single past, it is a weather system of desires, and purposes.

I had heard tales about the family for as long as I could remember. The historical was mixed in with gossip, and spicy titbits. Reminiscing was often about vanished times in England – bowler hats, pea soupers, sadistic Prefects. In the family repertoire were celebrations of eccentricity, the man who lived by Greenwich Meantime in Thailand, profligates and misers, the spleen and choler of privilege. Everything was faded and ragged, especially the generational cohesion and the sense of unity. And much of the shared recollection was recent. It rose gradually out of the 1920s and fizzled out in the 1960s. It was a short memory bump.

The Construction

The Thai house is a thing of beauty, well proportioned, elegant, and practical. It is also an artefact that describes the difficulties and dangers of life in the country. The Thai house is made of wood, which was once abundant. The parts can be floated to a suitable site on a riverbank for assembly. The structure consists of a kilted roof with deep eaves, which provides shade from the sun, and shelter from the rain. The rooms are made of panelled segments, which can be taken apart with relative ease. The timber is often teak, exuding an insect repelling scent. The house is held up by sturdy piles – creating an open-air living space beneath. In some parts of the country, houses have no staircases. Instead, the bedrooms are reached by a ladder that can be pulled up at night, as protection against tigers and other predators. In the flood season the elevated house becomes a refuge, when the waters submerge the dry land for weeks and months.

A house is not thrown up on a whim. There is a system at play – to build a house is a ritual event. The house is not simply a collection of materials; it will be a cosmos. Rites are conducted for the spiritual safety of the workers and surrounding community, as much as the wellbeing of the home and inhabitants.

Everything in the Thai universe begins with distinct intentional qualities. The chaos sets in afterwards.

I do not know how many ceremonies my grandfather Tula observed, or what exactly was specified in the Central Thai tradition of his builders. It is certain, in the initial building of

Tula and Chancham's Thai house, that offerings were made and a specific procedure was followed.

Andrew Turton provides a detailed description of the northern Thai process in his essay, "Architectural and Political Space in Thailand".[1] The following is a brief summary pertaining to house construction.

An auspicious day is chosen for the planting of the house posts, between the harvest and first ploughing. These posts, or stilts, are laid along the ground in parallel to the bodies of the Nagas, supernatural water and earth serpents, with the tops pointing towards the Naga heads. Offerings are made to the guardians of the cardinal directions, as well as to the rulers of the heavens and earth. All of this must be done in a strict hierarchical order. Next a type of exorcism of impropriety is conducted, which cleanses taboos and taints. Then comes an exorcism of the wood itself, done by inserting nails into the posts. After this the earth must also be exorcised, and offerings made to the Nagas. The final stage is the ritual binding of soul to the principal male and female house posts.

The physical construction commences with the laying of the pillars, which are erected in order of hierarchy, with each space predetermined by a ritual map.

Ritual house-building reflects Thai urbanism, the child of intertwined traditions.[2] The Khmer legacy is regal, and concerns the evocation of heavenly forms according to invisible and mathematical blueprints. The Mon is Theravada Buddhist, bestowing clarity and textual resonance, and the ready-made moated towns of early conquest. The Thai, also known as Tai, is pragmatic, malleable and martial. It borrows and adapts. A classic Thai settlement delights in proximity to flowing water. Thai cities are built in rectangles beside rivers, echoing a transitory past, the fairytale wandering of the Thai race down the waterways of the middle Mekong, to encroach on the lands of the star-gazing Khmers and Mons.

Nicknames

Chuen or Chuun. The transliteration cannot catch the Thai vowel. In Thai script, the diacritic over the vowel makes the sound of a falling tone uu. Chuen is a nickname, from the early 1600s. The first Thai nickname in the family, for the first to be born in Siam.

It was simpler to follow Ahmad, Chuen's father. His foreign name stands out, remaining even in his titles. Since surnames do not exist yet, the tracing of an individual will require knowledge of the titles conferred at a specific moment, and of linguistics and the historical arcana surrounding the defunct and shifting ranking system.

The titles, which come from the king, are descriptions of service that bear similarities to names but are impersonal. A title is a cessation of self, it can be taken away and reassigned. The chronicles do not record individuals, they set down the actions of office holders. The identities of the actors must be surmised by circumstantial details, and nicknames.

It is not clear how much the culture of Thai names has changed down the centuries. A modern Thai might have a formal name that is talismanic, and occasionally hidden to protect the bearer, or aspirational or pretentious, to confer good fortune. The nickname is for both public and intimate use, and these playful names remain in lineage books, for instance, Chuen and Chom and Chi. Melodic children's names prove durable down the ages when logically they should be lost with the passing of immediate relatives.

Chuen is then more faded than his father, and the bleaching out of the records will continue for several generations, down to his grandson. What is known about him can be summarised in a few statements.

Chuen was born soon after Ahmad's arrival in Ayutthaya. He was Ahmad's first son by his wife Choey. A younger brother, Chom, died in his teens, and there was a sister, Chi, who became a consort of King Prasat Thong.

Chuen was a royal page under King Song Tham. Chuen would take over his father's ministerial duties under King Prasat Thong and King Narai, with the title Chaophraya Aphairaja. He was acting Chularajamontri, leader of Ayutthaya's Muslims, between 1624 and 1630.[1]

Chuen had a son called Somboon, and a daughter, Luan, who joined her aunt as consort of King Prasat Thong, and bore the king a daughter. Chuen is said to have lived to the age of seventy, so it can be assumed that he died in the late 1670s or early 1680s.

Not much more is known about Chuen, or can be extracted from the existing records. The only detail that brings colour and texture to his life is peripheral. Prince Damrong noted, in his *Our Wars with the Burmese*, that royal pages had the right to wear silk undergarments.[2]

While the histories are reticent about Ahmad's son, more can be said about the life of his nephew.

A Persian embassy to the court of King Narai arrived in 1685. The account of their voyage, known as *The Ship of Sulaiman*,[3] provides a rare perspective on Ayutthaya and its environs. Waiting to meet the king, the envoys report details: the names of local Persians, their houses and hammams, the presence of a Greek adviser they call the "Evil Frank", Qizilbash guards with their Turkic ranks, the "Yuz Bashis", and the history of a man called Agha Mohammed, for whom a tomb had recently been built.[4]

As has been stated, Agha Mohammed Astarabadi was the son of Mohammed Sayyid, Ahmad's brother. It is not known if he was born in Ayutthaya before his father's departure, or back in Persia. In the 1640s Agha Mohammed arrived in Ayutthaya, presumably coming directly from Astarabad. He struck up a friendship with a prince called Narai, who was curious about the foreigners residing in the city, and often visited the homes of the Persian merchants.[5]

When King Prasat Thong died in 1656, Agha Mohammed played a role in the bloody coup that placed Narai on the throne. In one account Narai advances stealthily to seize the royal palace by hiding in a Persian religious procession.[6]

Agha Mohammed was rewarded with the hand of his cousin, Chi, one of the late king's consorts. They were to have two sons, Yi and Kaew, who would grow up at court. Kaew became Chularajamontri, leader of the Muslims, while Yi rose to ministerial rank, was made governor of coastal city Tenasserim and was recorded as having rebelled.[7]

After the coup, the leader of the Persians was a certain Abdur Razzaq, who is sometimes associated with Chuen.[8] When Abdur Razzaq fell from favour in 1663, Agha Mohammed became the most powerful man at court. At some point he provided Narai with a palace guard of 500 warriors, Qizilbash from Mazandaran and Khorasan who had been working as mercenaries in India.

Over the next decade, Agha Mohammed outfitted his own merchant ships, expanded trade generally and encouraged Narai to foster connections with the Safavid Court and the Persianate state of Golkonda in India.[9]

He grew powerful and rich. He is said to have built himself a large house, in grounds shielded by a high brick wall, that looked out at the river.[10]

Over time another adventurer supplanted him in the king's favour. This man was a Greek called Constantine Phaulkon, who convinced Narai to look to the French over the Persians. Narai dispatched a number of missions to France, and allowed the French to garrison vital ports.

After some thirty years of prosperity and good fortune in Ayutthaya, Agha Mohammed was accused of corruption. Narai had him executed in 1678 by having his lips sewn up with strips of cane. He was kept alive in this condition for a day.[11]

The Spirit House

The approaching road ascends a humped bridge next to the property, providing leafy views of the house roofs, its pointed gables and green glazed tiles. The house and garden are hidden behind trees, bushes, and a fence, that thickened and rose with the growing city, becoming in time a formidable barrier against the street.

The house number was 57, but at some point the local authority decided inexplicably to make it number 1, disjointing all of the other dwellings in the lane.

To the right of the driveway is a small spirit house. The shrine stands facing into the property, in a spot the house shade does not reach. It had been sanctified by a court Brahmin Tula and Chancham knew, and is an elegant handcrafted wooden structure, like the house itself. In the late 1990s it was changed for something more solid, and mass-produced, apparently on the advice of an expert who warned of consequences if our powerful guardian spirit was not re-housed.

Dad made it a point that we should always offer prayers and incense at the start and end of our stays, and to acknowledge the spirit when entering and leaving the house. If we ever felt something uncanny or frightening in the rooms, we were to go and reason with the spirit, who would mediate or pacify as appropriate. I loved the ritual, and the feeling of ceremony.

I don't remember Tula or Chancham paying much attention to the spirit house. When she told me that Tula had never seen a ghost but had always prayed to see the spirit of his mother, who had died when he was so young, I always imagined that he prayed for this visitation here.

One day, coming back to the house, I almost trod on what seemed to be a large log in front of the spirit house. It reared up and then fled into the undergrowth. It took me a few seconds to realise that it had been a large serpent. I called to Umpai, the gardener, but it was too late. The snake had vanished. I was told that it was another house-protector spirit that lived in the earth of this property.

Umpai and most of the other staff at the house are from Si Saket, a province on the Cambodian border. They speak a form of Khmer amongst themselves, and Thai in a strong provincial accent. Umpai is the brother of the lady who cooks, and another who cleans and washes. He is boy-like and always kind to me, carrying me around and playing with me, and later driving me around town and picking me up from the airport. He becomes convinced that he is gifted with spiritual powers. These sensibilities tell him there is another strong spirit in the garden. He makes offerings of red soda drinks and incense. The red of the sugary drink recalls the blood of ancient sacrifices.

Somboon's Eclipse

1685, not far from Lopburi, in central Siam.
He is silent. One among a crowd of courtiers, guardsmen, attendants and servants, a large number of people waiting mutely. Their faces are illuminated by torchlight.

He is called Somboon. He speaks only in hushed tones. The crowd is reverent, or afraid.

The French priests, who arrive later that night, will leave a record of the event. They are struck by the stillness of this multitude of people. They have no motive to exaggerate the quiet of the gathering that night.[1] The detail is innocuous, not worthy of history, but it is human, a small and tentative insight into the lives of people.

Somboon would already have been the Minister of Civil Affairs[2] for perhaps six or seven years, a position he had stepped into after the death of Chuen, his father.

Chuen and Somboon. Their lives are constellations, made up of points on an uncertain background. The bright spots are the achievements – titles, wives, offspring. Patterns can be discerned, similarities, almost repetitions: like Chuen, Somboon had risen up the ranks. He had two sons, Jai and Jit, and a daughter named Cheng. He had been a page under King Prasat Thong, and then Deputy Commander of Narai's palace guard, before taking over the Ministry of Civil Affairs. His title was Chaophraya Chamnan Pakdi. Perhaps he was corpulent in his mandarin robes, as the name Somboon, meaning abundance or wealth.

The French Jesuits were there to observe a lunar eclipse with the king[3] and had been to the location two days earlier. The site was close to a lodge where the king was hunting elephants. It was accessible by river, featuring buildings with a large open forecourt, a gallery, and a stately pavilion; presenting perfect views of the heavens, "at all hands".

The priests had been making calculations, on the "astronomical ring of Mr. Butterfield" and the "Parallatick Engine of the Sieur Chapotot"[4] as well as their pendulums and quadrants. Their measurements had started months earlier, far away, at the Cape of Good Hope. They were nervous, since their equipment needed steady ground, and their lodgings in Lopburi were wooden and shook.[5] Accuracy was essential, since their western science gave them the king's ear. In advance of the eclipse, the Jesuits had offered Narai an intimate presentation of their methods, showing him lunar maps and engaging in discourse.

Christianity had already arrived in Siam but had not taken root. Naturally the priests sought inroads. The Jesuits' stratagem involved building an observatory for King Narai, which would be manned by 12 "mathematical" priests. The alternative was more austere – to ask for a papal dispensation to emulate the ascetic life of the east, attempting to convert while barefoot and in Buddhist monk's robes.[6] They claimed this method was effective, but very uncomfortable.

• • •

The astronomical event occurred in the cold early hours of December the 9th. The penumbra had already started by 3 am when King Narai was invited to observe. The French offered the king a 12-foot telescope to watch the progress of the eclipse.

An engraving of the scene depicts the court and jesuits beneath a night sky pierced by diamonds.[7] The courtiers bow low in a train towards the king. Narai sits in his pavilion, his telescope pointing at the extant sliver of moon. The French are clustered to another side, one bears a box, the others are occupied with their viewing glasses. The scene floats – the people, star-gazing gallery and the heavens – above curls and peaks of river water.

In storytelling logic, this celestial event would be a foreshadowing of the king's end. Three years later, in 1688, another party of learned priests would arrive in Ayutthaya ahead of a series of eclipses.[8] Their ends were the same: to use technology to charm and entice the Siamese monarch, but by now King Narai was terminally ill, and the situation was very volatile.[9] Two of Narai's brothers and another potential heir named Mom Pi had been tarnished by a plot to seize the throne two years earlier, which had culminated in a massacre. The man who had precipitated and then seized advantage from this was a certain Petracha, who headed the military elephant division. To complicate matters, there had been rumours for months that the French, aided by Narai's favourite, Constantine Phaulkon, were plotting to colonise the country and convert its inhabitants to Christianity. Suspicions had been aroused when Phaulkon convinced Narai to let the French garrison a fortress at Bangkok, at this time a strategic settlement guarding the approach to Ayutthaya. He also sent a Frenchman to govern the important harbour town of Mergui on the Andaman Sea coast.

Phaulkon, knowing that Petracha was plotting a coup, attempted to convince the French garrison to send 80 men to engage the rebels before it got out of hand. However, local French dignitaries, who were distrustful and jealous, thwarted Phaulkon, convincing the French Captain that there was no rebellion afoot, and the whole thing was exaggerated by the manipulative Greek. Soldiers were not sent, instead a French officer was dispatched to find out what was going on, and carry a secret missive for Phaulkon, rolled up in the knot of his wig.[10] When this messenger arrived at Lopburi it was night, and he was surprised to find everything calm; the king was engaged in watching a lunar eclipse as if there was no trouble abroad in the kingdom.

A month later the whispers were rife that Narai was dying as punishment for turning his back on Buddhism[11] and people across the country were arming themselves in preparation for the coming succession fight.

Shortly after the solar eclipse of May, Petracha struck decisively. Mom Pi, many of his followers, and some French soldiers were overpowered and killed. The Persian palace guards, and presumably Somboon, whose uncle had created these praetorians, had supported Petracha.[12]

With this, the dying king was practically a captive in the palace and Petracha proclaimed himself Regent. After Narai's death Petracha rid himself of any remaining claimants to the Throne, and crowned himself king, taking Narai's sister and daughter as his wives. Phaulkon was arrested, and tortured to death, his beautiful Japanese-Portuguese wife condemned to perpetual slavery in Petracha's kitchens, and the French were besieged at the fort of Bangkok until a truce was arranged.

Kosa Pan, who had been Narai's ambassador to France in the 1660s, became Petracha's Foreign Minister before falling from favour. He was executed, after having his nose cut off as a humiliation. These decades were hazardous for courtiers, the histories abound with tales of high-ranking officials demoted to cut grass, or chained to corpses in punishment – flogged, tried by fire and water, and killed along with their wives and heirs.[13]

It is likely but not certain that Somboon outlived Narai. It is not known how he fared under the next reigns, whether the manner of his death was peaceful or violent.

The dynasty Petracha founded was to last until the fall of Ayutthaya. It was seen as inward looking after the cosmopolitanism of Narai and his intellectual eclecticism, but foreigners with their trade networks continued to thrive. Persian influence, in craftsmanship, architectural form and decorative motif, is easily discerned in its local evolution over these decades.[14]

The family of Ahmad did not vanish from court life, or commerce but it is likely they went into a mild decline over the next couple of reigns.

Petracha was followed by his son, Suriyenthrathibodi, also known as the "Tiger King". He liked to enter prize-fights incognito at village fairs and had a penchant for sadistic sex with underage girls.[15]

The following king, Tai Sra, whose name means Back of the Pond, had an almost sacrilegious passion for killing animals, particularly fish; he killed lustily, using snares, traps, harpoons, hooks, and bamboo splints.[16]

The Fork and Spoon

Up until my late teens, when I travelled to Thailand alone, my voyages were conducted in the family unit: Tanya, two years my elder, mum, always a bit anxious about staying in Bangkok, dad, with a brave face. Recollections are shared – hyphenated within the group – some almost indistinguishable from those of my sister. Tanya and I will squabble about our childhood: the sequence of events, the protagonist, the acceptable level of embellishment.

It is turning memories into narratives that does them ill, because that act brings judgement, a function of age. Childhood memories are the most sensorial, they emerge within that property of early life that bestows magic upon everyday objects. The early recollections are precious, tentative, and polymorphous – later come layers of meaning and interpretation.

• • •

1982. I am six years old. Dad is showing me how to eat using a fork and spoon, in preparation for Thailand. Fork in left hand, pushes food onto spoon, this one for mouth. I should always leave a little food on the plate; it is ill-mannered to finish everything because it suggests hunger.

Our plane lands at night. I look out the window at Don Muang Airport, the lights and the landing crew on the tarmac recall war and science fiction. I am carried into the little house at my grandparents', with its polished antiquity, and put to bed.

The weather is cool the next morning, a white light. My grandmother has bought *pa tong go* (which are deep fried pieces of batter, similar to Spanish *churros*) for our breakfast, to be dipped in sweetened condensed milk.

Chancham has a raspy voice, and Tula a sing-song way of saying things. I notice that he puckers his lips slightly when patting eau de cologne on his cheeks.

Chancham is in her late 50s. She is always on her feet, pattering about, talking, and alert. She wears Thai fisherman pants at home. Around the house, Tula wears collarless short-sleeved shirts, with patch pockets, a Chinese-style garment.

I get a toothache after eating a bar of chocolate at Bu Ot's house in Ari. Bu Ot is Chancham's younger brother. He supports an orphanage with his wife – I wander around its deserted playground crying from the pain – Bu Ot gives me a small porcelain lion from his home, as distraction, which I drop the next day. Tula glues its broken leg back on some days later. I have to be held down at the dentist's.

Everything is colourful and scented. There are snakes everywhere in the countryside. Bangkok is sun bleached, it shines, and the skies are blue. My sketchbooks and dreams are filled with golden places – recurring dreams that will bleed temples and palaces into the confines of my grandparents' house.

At the beach in Cha Am, a little boy lives in a nearby house. We are a few minutes walk from the sea, with no other buildings about, except the shack next door. He runs around naked, with a string belt of phallic amulets hanging next to his penis. He is my age, and I follow him into the woods; there are orchards, he is very at home in this environment, which is foreign and intimidating for me.

The sand on the beach is dazzlingly white. We get bitten by sand flies, the bites becoming infected and oozing puss. We play with hermit crabs in the shallows and discover a dead snake on the beach, killed by an old man with a rotten leg. He says that he was bitten after treading on a snake as a boy and his leg had never healed.

I pretend to be sick at a family gathering at home. I am afraid of my cousins, Inka, Kim and Carla, who are playing at the house, and I want to sit on my dad's knee. Tanya, more confident, rushes up and down stairs with them.

We go to the snake and crocodile farms. Dad borrows Tula's beautiful Fiat sports car to go to Pattaya. It breaks down on the way back in traffic. A young man gets out of his car to help push it and cuts his hand on the bumper. I am transfixed by the blood.

Umpai, the gardener, is at the back of the house. He gets coconuts down from the palm and then shreds the flesh with a special implement he has on the ground. We eat curry with that fresh coconut milk.

Umpai takes me on his bicycle to the small fresh-market near the house. Meat is laid out on a table, attracting large black flies. He buys some, which is wrapped in a banana leaf.

I have a security blanket. Uncle Tej asks me when I will give it up and I say, "when you stop having whisky every night," and turning to Chancham, "when you stop smoking." Dad had put me up to it. I think they might find it funny but they look horrified.

When asked by Chancham if I could learn just a few words of Thai everyday, I reply, "I have so much on my mind." She finds it charming and leaves me alone, to my detriment.

We collect stickers about Doraemon, a Japanese cartoon character. They come in long film-strips and we hang them from the frangipani tree where we play. Jaru, Tej's daughter, buys small white sweets that I confuse with the small white flowers of a garland.

Jaru's nickname is Peach. She has a poodle called Pooh Bear.

Peter Bunnag makes everyone laugh and flirts with a friend of my parents who had come to visit from London. There are small flashes of memories of other family compounds – attacking dogs with muzzles outside a relative's house, the story of the ghost that grabs your bottom when you go to the loo, and tale of the tokay-gecko that jumps on your back and won't let go.

I wet myself, while watching "Time Bandits" at an enormous cinema, which has endless rows of wooden seats. The film is about a little boy getting lost in the world of storytelling. The film is strange and terrifying. I don't tell anyone.

My favourite book is Dr Seuss' *Bartholomew Cubbins*. It's about a boy who can't take his hat off for the king, as each time he removes his hat another one appears. The boy is condemned to death, but as the hats get ever more precious they realise that he is valuable, like the goose that laid golden eggs.

• • •

I will wonder in later years about my dad's relationship to the family story. I don't question why he left the comforts behind, because I am a product of his Englishness, which implies some repudiation, and I cannot imagine myself uncreated. But with time I will find his lack of interest in the family history perplexing. He attempts to explain himself a number of times, and I sense a frustration with me, and varieties of pain or discomfort that remain private. On one occasion, he writes to me, "I have come to recognise, that one significant factor was my best friend's death in a car accident in 1966. He was called Giap and had graduated from the British Film School and was setting up a production company in Bangkok. We had plans to make films together along the lines of Satyajit Ray or Ozu, our favourite directors. I was to be the scriptwriter. He was waiting for me to join him in our adventure. When he was killed on the way back from Hua Hin to the capital he was just 23. Only now do I realise the depth of my shock and grief at this sudden loss of my friend and, in many ways, my mentor. From one day to the next my lifeline back to Bangkok had been severed. Our shared dream, fueled by youthful confidence, was the reason I was looking forward impatiently to finishing my studies and getting on with my creative life. I recall thinking at the time; 'what is the point now of going back to a country from which I had I been uprooted as a child and where I have never felt at ease?'"

Four Reigns

"There comes a time in a man's life when he feels the urge to set down in writing the modes and mores of a disappearing age." So begins Kukrit Pramoj's introduction to the English translation of his novel, *Four Reigns.*[1] Kukrit was a Thai polymath, and politician, serving as Prime Minister in 1974-5. He would have been in his early forties when he began writing *Four Reigns*, a novel that would become the classic work of modern Thai fiction.

It is pre-eminently nostalgic and I have been reading it before sleep. This means a few pages at a time, as I drift into fogginess. He wrote the book in serial form, like Dickens or Dostoyevsky. It comes in narrative bursts, just enough to fit his column in the *Siam Rath* newspaper.

The story charts the life of a woman called Phloi between the 1890s and 1940s, covering the reigns of Ramas V to VIII. I have been reading it to hear Chancham's voice. She wrote the English Version[2] under her nom de plume Tulachandra, meaning October Moon, an amalgam of my grandparents' names. In his introduction to this edition, Kukrit states that in order to maintain the feel of the book the translation needed to be a reworking; it is a translation of mentality, and sensibility as much as language.

It is a pleasant way to drift off. I hear her voice, I see her face, I can sense her through the sentences. Subsequently my sleep is troubled. The images that come to mind are sharp, filled with detail. Phloi is told not to tread on the threshold of the Palace gateway. It is forbidden. She cannot help but land both of her feet on the raised step, even though she has been telling herself not to as she approaches. I recall Chancham telling me to avoid treading on the threshold at her house. In the reading I pick up the rhythm of her speech, her phrasing of Kukrit's writing.

The work is a cognate of the Testimony of Ayutthaya, in its preservation and interpretation of so many lost moments and experiences. And it is an attempt to imbue tradition with life.

Chancham loves words, and the precision of language, but she is a poor teacher. She gives me sentences to learn in Thai but sometimes sets me up with a strange word. Her translations were done for pleasure – *Four Reigns* and *Prisna*[3] into English, *The Red Badge of Courage* into Thai, and some poetry, including a piece entitled *Mere Movement*, which touches on the student uprisings of the 1970s.[4]

Tula and Chancham come back to me outside of time. They are free of outmoded fashions, and quaint old things. They are revealed eternally, like landscapes. These versions of Tula and Chancham are composites formed and set within early memory and then added to and embellished later. The platonic form of Tula is then less detailed than that of Chancham, who I knew for longer.

Tula carries himself in a particular manner, his shoulders out, straight back, an arrogant stride. People say that he carries himself like a European but I cannot determine what that means. He has an angular face, and an aquiline profile. His nose is strong, and curved. He has a slight expression of surprise, a tenderness to the eyes, which also betrays a sardonic attitude. His voice is mid-toned, but not as deep and chocolaty as dad. He delivers words curtly. He has delicate hands, with long fingers. His skin is light brown and carries a sheen. He takes great pleasure in clothes, and is always well dressed. It is not the cut, fabric or expense of his dress, it is the aesthetic delight that is important. This joyfulness is written through his house, and especially in the things he makes; he spends hours working on carvings and objects of mother-of-pearl inlay.

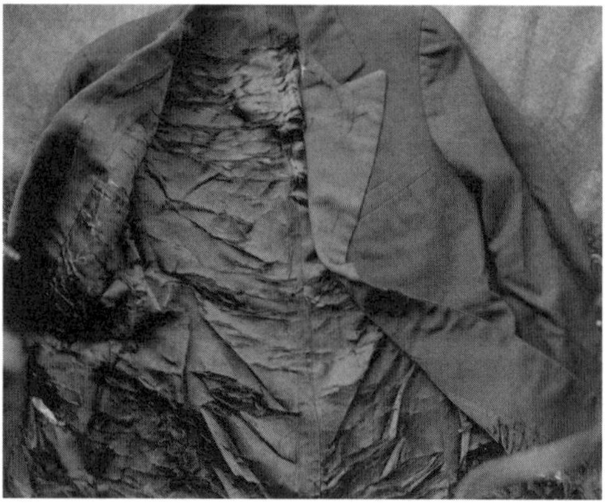

Chancham is like her handwriting, an expressive cursive, quickly penned, without effort but perfectly legible, in succinct bursts, and always entertaining. Like my father she has been known to sacrifice veracity for the sake of a well-told story or *bon mot*. Her voice is husky, with a vaguely American accent. Her hand gestures are expressive, but not in a depictive manner, serving rather as punctuations to thoughts and sentences. Her nose is a small concave, very East Asian. She has an expressive face, using her eyebrows and mouth to effect when recounting an anecdote. She cuts her own hair, and it looks great, is quite short, and young in style. The hair cutting she does from time to time, weekly, but never in an organised manner. She is not scatty but she is not one for organisation. She likes things to be fun and informal – like her dress sense, the items she uses as her bag, the things she keeps with her. She stands with one leg to the side, perhaps tapping a foot on the floor. She is not in the least bit shy, but she scares easily at certain things, and cannot deal with emotions. Her palms are deeply lined, but she has delicate fingers. She has little shoulders, that hunch slightly forward. She is not tall. She wears lipstick, which sometimes gets on her wine glass. She is rooster-like, in keeping with her zodiac sign. She can make everyday things elegant. She has a certain theatricality – the way she walks with a hand held up, calling attention to herself, words issuing forth, or about to. She loves to joke. I have never heard her say a bad word about anyone, even people I know she finds challenging.

She is patient with me. Reading *Four Reigns* in my forties, I feel a gentle reprimand, catching glimpses of myself in the wayward, rash young men at the edge of the story. The manner of storytelling is familiar – familial. I hear my father's voice too, inevitably I catch references beyond the story that relate to her life, small hints, private jokes – a character called Ot echoes my dad. Chancham describes him affecting a cockney accent when speaking English. The inclusion of asides about words gaining currency, like Sangkhom, society, Patiwat, coup or revolution, Wattanatham, culture, echo stories she told me. The Thai greeting Sawatdi was new fangled in her youth. Her teachers would tell them off if they used it at school, "don't you Sawatdi me, young girl."

I can't help wondering how she must have felt writing about Phloi's emotions at having her sons leave for schooling abroad, or about the passages regarding a son coming home with a European wife.

The original book was written before such events unfolded in our family – boarding schools, Western daughter-in-laws, rebellious sons. But the translation was made after these things had happened to Chancham. It can be imagined that Kukrit would have taken this into account when talking about the project with her, whom he knew socially.

She would receive some pages every Saturday, work on them for the week and then take them round the following Saturday morning. Chancham and Tula, and sometimes Tej, would go as a family to Kukrit's house off Suan Phlu. They would arrive there around 10.30 am. There would always be a large number of people at his house, waiting for various things, political or cultural, but gradually these people would leave. Kukrit would have two glasses of Pernod as an aperitif, and then they would have lunch. During and afterwards, Kukrit and Chancham would go over the pages and discuss the work.

They worked like this for years. Kukrit had been afraid that in translation the novel would be burdened by "footnotes and appendices", and "lose the affection and care that had been put into it while it was being written." The English Version fulfilled his desire. The book is more than a text, it is in itself the story of a literary and social relationship.

In a sense the book is about the medium of time, which softens, mellows, eases; and it is about things that take time, things that can only be seen against a long narrative background; and it asks a simple question of this sense of time, what happens when the structure against which time is measured is itself in the process of unravelling?

The Buddha's Footprint

It is hard to discern agency in the record books. The principal sources are chronicles oriented around the inner court, following dynastic narratives. They are not histories in the Greek model, connecting character to fate; individuals, even kings, sit flatly against the texture of time.

These chronicles are copies of copies, manuscripts found in later years that reproduce earlier texts, along with errors and misrepresentations. An American named Richard. D. Cushman, spent years translating and correlating the best available texts. He died just before completing the masterwork, which ends mid-sentence. Reading this work is an optical dance, like following a story across a temple wall, with its multiple focal points and impossible landscapes.

In 1612, around the same time that Ahmad helped to defeat the Japanese in Ayutthaya, a man called Bun, which means Merit, came across a strange indentation on the forest floor. He was hunting in the wilderness near a town called Saraburi, and what he saw looked like a large footprint in the hillside.[1] The king was informed that something miraculous had been found and set out on his elephant accompanied by four army divisions and many holy men.

Hunter Bun guided them along tracks through the forest to the hill. The footprint featured the outline of a wheel and was "endowed with one hundred and eight kinds of the One Hundred and Eight Marks of Great Auspiciousness."[2]

It was thus proclaimed that a true footprint of the Lord Buddha had been discovered on top of Suwannabanphot Hill, not far from Ayutthaya. A shrine was established and it became customary for the Kings of Ayutthaya to undertake pilgrimages to this sacred place.

Veneration of the Footprint was a religious duty, and a pastime. King Prasat Thong had beautiful residences built for royal use, along with pavilions for his entourage, which were protected against roaming tigers.[3] Narai constructed a road between the site and his royal capital at Lopburi.[4] One of Petracha's pilgrimages was so splendid that he becomes almost pharaonic, scattering gold, setting out on gilded barges accompanied by a host of glittering courtiers. At the holy place he had eight large fire towers lit, and spent his seven days of veneration exploring the famous "caves, streams, brooks, gorges, flue holes, and meandering tunnels."[5] The Tiger King, who fed people to sharks if they displeased him and took advantage of his noble's wives, was there in full military style. The culmination of his procession to the shrine was the customary alms giving. At the moment his foot reached the top of the temple staircase, underlings slid out of their hiding places in the trees, and after prostrating themselves to him, distributed alms.[6]

The excursion was political theatre, and ritual, all integral parts of court life.

While the sanctuary of the Footprint was evidence of continuity and stability, the mechanisms for regnal transition were as shaky as ever.

When King Tai Sra died in 1733, there was another outburst of chaos and violence. His brother, Prince Phon, the designated successor, was challenged by two sons of the late king, Aphai and Paramet. The younger princes had more followers and when the forces clashed it looked as if they would win the fight. At the last minute an officer from Phon's camp joined the fray. The warrior was called Chamnan Borirak, it is said that he had 4,000 soldiers, against the 30,000 of the princes, and yet he turned the battle and placed Prince Phon on the throne as King Borommakot.[7]

It is not known how the direct family of Ahmad fared in this struggle. There is a brief mention that some of the princes' high-ranking supporters fled to a temple, where they quickly ordained in the hope of saving their lives. Some Muslims, "Kaek and Cham", were sent to drag them out and kill them.[8] It is tempting to connect these assassins with Ahmad's family but there is no strong evidence.

In the succession battle the family had sided with King Borommakot. Jai, the eldest son of Somboon – Ahmad's great-grandson – is recorded as one of King Borommakot's guardsmen.

It is likely that Jai played a key role in the suppression of a rebellion that threatened the king in 1734, a year into his reign.[9] A group of Chinese, led by a certain Master Kai, plotted to seize the royal palace at Ayutthaya, while the king was on an elephant hunt near Lopburi.[10] Planning to install another king, 300 rebels crept into the palace compound at night and routed the guards who had been left to protect it. Jai, as Phraya Petchpichai, mounted a counter-attack, took back the palace, and, after killing the rebels, sent word to the king.[11]

Jai's fortune was to be sealed many years later at the site of the Buddha's Footprint. In 1750, after a severe illness,[12] King Borommakot decided to make merit at the Sanctuary as a gesture of gratitude. The family story tells that Jai was excluded from the courtly arrangements. When Jai asked the king what he had done to offend him, Jai was told that it was not his worth that was unwelcome, it was his faith. King Borommakot was a devout Buddhist and Jai was a Muslim. Jai asked to convert, and was allowed to do so on this auspicious occasion, when the king and court venerated the Footprint for seven days.[13]

Five years later Jai was appointed Minister of War, with the title Chaophraya Petchpichai.[14] He was the first member of the family to head this Ministry; until this point Ahmad's family had been associated with the Mahatthai, in charge of Civil Affairs.

Jai had four children; of his three sons, the eldest, Shane, remained Muslim, the next two, Sen and Noo, joined him as Buddhists. Shane became Chularajamontri, leader of the Muslim community. Sen and Noo held positions in the Ministry of War.

The War

Tula was sent to school in Rome in 1930, and by 1932 he was in France, where he lived in Poitiers for three years, with the Deville family. They would take him to Royan during the holidays to their place by the sea. Many Thais passed through the Deville house. Tula was there with aunt Patsri's father, Terd, who was older than him, and very attached to the place – even after Terd left to study in Paris, he would have his clothes sent to be laundered at the Deville's house.

Tula just missed boarding with Pridi Banomyong, Khuang Abhaiwong, Pibul Songkram and others who were to play a role in the ending of Siam's Absolute Monarchy. The connection between the revolutionaries and my grandfather is not clear, except that Tula referred to Pridi as "Acharn", teacher, and was close to Khuang in later years. But Tula was a boy then, and I was a boy when I knew him and I never thought to ask about his experiences in life. He only spoke French once in my company. It takes an effort to place him in France, although I have heard that he praised French *chauffage* (central heating), and that in the 1950s, taking the family on holiday from England, Tula would start singing Trenet's "La Mer" as soon as they crossed the Channel.

I have an impression of this young Tula as a wide-eyed child, but it is unlikely since he was quite unflappable. Patsri, who had been sent to the Deville's later, as a teen, had been unimpressed when she arrived in Paris, "I expected foreign cities to have taller buildings."

I have no stories from Tula's childhood, and only a smattering from Chancham's. Their anecdotal lives commenced when they met in the United States. They did not like each other.

By 1936 Tula was in America. He went to the Sitwell Friends School in Washington D.C, where Tom, his father, was Ambassador. Tula won the Washington D.C. district schools tennis doubles in 1936 with his friend Oleg Troyanovsky, the son of the first Soviet Ambassador to the United States. Oleg went on to become a diplomat, and was suspected of recruiting for the KGB during his time in the United States. In later years, after being splattered with red paint by protestors he quipped, "Better red than dead." Oleg was Ambassador to China at the same time as Tej in the mid 1980s, where Tula and Oleg were reunited, with a sumptuous feast at the Soviet Embassy in Beijing to mark the occasion.

Chancham was in the United States on a scholarship. She met Tula at the Embassy residence, where they were both staying. Their first encounter was after a bath, he came to tell her that she had left it dirty, and should clean it herself, to which she replied, "Well, at home we have servants to do that sort of thing," which was a lie. At the time, Tula had a blonde American girlfriend, who turned up in Bangkok during the Vietnam War married to a General in the U.S. Army. She once asked my grandmother, "Is Tula always so rude, or is it just me?" Chancham relied, "No, Tula is rude to everyone."

Tom had been concerned about the war spreading as he left Washington in 1940. He had Tula transferred from George Washington University, to complete his studies in Manila, closer to home.

Tula was already in Manila before Pearl Harbour. When the Japanese invaded the Philippines, Tula was evacuated by sea with a group of other Thai students. At one point an American submarine targeted their boat. They watched as the torpedo sped towards them through the water. As they stood praying, one of them had taken off his amulet chain and began beseeching the Buddha images, "Please, please protect us but please holy-ones don't fight amongst yourselves." His prayers were heard, miraculously the torpedo overshot them, and the submarine turned away. They were able to reach Vietnam and travelled overland through Indochina to reach home.

When Tula arrived back in Thailand, the Prime Minister held a welcoming reception at Government House, which included Chancham's group, who had been evacuated via a different route. They are both in the formal photograph taken on this occasion.

Chancham had been in the second group of girls to receive government scholarships to study abroad. On the 10th of October 1938, she took the train down to Singapore from Bangkok's Hualampong station, seen off by a crowd of friends and family. Her father accompanied her to Singapore, where she boarded the French boat, "*Jean Laborde*." It took 22 days to reach Marseille, via Colombo and Port-Said. She then took the train to Paris where she stayed for three days. She had her first croissants in Paris, and could remember their fragrance for the rest of her life. From Paris they journeyed to London, arriving on the 15th of November, and from there to Washington D.C.

She was majoring in English Literature at Goucher College in Baltimore when America entered the War. Chancham was given the choice to stay and contribute to the Allied War effort or return to Thailand. Worried about her parents, she opted to leave and went home by boat with a mixture of Thai and Japanese citizens. At Buenos Aires they were not allowed to disembark, and she got drunk for the first time as they were docked. A Japanese man decided that she was Japanese-American, hence her lack of language skills, and spent much of the journey trying to teach her Japanese manners, and telling her to quit smoking. Chancham played along, and he was very upset when he found her out.

Back in Bangkok, under Japanese occupation, they lived nearby: Tula at his father's house on Silom Road, and Chancham not far off, in Trok Phraya Phiphat. He could row himself over by boat, along the old canals. Chancham's youngest sister, At, deemed Tula to be sarcastic but even so he won Chancham's hand.

In 1942 Bangkok was underwater, there would not be such extreme flooding in Thailand until 2011. The historic inundation of '42 transformed the capital's roads into waterways. Tula and Chancham would meet and take a boat to explore the drowned city. They were the courting couple of the time, while the world was upside down, war and water without and within.

Once asked why she married Tula, Chancham replied, in her flippant manner, "It was the War, I was bored." I can hear her saying this in exactly the same way she told me she decided not to learn Spanish because she didn't like pronouncing "Zaragoza", "tharragothaa," or could never put herself to mathematics, "I couldn't stand logarithms." She would emphasise, "Logaarithmmsss," followed with a "hmm". Her eyes glazing back in time at an impatient schoolteacher.

After they got married, they moved into Tom's house on Silom road. Tula would make clothes for her, nice clothes were scarce and he had beautiful taste. A son, Tej, was born in 1943. There was an air raid shelter in the garage at the back of the garden, which they piled into during the bombing raids. The Allies bombed Bangkok on various occasions. They damaged the main railway station, many of the bridges, and on the 5th of June 1944 they hit Thonburi, destroying parts of the family temples, Wat Buppharam and Wat Prayurawong, and, in both cases, obliterating some of their Gothic-style buildings.

A few years before my grandmother died she told me that Tula had been engaged to a girl in the Philippines and he had given her a ring. At the end of the War, after they were married and had their first child, Chancham told him to go back and clear things up with his old fiancée. He went back but couldn't find her, she had been killed in the War.

For nanny Nark, the wartime occupation of Bangkok was encapsulated by one horrific incident. She witnessed an execution in the market, after Japanese soldiers had caught a thief. They forced the crowd to watch as they put a hosepipe to the man's mouth, filled him up with water and then bayoneted him.

Tom kept quiet during the War. His second wife, Lady Ruen, had been brought up and educated in Tokyo, where her father had been Ambassador in the 1920s.[1] Ruen spoke fluent Japanese, but there are no stories of any social interaction with the occupiers.

A first act of peacetime saw Tula jumping into a jeep with a friend and driving to Cambodia to see Angkor Wat. It is not clear if this was before or after his journey back to Manila. By this point, Tula was in the Democrat Party working for Prime Minister Khuang Abhaiwong. Tula and Chancham were soon to have a second child, Tew, my father. Chancham left her job at the Ministry of Finance, with its onerous arithmetic, and started working for the Americans at the United States Information Service.

The Pikul Tree

The pleasure gardens of Ayutthaya are shrouded in mystery, since they pertain to the inner palace – the life of the harem. Travellers to Ayutthaya in the 1600s such as Guy Tachard, Abbé de Choisy, Nicolas Gervaise, Simon de la Loubère and Dutchman Engelbert Kaempfer[1] left short descriptions of the parks around the old palaces. They describe beautiful orchards, cooling streams, gardens with towering trees under which the court received them. Except for a brief tour of the king's garden, they could only guess about the delights of the forbidden areas, overlooked by the private quarters of the palace.

Prior to airconditioning there cannot have been such a schism between inside and outside living. Gardens were once prestigious. It is known that the kings of Ayutthaya, Narai in particular, placed their pleasure grounds under the supervision of foreigners, the French designed the hydraulic systems for the fountains and other water-works; while Japanese and Dutch contributed their aesthetics to the parks. In the modern world of Bangkok, the outdoors is for the disadvantaged, and the culture of Siamese gardens is fading. Foliage is for snakes, and gardens come with an air of antiquity – and are therefore associated with ghosts and sweat.

To the left of Tula and Chancham's driveway, entering from the street-side, is a large pikul tree. English names for the pikul are Spanish Cherry and Bullet Wood. It has a folklore, in one story a girl called Pikul spills flowers from her mouth when she is sad.[2] The real-life flowers are cream coloured, small and cuplike, with crenulated edges. The blossoms speckle the ground beneath the pikul in its seasons. They smell of honeyed sandalwood and delight Chancham. The tree reaches above the house, spreading its branches across the drive and beyond the windows of the second bedroom upstairs.

The staff rig up a swing from the branches of the pikul. They occupy a bench there during the afternoons. In Chancham's dotage, she is wheeled out to sit with them, as they chat in their dialect. Sometimes, when it's just the two of us, I sit there reading to her. After a time she might nod for me to go on, or tell me that she's had enough. She is not speaking very much but she has moments of lucidity. It is hard to know what might come out.

At a dinner, Chancham is asked how old she was when she had Tej and replies, "I was 12." She was 22.

She gets sad in the evenings. We are told that this is common and is known as sundowning, when memories come flooding back in waves of poignancy.

Once or twice a week I take her out to dinner, sometimes with Peter Bunnag, who lives nearby. We might go to an Italian restaurant called Pan Pan, a perennial favourite; she has ice cream and red jelly for dessert.

In an earlier time, still active, and almost youthful in her sixties, Chancham rises at dawn. I get up to find her telling the gardener to move some potted plants here and there. When I ask what she is doing, she replies, "gardening without tears."

The garden has many beautiful and rare plants and trees, collected by Tula and Chancham over the years. I am blind to them because I do not know yet about Asian plants. There is a varietal of eucalyptus from Indonesia that dies slowly, though many are killed suddenly in floods, including the large frangipani that we played on with cousin Jaru.

Dad is on the lawn, he has his shirt off and has been exercising. He does T'ai Chi out here, and we knock badminton shuttlecocks around for fun when the ground isn't wet. The grass of the lawn is more bristly than what I'm used to in England, and itchy if you lie on it, the earth is blacker, and both stickier, when damp, and harder, when dry, than soil at home.

An Apsara, Khmer female deity, watches over a small pond. In the corner of the garden is a Thai folly structure, it might have been a meditation platform in its youth. It was found by a friend of the family in Bang Pahan, Ayutthaya, but now its steps and roof are slowly rotting and falling apart.

The pikul tree is the emblem of a majority Malay-speaking province in the south of Thailand. When we are not vigilant the gardener takes out his frustrations on the plants, hacking at things with a rusty machete. The tree has suffered a few times from his erratic pruning. I see him start to cut some low-hanging branches minutes after dad leaves for the airport. I run down from the workshop and beg him to stop, and he thinks I'm mad.

Tula's Fiat is parked beneath a shelter, just off the main driveway. It is a beautiful thing but needs a lot of care. Mostly it is out of service. The cook's son was born in it, stuck in traffic on the way to the hospital. He is called Fiat, and must have been born in the late 1960s. This raises a question. When did traffic become so intolerable? The Bangkok of the 1980s and 1990s are recollections of eternities spent in the car, behind vehicles belching black diesel fumes.

"Das auto ist kaput," tentatively, "the car is broken." This is the line Chancham mustered in German, when calling for assistance after a minor accident on the *autobahn*. Tula had been at the wheel and she did something rash with the door. It's a line that enfolds both the Fiat – elegant but *kaput* – and the problem with Bangkok's automobiles. The city is destroyed by cars. I imagine a trickle and then a flood.

In the 1970s, Tula had a bad car accident in Bangkok. He was injured, and stopped driving from that point onwards. In my era, Umpai, who gardened, was the driver. He had a terrible sense of direction, and, dreaming off somewhere, would often forget to make a crucial turning, or would take a left when directed to turn right – in excruciating traffic. Tula was constantly berating him, but Umpai wore an honest and well-meaning smile as he acted chauffeur.

The Ministry of War

The record keepers made black paper from pulped bark, stained with lime, which they wrote on with chalk, gold and gambodge ink.[1] For religious texts they used palm leaf, bound together in bundles.

The astrologers were sensitive to peculiar phenomena and the seasons of the heavens. Their methods were scientific even in the service of prognostication, rendering accurate dates within a replicable chronological system. Like a seismic reader finely attuned to nature.

The monks, in the cause of their faith, inscribed the present as iterations of past action. They shrunk mileage and millennia, picturing the permutations of a single spark as it ignited and burnt out; the experiences of an individual spread across countless bodily vessels.

Time could be measured against the life of an ideal being. Their cause was moral and sometimes contorted by the sophistry: a bad person in the present, born well, is still good, because to be blessed with privilege is evidence of merit accrued in the past.[2]

The Persian emissaries to Narai were amazed at the diligence of the Thai record keepers, everything was written down. It was in this reign that the histories underwent a transformation. From this point onwards the astrological and the religious styles of narration began to blend, bringing forth a tradition of royal chronicle.

In speaking of high culture and the deeds of great men, they would be creating paradigms that uttered tacit reprimands, and warned of the vagaries of life, for all.

• • •

Jai's move, in the mid 1700s from Islam to Buddhism was also a warlike shift. But it did not occur in one swoop, it was a migration that combined spiritual, professional, and conjugal elements. Jai's first wife, Cheng, was a daughter of Chaophraya Rattanathibet, the last Minister of War under King Tai Sra. Nark, his second, was a daughter of the Minister of War in the early reign of King Borommakot. The conversion to Buddhism, at the Footprint, then speaks of machinations.

The family will hold the title Chaophraya Mahasena, an epithet of the Minister of War, for a long time, almost successively. After Ayutthaya there would be other Mahasenas, but first came the Lord of Khlong Gleab, who was both Jai's cousin and son-in-law, and soon afterwards Sen, Jai's son.

Sen would die in the fighting at the fall of Ayutthaya. His biography, from the little that is known, has an epic flavour befitting the end of an era. As a young man he was Head of Guards for the Heir Successor, Uparaj – Prince Thammathibet.[3] The men must have been close because as token of good favour the prince gave Sen one of his consorts, a lady called Mom Bunsri, who became Sen's second wife.

Prince Thammathibet was a romantic figure, famous to this day for his erotic poetry – delivered in a distinctive metre that recalls the movement of a craft through water, the journeys and motions of love. His verse was melancholy and full of yearning for beauty, truth, purpose. A counterfactual sees Prince Thammathibet on the throne, steering the ship of state, a competent leader of a cohesive court. In this fantasy, Ayutthaya does not fall.

In 1755 Thammathibet uncovered a conspiracy[4] by some of his half brothers. In the ensuing investigation, he was countered with an accusation of love affairs with two of his father's consorts.

Found guilty, Thammathibet and the two ladies were gradually flogged to death, over the course of several days.

After the execution of Thammathibet the choice of successor lay between two princes. The more capable one was young and inexperienced, the elder suffered from a skin condition and was known as the Mangy Prince. The king foretold "disaster and ruin"[5] should the Mangy Prince, Ekkathat, take the throne, describing him as "lacking perseverance" and "dull and stupid". Accordingly he passed him over in favour of Uthumphon, the younger son. On King Borommakot's death, Uthumphon took the throne but gave up after a few months and fled to a temple to avoid strife as Ekkathat mustered his forces.

Ekkathat became king with little popular support. Soon after his accession a group of nobles[6] were caught plotting to depose him and were flogged and imprisoned. The kingdom stagnated, old alliances were weak, and reliable manpower was lacking.

Siamese decline was seized on by the Burmese. They had been fighting with their archrivals the Mons throughout this period. By the time Ekkathat was on the throne the Burmese had begun to launch raids into Siamese lands.

The rise of Burma had come about as a counter punch in a war with the Mons.[7] The two peoples had been fighting for dominance of the Gulf of Martaban region for centuries, lands between the Burmese and Siamese territories. An ancient Mon city at Hongsawadi, meaning "She who holds the Sheldrake", had been under Burmese control for some time. While the Burmese were engaged in fighting to the north, the Mons rose against an incompetent governor. The Mon leader was an exorcist, adept at incantations, who was believed to be invulnerable to weapons. He was soon replaced by a Mon general who occupied the Burmese capital at Ava. They captured the Burmese royal family, who were taken as hostages to Hongsawadi.

The Burmese were soon to rally around a hunter, who had fought Mon tax collectors and gathered a formidable fighting force. In retaliation for the Burmese uprising, the Mons executed the Burmese royal family. Subsequently the hunter warrior was made king of the Burmese, his messianic charisma evident in his royal name, Alaungpaya, Embryo Buddha.

Alaungpaya drove out the Mons, large numbers of whom fled into Siamese territory. As the fighting spilled into Siamese lands it became clear to the Burmese that Ayutthaya was in disarray. They took Siam's vital ports of Mergui and Tenasserim on the Andaman Sea coast and pushed across the peninsula, meeting no serious resistance.

Sen was by now a high-ranking officer in the Ministry of War, and nine years of fighting had begun.

King Ekkathat was paralysed when the Burmese began to march on his territory. He called Uthumphon out of the monastery to lead Ayutthaya's armies, with an agreement to share power.[8] Uthumphon freed the noblemen who had plotted against Ekkathat in 1759, and sent out troops under his main deputies, placing the army under the command of Chaophraya Mahasena, the Minister of War – who at this point seems to have been Khlong Glaeb. Mahasena was to be killed at an engagement near the Monastery of the Nonsi Tree,[9] struck by spears while charging on his war elephant.

By 1760 the Burmese were outside Ayutthaya's walls but Alaungpaya was injured when a Burmese cannon exploded, and died on the homeward march. Having repelled the Burmese, Ekkathat reneged on the agreement with his brother. He took back complete power for himself and Uthumphon was forced back into the monkhood.

The Burmese would return five years later, with Sen now Minister of War.[10] The Burmese did not attack directly, but first subdued Chiang Mai and Luang Prabang, blocking Ayutthaya in the north.

Sen took 12,000 men to hold the enemy at Nakhon Sawan, in the centre of the country, while his niece's husband, Sua, the Phraya Amat, was sent to Chainat with 15,000 soldiers.

A second Burmese army made its way across the peninsula and

up from the south, taking large swathes of Ayutthaya's western territories. The Thai forces were pushed back on every front. In 1766 the two Burmese armies met, Ayutthaya was encircled. The Burmese were to build raised camps all around Ayutthaya, enabling them to hold the siege throughout the rainy season floods.

The chronicles record omens that pulse with intensity: the rivers of Ayutthaya ran red three times,[11] a bird impaled itself on a royal spire,[12] sacred images fell apart or shed tears and the figure of a warrior king was heard stamping his feet in fury.

In desperation, King Ekkathat sent Sen to negotiate.[13] He was told that historically Ayutthaya belonged to Burma, she must give up her rebellion and admit vassalage. When Sen relayed this message, the king yelled, "lying nonsense!"

The final words about Sen come from Burmese sources, who referred to him as Banya, a transliteration of Phraya, meaning Lord.

"Though they knew they would be defeated, the Siamese ministers Banya and Banya Kuratit still tried to defend the city. They reorganized 10,000 Siamese troops and commanded them to fight back against the Myanmar army. The two ministers came to disaster because they could not rely on their troops just like the boatswain of a crashed boat whose bow and stern have been demolished. It was the same as grass, litter, and silk-cotton blossoms that must be blown away in a storm.

"Just as Garuda swoops down on Naga, the Myanmar armies overran the city and palace of Ayutthaya, known otherwise as Ayujapura, dwarawati, or Yuan, on the night of the 10th waxing day in the month of Tagu, ME 1129 [8 April 1767]."[14]

Sen was killed in the fighting. King Ekkathat died of starvation attempting to flee, and Uthumphon was taken off to Burma along with thousands of war captives, who included Sen's daughters, Pao, Paen, and Thong Dee. The fate of his two wives, Puang Kaew and Mom Bunsri, is unknown but his two sons Bunma and Bunnag were still alive and free, in the Western Provinces.

• • •

Everything burned. A fire had destroyed much of the city before the final days. When the walls fell, the enemy brought more fire, and heaped untold misery on the inhabitants of Ayutthaya, those who had survived the disease and starvation of the long siege.

It is doubtful that anyone was thinking of the written archives of the city as it fell. They would not have thought about the three centuries of written documentation that were turning to ashes, of the manuscripts and palm leaf books discarded, scattered, and defiled in the two palaces, the many temples, and ministry buildings.

The paroxysm of violence and wanton destruction would be soothed by forgetfulness, and amnesia for the horrors of war meant also an escape from the hysteria of state activity.

Returned to nature were countless catalogues of energies spent, copies of decrees, charts and logbooks that were both temporal and secular, the histories in their various forms, and unknown curiosities.

All was burning, with the fire of passion, hatred, delusion, the fires of birth, decay, death, grief, lamentation, pain, sorrow and despair. But as ever, the end was also a beginning.

Khlong Bang Nang Cham

Tula chose the land because it was situated beside a beautiful canal in lush countryside. In the early days, the farmer who sold the land was still there growing rice in the fields surrounding the property. When the rice was harvested there were haystacks, and buffaloes grazing in the fields. The canal beside the property was called "Khlong Bang Nang Jeen" (Chinese Lady Canal) which was soon nicknamed "Khlong Bang Nang Cham" (Lady Cham Canal) by Chancham's friends. The house was completed by the mid 1960s, and had a large pavilion set next to the canal. This "Sala" a gift from Chancham's best friend, Princess Sudasiri, a granddaughter of King Rama V by Queen Saowabha.

The family, staff and guests enjoyed swimming in the canal. It was clean and refreshing. They could take one of the boats and paddle it to the local market. There was always a risk of flooding in the rainy season, but the water flowed freely and gently in the canal all year round.

By the late 1970s things began to change. A bridge was constructed next to the house, giving direct access to Sukhumvit Road. It was poorly constructed but functional. There were large holes in it, and one day Chancham fell through, breaking her leg. The canal system was blocked off and later its banks were enforced with cement, so the house's garden was cut off by some feet from the canal. The concrete embankment began to serve as a walkway, so fences were put up to stop people wandering in, or looking into the house.

The water was now stagnant. It turned black, bubbled and smelled strongly. It became pungent, like an open sewer.

Occasionally children would jump in if it was especially hot, and a boat might pass by, but it was dead, and a place for those heading that way.

Around 1999, it was visited by a strangely handsome young man, with long hair, who wore black fisherman trousers. He would walk down the alley and come to swim in the toxic canal. He sang a sad song, about all the fish and the birds being dead, and would come out of the black water covered in silt. I only saw him for a few months.

As a child, before that, I would dream that one day the canals would be opened up again and the water would flow.

My grandmother would say, "never mind, everything changes", and try to avoid the topic. One day she said to me, "you know, I hear people, particularly foreigners saying, 'Oh it was so wonderful in the past, if only things had been better conserved.' But really it was always like this, always a mess and rather ugly." Chancham didn't like dwelling on the things that made her sad, or brought up emotions.

She told me that when she was a child there was still a crocodile in the Chaophraya River. It was old and large, and quite lazy, and lived beneath the Memorial Bridge. One day a Chinese man who was very unhappy in life, decided to end it all by jumping off the bridge. He had forgotten that there was a crocodile nearby, but remembered when he hit the water and started calling out, "Please help me, I don't want to get eaten by Uan (Fatty). I wanted to die but not like this. Help me." He was fished out safely, to the onlookers' amusement.

As she aged, more memories came to the surface. Her mother had been a famous gambler and had bankrupted the family several times. At some point, when Chancham was a girl, the family had been obliged to move to a small house, next to a canal. Chancham used to listen to the neighbouring family fighting, the husband was a drunk. Chancham was amazed by how often they would row and for how long, with every detail broadcast. One day she saw a dead baby float past in the canal. Seven decades later the memory still upset her. I don't think she had shared this with anyone until the moment we talked about it.

Chancham had been born into immense wealth. Her mother was the favourite daughter of a tycoon-like figure, who had an enormous Italianate house at the corner of Silom and Rama IV roads. Chancham's mother had inherited a great fortune, all of which she lost at cards, literally gambling on her deathbed.

Water and Time

The most familiar ritual.

Fire, ash, water, words, time.

The name of the deceased is written on a piece of paper. I set fire to the slip of paper, turning it slowly to make sure the whole piece catches. I drop it into a bronze cup and watch it curl and turn to ash. Then I pick up the vessel of holy water. While the monk chants I begin to pour. It is hard to judge the flow; the vessel, also made of bronze is heavy. I must try to empty out the water by the end of the prayer. By now the cup is full of ashen liquid, bits are floating on the surface. I go outside and pour out the substance by a tree.

Water filtering down from the mountains, out of the highland forests, trickling through to wide brown rivers, which carry on down to the gulf, sediment building into the wide expanse of the delta.

We sit and watch this unfolding, this non-action.

I was on holiday when we first met. I was 18, it was 1994. Tung had longish hair and a warmth in his expression. We went out in his pickup truck to play pool, somewhere across Bangkok. He told me the owner of the pool-hall was a bigamist. Then we went on to some bars. After that, we would meet every time I was in Thailand.

Tung is a painter, for a time he had an open-air studio, where he had erected a lone column of teak at the centre of the space, like a city pillar. He would paint at night, picking up the weather, the atmosphere of the sleeping city. He had a sparse bedroom off to one side, simple life then, used tubes of oil paint, canvases, bottles of whisky.

Forward in time to 2000, or maybe it was 1999. Tung had taken me up to Ayutthaya on a day trip. I had my Super 8 camera with me. A few seconds from the day still exist. We visited a house by a river, somewhere in the countryside, and lunched watching the water passing in front of us. Tung said, "This is enough for me. I couldn't live by the sea. It is too emotional. This pace is enough for me." We walked in the woods after lunch, on a dirt track through verdant nature.

We are still good friends. Tung is a good storyteller, with a wealth of ribald and darkly comic stories, like the tale of the restaurant owner who was so rude he'd get into fights with clients and eventually shot someone after taking their order. Or euphemisms and code words for obscene acts and the slang for the wispy, semi-visible hair that rises up a torso from the pubic area. He would take me to a noodle stall and tell me that this was the street where the intelligentsia and artists would hang out in the pre-war years, or reminisce of getting on a bus after classes when he was a student, having something to eat beforehand and sleeping blissfully through the traffic jam ahead until he reached home.

Tung knows how to see the treasures in the junk heap. Maybe he is the first person I befriend in Thailand who can open my eyes to everything else, beyond the obvious things of worth. And there is a lot. It is beyond me. The folk heroes, the pop culture, the streets and buildings; all these events that happen to normal people that are deeply poignant, poetic, disturbing, beautiful without needing to be acknowledged and sanctified by other standards.

He is not mystical. His world is of the senses, even so he became a monk for a time. We go to visit his temple after he de-robed. It is humid, hilly, forested. He felt despair afterwards shared by another former monk, the dread of the quotidian, having to buy toilet paper.

We look back at looking back and we stand and look back.

A Decade of War

The collapse of Ayutthaya in 1767 is just within anecdotal memory. Those figures who lived through the last days of the city, and were there almost two decades later at the founding of Bangkok, sired large families. They took many wives, and their family trees branched wide, intertwining inextricably. The lines of descent became increasingly important, people claimed rights and government office according to blood. There were so many claimants by the mid 19th century that official records began to be kept to verify the lineages.[1]

Connection to the past was precious, enforced by storytelling and conferred by association. There were no family names, one was known or unknown. To appear in an anecdote, or to present a new one, was to be placed within a potent narrative. This political necessity kept the past in memory.

A century after Ayutthaya's end, King Rama V commissioned one of his nobles to write histories of the first four reigns of his dynasty. The historian was Kham Bunnag, Chaophraya Thipakorawong. His chronicles would begin in the period of strife before the founding of Bangkok. In writing his histories, he relied on official documents, the existing chronicle material and the memories and anecdotes of his family and acquaintances.

Kham's grandfather appears in the opening pages of his Chronicle of the First Reign.[2] Kham will use the honorific "Mom" when referring to the man named Bunnag.

Bunnag was born in 1737 in Ayutthaya. His mother, Mom Bunsri, was a former consort of the Heir Successor, Prince Thammathibet, who had then been given to Sen, Bunnag's father, bearing him a single child.

Bunnag would have been 13 years old when his grandfather, Jai, became Buddhist, so it is possible that he was raised initially in the Shia faith of his ancestors before the family conversion.

There are apocryphal stories that his lifelong friendship with a man called Thong Duang began at a temple school they attended. This friendship was to be a dominant factor in Bunnag's fortunes. Thong Duang would one day be king, and the founder of the Chakri Dynasty.

How Bunnag came to be in the region of Petchburi at the end of Ayutthaya is a mystery. His father was the last Minister of War. It can be imagined that he sent his son out of the city to save him before the Burmese encirclement. It could equally have been that Bunnag was involved in defensive operations and had been stranded outside the city.

Bunnag appears in the records alongside Thong Duang, who was also in this western part of Siam, bordering Burma. Thong Duang was Royal Commissioner (Yokrabat) of the city of Rajburi and had married into a powerful local family, referred to as the Bang Chang family,[3] who like his forebears were ethnic Mons.[4] It is tempting to speculate about whether Thong Duang's Mon blood was a factor in his connection to these environs, with its large Mon population, a people so integral in the struggles between Ayutthaya and Burma.

As we have seen, the Burmese invasion came from several directions, from the north, south, up the peninsular and west over the Three Pagodas Pass. In one of the waves of attack, the Thai forces made a stand in the Western Provinces. They held back the Burmese at Rajburi for days before realising that their position was hopeless, at which point they poured liquor down their war elephants' throats, got drunk themselves, and launched a final frenzied attack.[5] They were defeated. The Burmese swept through, and the locals fled to the forest and hid there until the enemy had passed.

Bunnag would have heard about the fall of Ayutthaya, the death of his father and the unknown fates of his mother and relatives.

The Burmese installed an army of occupation, but withdrew after a short time due to their own domestic problems. However, there was no central power among the Thai cities and principalities, various claimants and opportunists fought each other. At the same time, there were additional invasions and disturbances within and along the Lao and Cambodian border regions.

In this turmoil, a general of obscure origins emerged called Taksin. He set up a new capital at Thonburi, down-river from Ayutthaya, and rallied a large faction of Ayutthaya nobles to his cause. By 1768 he began calling himself king. Over the next few years Taksin, aided by various military commanders, stamped out resistance and wrested back Ayutthaya's mandates for his new state. One of his earliest followers was Bunma, Thong Duang's brother, who had been in Ayutthaya at the end. Bunma was a talented fighter and leader, and he soon brought Thong Duang into the cause.

Bunnag did not like Taksin, for unknown reasons, and refused to serve under him, but he remained close to Thong Duang. He is recorded as serving in Thong Duang's military staff through the wars of the Thonburi era and had "accompanied him in many military campaigns and served with distinction."[6]

In 1778 Thong Duang and his brother Bunma were sent to stabilise the Laotian principalities, which were drawing the Burmese into their internecine problems. The two brothers caught Vientiane in a pincer, one force coming up from the south and another west across the Khorat Plateau. They defeated the Prince of Vientiane and marched thousands of Lao down to Saraburi, in central Siam, where they were settled. The two palladia of the Lao people, the Sacred Prabang image and the Emerald Buddha, were taken away to Thonburi.[7]

A hazy anecdote reports that at some point Bunnag was left in charge of a treasury, presumably while Thong Duang was on one of his early campaigns in Cambodia or the northeast. During a period of danger, Bunnag hid gold somewhere in the countryside of Rajburi. After retrieving the treasure, he was ambushed by bandits and in the fighting his wife, Lim, was killed. Bunnag had two daughters with Lim, the youngest of whom, Thani, was given as consort to Thong Duang, and bore him a son, Prince Surin.

Upon Lim's death, Bunnag married into the Mon family of Bang Chang. He took Lady Nual as his wife, the younger sister of Thong Duang's wife, Nark. Bunnag was now brother-in-law and father-in-law to a future king.

Taksin had been gradually assuming religious airs and privileges;[8] by 1779 he was openly suggesting that he was on the path to enlightenment, would soon be able to fly, and that his body was displaying characteristics of sainthood.[9] Among those he flogged for disagreeing were many monks, and possibly Thong Duang.[10]

The King of Thonburi was overthrown in a Palace Coup and executed in the ritual manner befitting kings, namely beaten to death with sandal-wood clubs. Thong Duang became King Rama I, while his brother Bunma was made Uparaj, or Heir Successor. A new capital was founded across the river at a place called Bangkok.

The Marble Dining Table

1990s. I arrive at the house and step out of the car; five or six small dogs come rushing at me. Addled by the flight, I walk from the gravel driveway beneath the pikul tree to the open-air downstairs space, stretching under the eaves of the house. My eyes adjust. Chancham comes towards me, one hand raised in the air, with a finger poised. She is wearing her house clothes but looks elegant, the loose trousers knotted elaborately at the waist, and bangles on her wrists. I give her a hug. She has some papers on the marble topped dining table behind her – a cryptic crossword, a letter, a translation.

1980s. I see Tula sitting at the table. At this point they are taking their breakfast here. He has a myna bird which is hopping about on the table and being fed paté on morsels of bread. The bird is known to call out, "Mae ben rok prasat, Por ben rok prasat," or mum's having a nervous breakdown, dad's having a nervous breakdown. The bird arrived at the house with these lines, which Chancham and Tula think is hilarious.

Tula is charmed by the bird; he comments on its actions, growing birdlike as he leans towards it. He allows it to stand on his shoulder, a sign of the tenderness with animals he can lack with people.

This dining table is where he famously pulled his chair out during dinner, turning his back on the guests and proceeded to feed his dogs. Chancham lightened his behaviour, turning it into a theatrical feature of the house. The action loops in time, in the retelling.

The space here is designed around Tula's body – the house like an enormous set of clothes. Where the overhead beams are set low, for structural purposes, they have been fixed just over Tula's six feet so he doesn't bang his head.

The table is next to a small square pond, inhabited by carp. These fish are aggressive. They look out of the water angrily, back up with their fins before suddenly flexing themselves out of the water to bite at people. I witnessed them hurling themselves out of the water onto the ground more than once.

In the pond, a Grecian deity stands shaded by an umbrella of papyri. On one of their trips to visit us in Athens, Chancham and Tula tried to find a partner for the nymph, without luck. Instead, Tula discovered an eau-de-cologne in a pinecone-shaped green bottle at an Athenian pharmacy. The scent transported him back to his youth in 1930s Europe.

The dogs charge in a pack throughout the grounds and this open area, with one always called Silom, a cocker spaniel from a dynasty that began in the 1960s. For a time we live in terror of a mean former street dog, Pa Thong Go, who looks like a teddy bear but bites.

In the afternoons, of my student years, Chancham might invite me to a drink. We chat over our glasses for hours. She recalls a novel that touched her by a Soviet Georgian author in which he described his childhood by way of light. She mentions her playful ambition to write screenplays, one would have been about a tram driver in old Bangkok, the other was located in a clock shop, and had temporal themes.

She talks about T. S. Eliot's *Love Song of J. Alfred Prufrock*, reciting her favourite stanza, with its modest disclaimer, "No! I am not Prince Hamlet, nor was meant to be." Chancham calls herself, "an attendant lord," "full of high sentence, almost at times the fool." The house is her theatre set, "to swell a progress, start a scene or two". We listen, at another quieter time, to Eliot reciting his *Four Quartets* on a cassette tape I discovered in Greece – Eliot's clipped tones echoing through the half-empty house.

The table looks across to another smaller one, set beside a screen of climbing plants. On top of a dusty floral table-cloth is a copy of Cushman's *Royal Chronicles of Ayutthaya*, and a book on the princely offspring of King Mongkut.

The extremity of the downstairs area, as it gives out onto the garden, speaks of bodily objects – Nanny Nark's rocking chair, and two Chinese seats which resemble reclining ladies. In a nearby shaded nook, are up-pointing breasts in wax of varying shapes and sizes: works by Chancham's niece, Pinaree Sanpitak.

To another side of the table is the entrance to the library, with a bathroom on one side and a large bookcase. On the wall facing the bathroom are various framed items: paintings by Sumet Jumsai, and Chatchai Puipia – an Italian street-scene, an elephant – and a newspaper article. This is Kukrit Pramoj's column and jokes about parents having trouble with their wayward children, recounting the story of dad getting arrested as a student at Hyde Park, during an Anti-Vietnam War march.

I turn to see my dad looking a bit blanched next to a table. The wall framing him is covered with dozens of Thai hats, made of bamboo and rattan. He puts down a letter, stumbled upon in an old drawer. It is an ancient thing he wrote to his parents, the painful document in which he declared his freedom from Thailand, and passed judgment on his parents. "I can't imagine what this is doing here, I must have written it a few years after Cambridge – I feel a bit ashamed reading it."

Chancham sidling up, waves her hand, saying, "never mind," to avoid a scene. I hear her husky voice generally. She might jab me with her finger on the arm, as she had the habit of doing. "Well darling…"

It is Sunday, when Chancham holds a "noodle party". These gatherings are famous amongst the circle. She has had the staff set up a noodle stall, with its vat of broth, condiments, various types of dry noodles and meats and seafood. People are having bowls made up according to their taste. The atmosphere is easy-going, seemingly without hierarchy or protocol, bringing together the family and her old school-friends. This collection of familiars could form a *dramatis personae* of fleshed out history – being the offspring of a clique or two who played state-building roles in old Siam. History's rivals and enemies now jostle each other for lunch snacks and condiments.

I am talking to aunt Patsri, standing next to the table. She explains that although she is closer in age to my father, she is considered to be of my grandfather's generation. "I am 7th generation." She insists, "But I look so much younger because I am well embalmed, from all the whisky." She has a twinkle in her eye and lets out a laugh, that is tender and naughty like a schoolgirl.

Pitya Bunnag is here looking birdlike. He drinks coffee saying that it is good for him, as it stimulates his heart. He mentions his archaeological research – delving into Southeast Asian penis ornamentation, which he explains over a sheaf of papers illustrating varieties of subcutaneous decorative barbs and baubles.

I picture Yukio Mishima passing through as a houseguest, he did exercises in the garden, and Jim Thompson, dining here on his last night in Bangkok before his disappearance. He arrived in a huge convertible, in the company of an American lady.

Family friend, Nui, breaks into laughter over a childhood story from England; he recounts the moment Tej, who was the eldest of the bunch, accidentally jabbed someone in the bottom with his umbrella – which Tej had been wielding with great affectation. Nui was part of the clan who passed through "Flat Broke", as Chancham christened their 1950s apartment in London.

The view from the table is of wooden house poles and their carved decorative brackets, so many tree-like verticals that it resembles a copse. An enchanted grove, with many seating areas for conversation and merrymaking, it is a jolly space, for a young couple and their friends. As the crowded weekend parties and dinners start to subside, the place becomes melancholy and deeply shaded.

The epicentre of the perpetual party is that round marble table. At the centre of the table is a Lazy Susan, which mesmerises me. For a time, a tame gecko lives beneath this rotating plaque, darting out and trying to steal food off plates.

At night, mosquito coils are lit under the table, and with the overhead light it is transformed into an island in an ocean of shadow. The Thai night is total, it comes fast, and the city is suddenly quiet. Life outdoors, no airconditioning, some sounds buzzing in from the neighbourhood, a voice, a waft of a television jingle, a passing vehicle – a hypnosis.

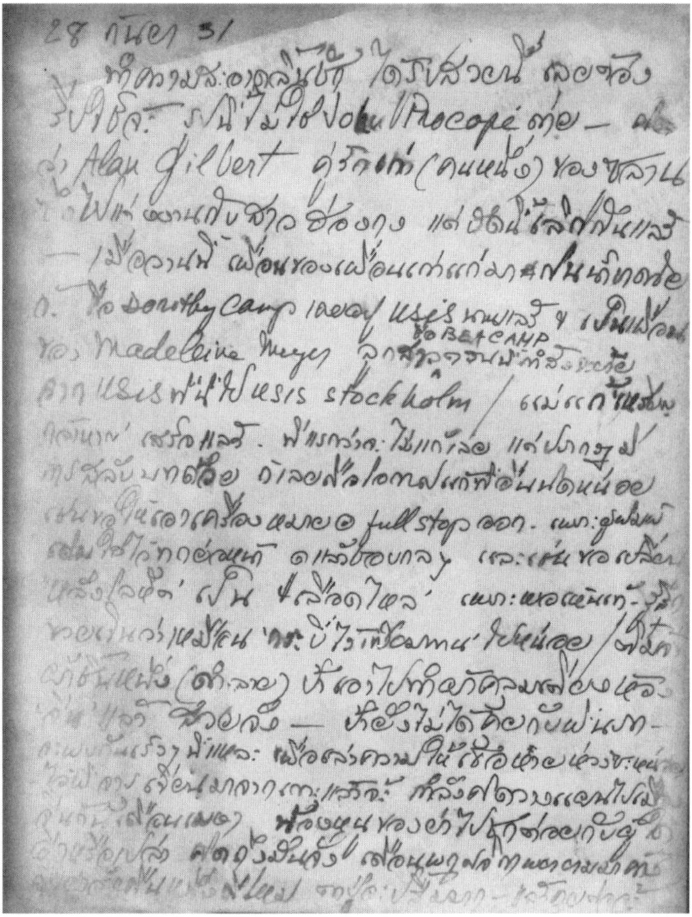

Mom Bunnag's House

The histories are clearer now. Ayutthaya was a fairytale, with elephant duels and chased gold swords. The mythic past evaporates in the clouds of musket and cannon fire that ended the old city. It is less vexing to follow the stories of individual lives, since Bangkok is early modern, and will rely on technologies not too distant – its tales voiced by people not too outlandish.

Ayutthaya is a place of ruins, taken back by the silt, and creeping nature. It gets dug up, explored, analysed, pilfered, what can be known of the old place via its material remains has largely been brought to light. Bangkok, on the other hand, is here, underfoot. Bangkok's sites of historical record are somewhere, some jutting out, others interred, submerged, waiting for excavations that cannot commence for the pace of life. The story has not ended, thus cannot yet be fully spoken.

• • •

Bangkok was founded on the 21st of April in 1782, when a ritual pillar was planted in the earth. This new capital was across the river from Taksin's city of Thonburi, on an outward bend in the river, on the eastern bank. It was more defendable against Burmese attack from the west. The city was planned and built according to the memories of Ayutthaya. One foreign traveller,[1] some decades after the foundation, remarked that although the city had many names, the only one used by locals was Sri

Ayutthaya. They had rebuilt the lost city; Thonburi was to be a pause, or anomaly, in one long continuation of power.

Bunnag was ennobled at the start of the new reign, with the title Phraya Outhai Tham. He was head of the Royal Pages Department and the king gave him land next to the palace to build his compound. To one side of his property was the home of Princess Narinthorn Thewi, a half sister of the king, nearby was the residence of the king's mother.[2]

It was customary for high-ranking officials to live close to the king so they could defend him. This became Bunnag's principle duty when he was promoted to Chaophraya Yommaraj in 1785, Minister for the Capital.

Bunnag was sent back to Ayutthaya to assess what was left in the fallen city. He was to bring back sacred objects and salvage materials to be used in the construction of Bangkok. He oversaw the building of parts of Bangkok's early fortifications, the erection of the new throne hall, and the crafting of the throne from precious wood. It is conceivable that during his time in the ruined city he visited his former home and the house of his father, bringing back things of significance from which to build his new mansion.

In 1787 the Siamese launched an attack on Burma. Bunnag was active in this campaign, and saw heavy fighting around the coastal city of Tavoy. He fought alongside his cousin, Phlii, who was Chaophraya Mahasena, Minister of War. Phlii was a son of Khlong Glaeb, who had held the Mahasena title in late Ayutthaya.

After the Siamese took Tavoy, the situation was calm until Phlii had some local men flogged, which started a rebellion against the Siamese and a massive counter attack. Bunnag and Phlii's position was over-run, and Phlii was killed. The Burmese were so violent with his body that little was found of his corpse after the battle.[3]

Back home, Bunnag took more wives. Women named Gong, Ming, Chim, Tu, Chan, Uam, and Tim joined his main wife, Nual, in the residence. Polygamy was an institution with many rules. There were hierarchies, and gatekeepers and procedures to follow, which may have staved off some of the complications and jealousies inherent in such situations. No records exist of Bunnag's relationships with his many spouses, or of how he might have decided to direct his affections.

A brief glimpse into the culture of the noble bedchamber can be found in accounts of the Heir Successor's Palace, it might be surmised that the practices were held alike, at least as guidelines.

The female body though desired was fraught with spiritual dangers. Sexual congress and taboo substances, such as menstrual blood, could sully the sacred protections guarding the male bed. Hence a secondary bed was used for lovemaking. The designated lady would wash and perfume her body and clothes, washing her lower body with scented water. Politeness prevented her from pointing her feet towards the head of her lover, so she waited for him with her feet turned back and her hands in a prayer position.[4]

Bunnag's main wife, Nual, gave birth to ten children, with Bunnag siring over 30 children in total. Notable among the children of his main wife, would be Dit, his fourth son, and Tat, the sixth.

Dit was born in 1788 and the following year, in an omen that would not have been lost on the populace, the Throne Hall his father had built was burned to the ground after being hit by lightning.

In 1793 Bunnag became Chaophraya Akha Mahasena, Minister of War, and was to reside at the compound he had built until his death in 1805.

In 1818, some 13 years later, Rama II decided to expand the private areas of the Grand Palace southwards. Bunnag's houses and land were taken back by the crown, becoming part of the Inner Palace. It might be wondered whether Rama II's construction plans also displaced his aunt, Princess Narinthorn Thewi, Bunnag's neighbour. The Princess kept diaries that were later to be edited by King Rama V.[5] She was the source of a persistent rumour that Bangkok had been born under ill-favoured stars. It was said in whispers, from around 1827 onwards, that the dynasty would last for 150 years, until 1932.[6]

The Southern Wall

The Covid upsurge of early 2021 has transformed Bangkok's traffic situation, everything is suddenly nearby and accessible. The city becomes large and varied, and there are less people on the streets, which are quieter and calmer.

On a whim, I drove over to the Grand Palace. It took a mere 20 minutes from Saladaeng. I parked near Tha Tien and hopped out to take a few photographs, thinking about ancestor Bunnag's residential compound.

At the far end of the palace complex at least one building by Bunnag still stands. This is the scripture library within the enclosure of the Royal Chapel. It is a Mondop, an enclosed square structure with a multi-tiered roof topped by a spire. The original was made of wood and had burned down during a Palace celebration. Bunnag built the new Mondop while he was still Chaophraya Yomaraj, Minister of the Capital. Bunnag would have rallied a large team of officers with titles like Phra Rajasongkram, Luang Changwang, Luang Wichit Narumol, Khun Phakdirojna, Khun Inphichit – engineers, wood joiners and carvers, metal casters, specialists in decorative motifs for roofs and gables – experts whose names have largely been lost to time.[1]

The total area of the Grand Palace is enormous. I stood across the road from the southern wall framing my pictures. There was no traffic, so I was able to get some car-free shots of the long wall. The ground in front was covered, between wall and road, by very neat grass lawns and an immaculate sidewalk, of patterned tiles. The long boundary wall was a searing white, and punctuated by some defensive towers. A tree was in bloom on the other side of the wall.

As I took photos, police passed by on scooters a number of times, on their beat or to check on me. There were no passersby, or tourists, although some building works were going on at Wat Pho.

The wall is effective. There is no reasoning with its glare and perfection. Nothing can be seen, or surmised from the material. Everything around the wall has been controlled, there is no moat with bears, or water, or even banks that burst into wild flower, as at a French chateau in spring. Here, the only blossom is on a tree up above. At street level we are pushed back by the blankness of this structure. The past is walled off, tamed like nature. The wild aspects of history, with its unruliness and embarrassments and ambiguities, are behind the unmoving curtain.

• • •

Later that day, I have my dad on video call from Spain, where he lives with his wife Denys, and has been throughout the year of pandemic. He is sharing a rediscovered memory. It was 1974, in the months before my sister Tanya was born, Tula asked him to come out one night, saying, "I have to go and see someone for myself." It was perhaps the last time he remembered Tula driving himself. They drove over to Thonburi, arriving at a shack – it was the rainy season, and they had to enter via slippery planks. Inside it was crowded, with people sitting on the floor before a spirit medium. This was a small, strange old man, who went into a trance and completely transformed, telling people things they had come to find out. Tula got bored and started to smoke. He recognised someone else there from the Palace, where he was still working.

They started to gossip quite loudly. Tula got more and more excited by the story he was recounting. He told it from one side and then another, laughing at his jokes and asides. Dad started to feel embarrassed but there was no stopping his father. The supplicants in the shack began to prick up their ears, then they lost interest in the medium and started to listen to these two men talking, and follow their gossip. The medium and his wife were left alone, and sat wondering why they had lost all the attention.

Although Tula was not superstitious, he went to see the new royal astrologer at the time and came back saying, "he's very good. I tried to trick him. I gave him my mother in-law's chart, instead of mine. The man looked at it for a long time before saying, 'This is very strange, this is a woman's birth chart, but one who is very masculine and a gambler'."

Mnemonics

The Ancient Greek poet Simonides of Kea is credited with the invention of the memory palace. The story goes that he was at a crowded feast when he was informed that two young men needed to speak to him and were waiting outside. By the time he got there they had departed. As he stood looking for them an earthquake struck destroying the banqueting hall behind him. Everyone inside was killed. Simonides found that he could identify all of the revellers by recalling their relative positions in the room. A mnemonic came from this morbid affair. Memory functions best in relationship to space.

The technique of the memory palace is simple, and highly effective. A familiar building, or a pathway, is remembered in as much detail as possible. Mental stops are inserted as the mind journeys through these places, jarring or outlandish features can be added, which bring forth memories, or keep them readily accessible. With practice, thousands upon thousands of small things can be recalled.

The Welsh and English once had a parallel tradition. They called it beating the bounds. The objective was for the community to remember the exact boundaries of their territory. On certain feast days, children were walked to location markers at the borders of the district, an old tree, a stream, a ruined wall. They were beaten at each marker. The pain combined with the walk and the sights created indelible maps.

These mnemonics summarise the nature of popular history.

The past is remembered via strange details, places and monuments that loom before the eye, and from pain.

This way peculiar and troubling stories gain oversized representation in memory.

• • •

Dit was Bunnag's fourth son, and would have been 15 when the city was shaken by a series of unfortunate events. These things happened not far from Dit's home, which at this point was next to the Grand Palace.

A kilometre of so to the north was the royal compound of the king's younger brother, Bunma. This prince had been a brilliant general. He joined Taksin's army, to fight the Burmese, before Thong Duang, as the later king was then known. Indeed, Bunma was with Taksin before any of the other Ayutthaya nobles, and had been an active general through the turbulent times before the founding of Bangkok. During his brother's reign Bunma had built up a large following, with many trusted and battle-seasoned lieutenants. He had his own army. When Thong Duang became king he made Bunma his Uparaj, or Heir Successor. It is debateable whether or not Siam was a diarchy, but there is some evidence to suggest that the office of the Uparaj was close to kingship; it had its own revenues, envoys, bureaucracy, military, and conducted important ritual functions.[1] Tension between the one crown and the other was part of the inheritance of old Ayutthaya.

In 1803, Bunma is said to have fallen sick. He feared that he had been poisoned or that black magic had been cast on him. As a warrior he was an adept at incantations and magical formulas. He recited a mantra and told himself that if he could drink his tea all would be well. He did so without mishap but soon vomited.[2] Bunma went to Wat Mahathat, where he presented his sword to the Buddha. He lit candles on the flat of the blade as he made this offering. No sooner had he done this than he was afflicted by extreme pain, so much so that he tried to kill himself with the sword but was restrained by his son.

Bunma was wracked with rage and sorrow; he had fought so valiantly for the nation, he had achieved so much. The enormous palace complex that he had built would be for nothing, it would not be his for much longer; his rank of Uparaj not being hereditary, all that he had done would pass to other people. Before dying he cursed the ground of his palace against future inhabitants that were not his children.

His sons and supporters were distraught and furious. They blamed the king, hatched a plot and armed themselves. They were said to have practiced black arts at Bunma's palace, causing a number of their followers to die. These corpses were buried, along with things of power in the palace grounds. The king got wind of this treason and had the conspirators and their families put to death.

It is not known how Dit responded to these events. In later life, as a man of power, he would also create his own ghostly myths.

• • •

There is a folktale about the city pillar in the eastern city of Trat.[3] Dit was campaigning against the Vietnamese in the eastern gulf. It was 1848. His fleet had been sent out in support of the land armies under his friend and comrade-in-arms, Chaophraya Bodindecha. When he landed at Trat the Vietnamese scattered. He held the city for a time, during which he decided to build a temple and lay two city pillars.

A Thai city radiates out of its omphalos. Like Leonardo's idealised man the navel and phallus are interchangeable, links between sacred and profane. A pillar is laid, during a brahminical ceremony, at a specific time and place. The pillar is a first chosen cut, or foundation stone. It pierces the earth and the air simultaneously. The laying of the pillar is the moment of birth.

Before Dit's pillars were laid, an announcement was made that they would be looking for men to be sacrificed as guardian spirits. Naturally that night, when the soldiers passed with their calls, the townsfolk kept quiet. The soldiers began to knock on the doors of houses and two men answered, their names were Man and Khong (meaning Stable and Enduring). They were buried alive beneath the two pillars. From then on the pillars conferred protection and happiness on the city.

Later when the French occupied Trat, a French officer decided to have the pillars torn down, as they were deemed a gathering place for rebellious locals. After trying unsuccessfully to shift the pillars with the use of an elephant, he gave up. A short while later he met with an accident and died.

Each year, on the anniversary of the laying of the pillars, the townsfolk enact a ceremony which culminates in a boat passing the canal beside the pillars to cleanse the spirits of the place. The boat floats out to sea and sinks.

A Tour of Thonburi

I left home in the dark of a Sunday morning. It was almost chilly at this hour and just beginning to get light as I parked and got out of the car at Wat Prayurawong, the main family temple. I had been there many times, for family ceremonies, and at least one cremation but never to explore properly. The most prominent structure in the temple compound is a towering white Singhalese-style stupa, which can be seen from the Chaophraya River, and in Bangkok proper, where it looms mirage-like directly at the end of Sanam Chai, as that road heads west along the edge of the Grand Palace. In the 1980s, pre-restoration, the stupa of Wat Prayurawong leaned precariously to one side, and was grey with city dirt and tropical fatigue. Now brilliant in the sunlight, the new white coat shrouds a family past, almost all of the dedicatory inscriptions on its exterior have been covered up with plaster and paint.

By the gates of Wat Prayurawong, as the temple begins, is a small park-like area. This temple garden features a rather pungent turtle pond surrounding a miniature mountain.

The park was largely the work of two men. Dit, my ancestor, who built the temple and the artificial mountain in the 1830s, and Pon, his youngest son, a flamboyant figure who would eventually be known as Chaophraya Bhaskorawong. Pon's numerous inclusions to the park came half a century after its creation, and suggest a political significance, and a desire to redesign a narrative.

As I passed Pon's pavilion at the garden entrance, I pictured him as caricatured by Vanity Fair in 1879 – dressed in his sartorial invention, a jaunty combination of billowing Siamese trousers and European dress jacket.

Close to this shelter, once called "Sala Farang", is a bizarre object made from three down-facing cannons embedded in a hefty block. This commemorates an accident in which several people were killed at the temple's inauguration after an old cannon that was being used for fireworks exploded. It was made by Dit in 1836 and originally displayed beside the temple's stupa, but Pon relocated it to the garden.

I searched in vain for the bronze busts of Bunnag patriarchs I recalled from childhood. Instead I noticed a row of empty plinths, now covered with flowerpots. While I was exploring, a monk called to me. A large old turtle had wedged itself into one of the bushes, I helped to pull it free and release it, with the monk whispering, "sathu, sathu," in gratitude.

At the other side of the garden, which is not large, is a small gothic-style chapel with flying buttresses, and spires. A monk at the temple, called Phra Ieng, who deals with Bunnag family matters, had told me that the building's Buddha image was in fact a disguised sculpture of ancestor Dit.

The light was still dim as I stood before the seated figure that dominates the structure. Hovering halo-like behind the statue's head is a wall plaque. I strained in the gloom to read its ornate English calligraphy, "Sacred in the memory of Somdech Chow Phya Parama Maha Prayurawongse (sic). The Great. Erected in filial piety by Phya Bhasakorawongse. 1885. "

The statue, becoming secular, presented an earthy and worldly form, with even the gold-leaf, so typical of Buddha images, shifting in meaning. The statue's robes were no longer ascetic but sumptuously draped over the splayed legs of a magnate, whose hands and feet were weighty in experience and power. Made 30 years after his death, I wondered if an original statue of Dit had been repurposed, or if the craftsmen had worked from another image, since lost, representing a faithful version of the patriarch's face.

I soon left, mutely and uncertain. At a small gateway, I exited and crossed a road, in order to take a photo of the artificial mountain, now catching the morning light. I then turned towards Memorial Bridge, with my mind on the family migration from the Bangkok side of the river to these parts. It is known that after "Mom" Bunnag's residence beside the Grand Palace was taken back by the crown, his two prominent sons, Dit and Tat, moved across the river. Dit, my ancestor, built his house where the main supports for the bridge now stand.

I speculated that when the family property in Bangkok was destroyed, Dit must have tried to salvage materials. His father, Bunnag, had built that compound, and would himself have brought things down from Ayutthaya to erect his houses, things from ancestral homes in Ayutthaya, parts of the old city that had value and significance.

I had been reading what I could find about the old properties, and was discovering the subject to be a treacherous terrain, crossed by labyrinthine pathways. It is not clear which lands were owned by the old Ministries of Trade and War, the "Phraklang" and "Kalahom", positions held in a semi-hereditary manner by the Bunnags, and which plots belonged to the family in a more conventional sense; it might even be said that by design the family belonged to the Ministries of this epoch, and vice versa. The line between the two seemed impossibly blurred, with interpretation inviting anachronistic judgment – what was clear was that the area was developed and exploited thoroughly by the families of the "Somdets" Ong Yai and Ong Noi (Dit and Tat Bunnag) between the 1820s and early 20th century.

The first family home on this bank of the river was Dit's mansion, which stood roughly between the years 1818 and 1930, and was in turn taken back by the state through imminent domain. I wondered if the rubble from the old buildings was used in the foundations of the bridge, or in the filling up of the canals, that were now beneath the roads running through this area.

As I made my way down the bridge steps, a young man came running at me, his eyes narcotic bright. He paused before approaching. I sensed ill-intent, and I quickly turned, pointed in the air and exclaimed, then dashed back up the steps; my eccentricity baffled him, he smiled and ran on past in fresh distraction, to some other unforeseen trouble.

I surveyed the zone around Memorial Bridge, which was taken up by the large piles of the structure, an underpass road, and a small park. Sheltered by the bridge, a homeless man was installed with his meagre possessions by the river-wall, water lapping beneath him. I turned to the sun-filled park to behold a girl sitting as though stunned by sadness, a teenager exuding unknown tragedy – unwholesome in the morning glow. Gazing between shadow and light, I thought of British envoy Sir John Bowring meeting Dit in this place, which was then a palatial residence. Bowring took note of a stone pillar in the house, with its carved inscription, "Peace be at thy gates." Nowadays, the park and some of the railings bear Dit's crossed pike emblem. This was all that remained, it was now a municipal space, neutral, unwelcoming.

I knew that in 1822 Dit had housed British envoy John Crawfurd by the river, at a place with its own pier. This was where I walked to next, heading north upriver – mindful of a piece I had come across in the *Journal of the Siam Society* written by R. Adey Moore in 1914. The article included essential details about the district that had been told directly to Adey Moore by Pon.

In the mid 1820s, a parcel of this land was rented to Scottish merchant-adventurer Robert Hunter, who set up his trading operations on these premises. Hunter had arrived with a cargo of muskets, which the Siamese bought and used against "Chao" Anu's Lao forces in the War of 1826-1828. The property was called by some the British Factory, and by the Siamese "Hang Huntraa", Hunter's Warehouse. It featured a simple European-style house between rows of brick "godowns". Hunter used the site for all manner of trading activities until 1844, when he was banished from the kingdom. The buildings were then repaired and set aside for receiving foreign dignitaries – Sir John Bowring stayed there in 1855 while negotiating the trade agreement. A party of Austrian envoys were housed in these digs in 1869, after which it was rebuilt again. Adjacent was another plot of land which was rented to the American Missionary Dr. Dan Beach Bradley for a time, until eventually the entire tract, comprising the former Residence for Foreign dignitaries and Bradley's original home, went to Pon, who built an even grander residence on the riverside, making use of parts of Hunter's original building. The breathless history of the plot, which is absolutely unremarkable these days, ends with Pon's house taken over by the Department of Irrigation, and the riverside mansion torn down.

On this site now stands the Crime Suppression Department (presumably the heir of the old Irrigation Department), it is a blocky and towering edifice from the 1990s. As I passed, men with crew cuts dressed in semi-official mufti were standing around chatting in the shade of a side alley.

Across from here, as I went, was a vacant plot of land, walled in by rusting corrugated iron. Some of the sheets had slipped; I glimpsed a verdant, overgrown patch of land, strewn with rubbish. The rest of the area was built up, covered in poorly constructed shop houses. There was nothing old or durable standing, apart from some trees dotted about in the urban sprawl.

I headed back to the temple, where uncle Tatiya was waiting for me by the car park. He is a tall and distinguished looking man, he has the rank of Admiral, is a Munich-trained dental surgeon, and the family memory.

Brushing off my blather about my impressions of the locale, Tatiya handed me his father's funeral book, which included a history of the temple. Not wanting to waste time, with so much to impart, he began by steering me into one of the viharas, a large monastic hall. The room had been restored some years back. The walls were white-washed, plain, the centre piece an enormous stone Buddha image, to which, Tatiya said, people pray to get pregnant. The Buddha image was a twin to another at Wat Suthat across the river, both brought down by Dit from the ancient city of Sukhothai during the reign of King Rama III.

Standing in front of the entrance to the hall, he pointed up at the decorated door lintel. It featured a phoenix, a family symbol in its relationship to fire and the sun. Within the design were swords, axes and symbols of power, intimating the temple's worldly functions. Dit's family and their allies would be ordained at the temple, it was a way of sanctifying and solidifying political connections.

Again, we left the temple park through its small gateway, this time lost in a conversation becoming locomotive, our speech powered by anecdote and opinion, the streets rolling with names and impressions – brilliant Pinklao, who had been the Second King of Mongkut's era, Damrong's account of the Front Palace Incident, Kukrit Pramoj's book *Skeletons in the Cupboard*, Kham residing, childless, in Nakhon Pathom, family blood connections to King Taksin through the Komarakhun Na Nakorn family. In the spirit of our conversation, time disappeared. Tatiya told me about exploring Wat Buppharam, another family temple, with Tula in the 1980s as if it had been yesterday.

Tatiya had some old maps to aid our journey through the past. We stopped near the river for him to point out the less obvious changes that have occurred over the years – in particular the loss of antique waterways, which would have made more sense of the district's plan, enabling easy access to the temples and houses from the great transport artery of the river. I inquired tentatively about the rift between the branches of the family, a schism between Dit and Tat I had heard attributed to professional rivalry, financial misgivings and possibly the hand of Dit in the execution of Tat's first son. Sanit, who would by tradition have been Tat's main heir, was put to death for an affair with a royal lady. More tangibly, it was well known that Dit's son Chuang had acted against Tat's trade interests, but if there was a political distance between the two families, there was also much shared blood.

To prove this point, as we came once again to the old bridge, Tatiya pointed out the property to our left. The area represented the extremity of Dit's lands, and had belonged to a family who were descended from both Dit and Tat; the territory was now occupied by forlorn buildings which gaze at the bridge's U-turn, therefore signifying a merging of geographical and genetic heritage.

The knowledge imparted to me added texture and exquisite detail, but not clarity. As we departed the bridge area, Tatiya asserted that, long before its demise, Dit had built a second home for himself at some point, but its exact location was a mystery.

We walked towards Wat Pichaiyat, the temple of Tat, Dit's brother, stopping along the way at Wat Anongkharam, built by Tat for his mother. At Anongkharam a Chinese ceremony was underway, prayers beating out of a large sound-system in the courtyard, and a small crowd of devotees all dressed in red. By the entrance, a sad laminated photo of the place in the old days – of this street scene, only two stone pillars connect past and present. At Wat Pichaiyat, climbing the Prang, its Khmer-style stupa, a sudden splatter of pigeon shit landed at our feet – as if a warning from one branch of the family to another.

As we walked, the sun got stronger. I was now sweating, and grateful for the hat I decided to bring. Tatiya talked about the peculiarities of Thai history. He pointed to the long canal running beside us, Khlong Somdet Chaophraya. The canal must have been dug during the reign of Rama IV or V, and yet no records seem to exist documenting its construction or purpose. Although popularly believed to have been built for the shipyards, its function was unclear, since the docks were much closer to the main river, and would not have needed this backwater. As we meandered along the noisy street, Tatiya observed that people were willing to believe that there was a curse of King Taksin on Bangkok, but they were not willing to look at, or trust, actual historical records and documentation. There was more interest in prolonging ghost stories than in preserving the smaller monuments of Bangkok and Thonburi.

Our journey ended at Pajjamitr Fort. Built by one of our mutual ancestors, Chuang, it had once controlled the strategic bend in the Chaophraya River, in the star-shaped style of Vauban. Only a small segment remains, it has long since lost its command of the river, being now boxed in on all sides by buildings. Today the space serves on one side as a parking lot and the other as a miniature public park, boasting a number of built-in exercise machines.

Dit's Life and Times

Dit's life straddles the 18th and 19th centuries, the leap between the two being greater than the years. The changes that were to occur from the beginning of Dit's life to the end were equal to a millennial shift.

But he is not a passive object of time's vicissitudes; his ambitions and personality would bend the era to his needs. Dit is the family patriarch, without whom there is nothing. His achievements were considerable. Together with his brother, Tat, he carved out a large family fiefdom on the western bank of the Chaophraya River, opposite Bangkok, and transformed trade and Siamese maritime activity. His success came largely without the direct patronage of his father and uncle, who were both dead by the time he was 22. At 34 he was Minister of Trade, and by 36 running the Ministry of War concurrently.[1] He built himself a mansion, a temple, warehouses, shipyards, and residences to receive foreign dignitaries, and in Chantaburi he constructed fortifications. He married Lady Chan, the daughter of the Minister of Lands, and first cousin of his friend, the general Chaophraya Bodindecha, Singh Singhasaeni. Dit took other wives called Rot, Yai, Prang, Ges, Tabtim, Pung, Gorn Thong, Sai Bua, Tap, Sun, Klai, Run, In, Pan, Muang, Sap, Tomya, Kaew, Bua, Yeam, Plap, Pum, and Klan. King Rama II gave him Ges and Pung, while Rot and Yai had been given by princes. In his later years Dit was known as Ong Yai, which means Elder Prince, and he was the first to be granted the use of the solar chariot as his seal.

The lists of events, and dates, and building works cannot adequately conjure a feeling of his times.

Imagine a book.

The book is a scruffy thing, many pages are missing, the cover is ragged, there are spaces where some of the images have fallen out. The frontispiece is a hand-drawn portrait, the only actual picture we have of this great man. This drawing has been touched up many times over the years, the lines and shading are heavy handed, accentuating the older man's stern visage.

The album features yellowing clippings in English. The entries begin in the 1820s and end in 1855.

In the first of these Dit is about 33 years old and the year is 1821. He is the acting Minister of Trade, with the title Phraya Suriyawong Montri, which means counsellor of the lineage of the sun. Dit is meeting the British envoy John Crawfurd. He provides Crawfurd and his entourage with accommodation on his property. They are far from happy with the building, which is small and enclosed, and not nearly as pleasant as Dit's own home.[2]

It is remarked[3] that Dit will not suffer to have the foreigners above his head, and visits their house through an upstairs window by way of a ladder, in order to avoid ascending from the floor beneath their impure bodies.

Crawfurd's party is surprised when later Dit is seen grovelling before his patron, Prince Chetsadabodin, who will soon be King Rama III.[4] Foreigners are generally taken aback by Siamese protocol – they find it overly subservient.

On another occasion, Dit receives the envoys at his residence. Here he is haughty and proud, he makes them sit on the floor and talks about the purchase of arms through British India.

Crawfurd is visited by a Lao prince, called Anu, who bows respectfully in the direction of Dit's home. It is thought he was there to buy guns from the British, which he intends to use in a rebellion against the crown.

A snippet from a later traveller, Frederick Arthur Neale,[5] is several pages away in this book. It is now 1840. Many years have passed since Anu's war against the Siamese. The speed of Anu's campaign had taken Bangkok by surprise and sent them into a panic. By ruse, Anu managed to seize Khorat, Bangkok's military headquarters in the northeast, and at the same time dispatch crack troops to free his compatriots in Saraburi, who had been settled there by Rama I. The Siamese defeat him; led by Bodindecha, they have better guns, and drag Anu back to Bangkok. Anu is blinded and put in a cage, which hangs just above the river. He is tortured for days until he gives up the ghost. Many of his relatives are also executed. Neale recounts how the stretch of river bank, which is directly across the river from Dit's house, is considered cursed; the Siamese will not tarry there, nor moor their house boats around this location.[6]

The next entry is from a newspaper, the *Singapore Chronicle* of the 22nd of November 1832. The piece is penned by J.H. Moore, an Englishman. It describes the arrival of captured Malays at the warehouses beside Dit's mansion. There are thousands of them, it is a sorrowful and distressing account of a people taken in war, maltreated and destined for slavery. Many of them are settled on Dit's land. They will form a community called Ban Khaek, Muslim Village; among their number are many skilled goldsmiths.

There is a companion piece by J.H. Moore in which Dit is described, in highly unflattering terms, in the preceding Malay campaign. He has been sent to quell rebellion, and devastates the region.

The next two pieces are by Americans, Edmund Roberts and W.S.W. Ruschenberger, in Siam on treaty missions in 1833 and 1836,[7] respectively. Roberts records Dit as 55 years old, when in fact he was 45. He is described as heavy and unwieldy, sitting bare-chested on crimson velvet cushions. In front of him are gifts from the king. He is now Lord of both Trade and War, referred to as Phraklang. On the walls of his reception room are English prints of battles and pastoral scenes, alongside Chinese screens and mirrors.[8] He invites Roberts to a family ceremony, a ritual hair cutting for two of his sons and a nephew.[9] The Americans are expected to help with the refreshments and provide wine.[10]

In another work by Roberts, entitled *Embassy to The Eastern Courts*, Dit is described passing by each morning at half past eight, on his boat. He is seated on a palanquin in the vessel, ready to be carried straight from the boat and onwards to court. He is shaded by umbrellas and attended to by slaves. As he goes, people crouch low in fearful homage.[11]

The American missionary, Howard Malcolm, stopping in Bangkok on his grand tour of Asia in 1839, has Dit asking questions about the death of the Burmese monarch, and showing off gem stones, all accompanied by a Siamese orchestra, "playing in a manner far from disagreeable".[12]

A scribe keeps record of every word uttered. Meetings are noted down, and read back for accuracy. These minutes are kept, presumably, against frail recall, and prejudice. The king's ministers are his embodiment, they save him the discomfort of audiences and they spare time. The records are for repetition, but it is not known if they are for posterity. Malcolm sees the scribe using Latin script to write Thai, later he remarks that a printing press, equipped with typefaces imported from Italy, produces Thai books in these Roman transliterations.

The city is a place of business, full of jostling boats, commerce, bustle, graced by transcendence and weighted by stretches of ennui. From Ruschenberger, comes a delight in the lighted torches of "sweet smelling agila wood" that illuminate the pathway as he leaves the home of Tat, Dit's brother.[13]

Neale first encounters Bangkok at night, with its myriad lanterns swaying from floating houses and temples, "the most striking, the most beautiful panorama I had ever witnessed."[14] He wakes the next day to disappointment, "the town looks as a supper room does the morning after a ball; there was nothing left of the feast save the odds and ends; jellies had melted to nauseous-looking water, and gaily-ornamented cakes crumbled into indescribable pieces of nastiness. So it was with Bangkok, as the first light of morning enabled us to obtain an obscure glimpse of the long range of floating houses that lined the river on either side. By night they looked gaudy enough and sufficiently brilliant in our uninitiated imagination to have risen up into stately palaces, glittering with the golden light of the sun's early ray; in the morning they appeared a nondescript confusion of cabins, pagodas, junks, canoes, vessels, fishing-boats, rafters, and rafts, and heavy-looking piles of bamboo and timber".[15]

Neale lives on Dit's property; he drinks, he is bored, he waits for the afternoon breeze, on which he bestows the Anglo-Indian nickname "the doctor". Seasonal storms rage through his text with Munchhausen-like intensity, pulling doors out of their frames.

The last words about Dit, in this scrapbook, come from Sir John Bowring, in 1855. By this point Dit has the exalted title Somdet Chaophraya Prayurawong. He has only months left to live.

"Paid, at five o'clock, a visit to the Somdetch. Soldiers presented arms at the entrance of his palace; and in the inner court were guards, clad in yellow, bearing pikes. The Kalahom and Phra Klang were there. Tea and sweetmeats, and cigars, as usual, and crowds of prostrate attendants of different ranks. There were twenty or thirty children, almost naked, at his right hand. He is sixty-eight years old, and he told us he had one hundred living descendants, many of the fourth generation. He spoke of trade as the source of riches, and said he had five ships, trading with China, Singapore and Java. He said he had not received any orders from the king on the subject of the Treaty. He asked if I had seen his temple and gardens, and promised to send us a guide to accompany us thither to-morrow morning at six o'clock. He grew coffee and would send a sample."

"April 7. We walked around the Somdetch's garden; it is large and wild, had a good deal of coffee growing of which he sent me two bags as a sample."[16]

The Upper Terrace

The way to the upper level at the house is via an argument. According to anecdote, Saengarun Ratkasikorn of Chulalongkorn University's Architecture Faculty was an old family friend, and rather temperamental. He designed most of the house but ran out of inspiration for the stairs. He could not agree with Tula, who ended up having to design the three staircases himself. Perhaps this explains the disconnection between the two halves of the house.

Upstairs is a large terrace. It is effectively an elevated courtyard measuring about 20 by 20 metres. Buildings enclose three sides. The square is completed by a small pavilion sheltering a rain-drum, and a walkway to a building beyond. As a boy, I used to play by the rain-drum, tracing its bronze features with my finger.

The terrace is paved with hexagonal terracotta tiles, at the centre of which is a fenced off light-shaft, giving onto the fishpond below.

The space is exotic in a heady, intoxicating manner – hemmed by the kilted roofs of the houses, with their dragon scales and flourishing wooden "sky-tassels", those distinctive Siamese finials. The top of a tree joins the terrace beside the rain-drum. Its dark green leaves have serrated edges and a sandpapery texture. Tula told me that people once used this kind of leaf to brush their teeth, which was why they had such white teeth, and that cousin Jaru had attempted to clean his television with them and had completely destroyed the surface of the screen.

Large antique pots adorn the edges of the terrace, and small potted plants: euphorbias called "crown of thorns", or "Bouy Sian" in *Siamesed* dialect Chinese – meaning "Eight Divinities", that will confer good fortune. There is also a bench and those contentious flights of stairs leading down at three corners of the terrace.

Sunsets are spectacular – the silhouetted Thai forms of the roofs framed by celestial panoramas of peach, apricot, rose, and sometimes those seams of mother-of-pearl clouds that I have only seen in Thailand.

The outer wall of the shrine room, next to the entrance to the drawing room, featured panels of carved flowers, in bas-relief. Dad had done one of them; in one of those rare moments when he could sit and do something amicably with his father, who did the other carving there.

When it rains the staff let large, dark green tarpaulins down to protect the exposed antechambers to the rooms. It is always menacing entering behind these heavy curtains, the trapped space between the tarp and the door is still and dark.

After dinner, Tula would walk around the terrace, claiming its health benefits. He conducted this in silence, in a serious manner, making many circles of the sky yard. This post-dinner circumambulation became a tradition after Tula died, and has been carried over to my dad's in Catalonia, performed with jocular deliberation.

I remember, on one of those first visits, Chancham letting the dogs out of her room, opening the heavy teak door, the dogs hopping over the ledge and running across the brightening morning terrace.

By the final years the terrace stairs are fenced off. The dogs have taken to peeing on the drawing room veranda, which is not water tight, and urine drips through onto the seating in the downstairs area. The easy solution is to rig up a low barrier made of plastic corrugated sheeting and bamboo. The dogs are barred but it is ugly and adds an extra, awkward, hurdle to get up and down stairs. However, by this point I am the only person using the upper part of the house.

On one trip I had stayed longer than usual due to a tragedy. Dimitri, one of my oldest Greek friends, was killed in a terrorist attack in Bali. He was on the way to see me. I went over to Bali, the day after the bombing, in the hope of finding him, it was chaotic in the first days, but it was too late. When I got back to Thailand I was not in a good place – I got into the habit of doing evening exercises on the upper terrace of the house to clear my head. I would use a skipping rope to work up a sweat. Chancham told me that, as a girl, she used to watch her uncle doing his exercises. She mimed his motions as she spoke. He was a tough man, who had been a student in England in the 1950s. He was macho, and would often get into fights. After an incident, involving dragging another Thai student behind a car, two policemen were sent to arrest him. He fought them off, but one of the bobbies knew Judo and overcame him. He was deported and ended up in the Thai Army commanding a tank corps, or so the story ends.

Chancham's mimicked callisthenics recall the "exercises" she did on long-haul flights, movements she said were essential for her fitness and well-being, and consisted of rolling motions of her hands and fingers, from the wrist, back and forth.

Dit's Folly

When one of the Royal White elephants died on the 19th of June 1824, King Rama II was shaken by the bad omen. White elephants cannot be bred. They are found in the wild and symbolise divine favour, and royal legitimacy. The presentation of such a sacred being to the king is a great honour. Only the most meritorious of individuals can hope to own a White elephant.

Other elephants are classified as "Samkan", or special, with unusual features such as darker skin or elegant tusks but the White elephant is the most sought after by far, and its verification and appraisal is an exhaustive process. The Siamese consider their methods of selection to be more stringent than that of their neighbours. It is not simply a matter of pigmentation. In order to qualify, the elephant is evaluated and measured to a precise degree. If such creatures are inducted into the royal stables as calves, which is rare, they might have lullabies sung to them. They receive noble titles, and are fed special food.

To offset the misfortune, heralded by the elephant's death, King Rama II sent his son, Prince Mongkut, to be ordained as a monk.[1] At the time, Prince Mongkut was his likely successor, but an elder half brother, Prince Chetsada, was more powerful. A few weeks later the king sickened, he soon lost the power of speech and passed away on the 21st of July. A council was convened and it was decided that Prince Chetsada would be the next king. Prince Mongkut remained in the monastery for 27 years, for the entirety of Chetsada's reign as King Rama III.

Dit had been close to Prince Chetsada since childhood. They were the same age and cousins. After a joint coming of age ordination at Wat Phlap they worked together in the trade department, where Prince Chetsada was Minister. Dit was his director of port operations, and together they embarked on a number of ventures involving the outfitting of merchant ships and lucrative trade with China.[2]

By 1819 Dit was acting Minister of Trade, integral in the treaty negotiations with the Portuguese that year; the land grant for the Portuguese consulate was signed over by Dit. In 1822 Prince Chetsada passed control of the Trade Ministry to Dit, who would be called Phraklang, as the Ministry was known, until his death in 1855.

Dit and his brother Tat were instrumental in the accession of Prince Chetsada. They promised to bring their men to Chetsada's aid if the succession was contested. The brothers were rewarded for their actions, becoming King Rama III's dominant ministers. But the elaborate, circular, pattern of Dit and Tat's actions was only visible many years later, when they brought their forces back again into the game of dynastic succession. Upon the death of King Rama III there was a fear that the king's sons would try to retain the throne, but Dit and Tat now threw themselves behind the cause of Prince Mongkut.[3]

Mongkut, as King Rama IV, elevated the two brothers to the princely rank of Somdet Chaophraya. Dit would be known as Ong Yai, elder prince, with regent-like responsibilities over the country. Tat would be Ong Noi, younger prince, regent of the capital.

• • •

Candles burnt perpetually in the bathroom of King Rama III's Chakraphatphiman Throne Hall. A mountain of melted wax had formed in this room. Dit was entranced by this object and had it replicated on a gargantuan scale in stone, in the northeast corner of his temple grounds. The ceremonial hill is 20 metres high, irregular in shape, and is adorned with grottoes and decorative trees. It is at once a sacred mountain and a feature of classical Thai pleasure gardens.

Frederick Arthur Neale, in his account of 1840s Bangkok, wrote that King Rama III liked to work at night, while it was cooler.[4] It is tempting to see the structure as a monument to all the candle-lit work Dit did with the king over the years, and as a symbol of gratitude.

The mountain can be read in multiple ways. It is a curio, a monument to royal service, and a cautionary gesture. The mound of wax is magnified, dwarfing the visitor, signifying a greater and larger power above – making the individual a plaything to be grasped, devoured or given succour by the giant's hand.

Lunch with Tej

My uncle Tej is an historian. We are having lunch in a French restaurant not far from his office. He listens to me with amusement while I try to sketch out the outline of the Bangkok curse. The laying of the city pillar was tainted, a rumour spread some time after the event that the dynasty would last for 150 years. This had been triggered by a lightning strike on the newly constructed throne hall, and was attributed to Princess Narinthorn Thewi, who was an elder sister of King Rama I. In the early 1930s, with the fatal approach of 150 years, two buildings had been commissioned in the hope of warding off bad luck, the Memorial Bridge and a building in the grounds of the Red Cross compound where Tej works.

"I have never heard about the Red Cross connection but I will look into it. Best if you write all of this down and send it to me and I will try to get back to you. Better still include notes, but it might take a while because I've been asked to write the introduction to a book on the foreign policy of King Rama III," he tells me.

• • •

That morning I had arrived at the Red Cross compound 20 minutes early. I wanted to locate the building relating to the old prophecy. The folklore is hydra-headed, a confused and persistent creature of fabulous dimensions. One version includes human sacrifice, another tells that the ritual founding of Bangkok was blighted by the appearance of four snakes, which slithered beneath the sacred city pillar as it was laid. The blood of the snakes had sealed misfortune into the city's future. The serpent tale connected dynastic doom to the Chinese zodiac of King Rama VII and four of his closest advisers, all born under the Snake sign. Rumour had it that the snake farm building at the Red Cross had been put up as a propitiatory act by King Rama VII's four companions to avert disaster.

I walked around aimlessly hoping to stumble on a plaque, or a clue about the ritual structure. At the snake farm the guard was waiting by the turnstiles for visitors to the show. The place was empty. Finding nothing, I recalled a trip to the snake farm in 1982. I am a child. The crowd leans over the pit to see the show, I watch a cobra winding its way up a ladder by my feet. In this garish memory, the huge hand of a faceless official snatches it away in the nick of time.

Across the way and some flights up, I found Tej sitting behind his desk. The office had a few things on display. To one side there was a large engraved marble plaque, I didn't get a chance to read, and at the end of the room a framed document displaying calligraphic script, which looked almost like a graduation diploma. It was from Pope Francis to Tej.

Tej seemed thinner, and frailer than when I had last seen him in passing at a cremation. He is in his late 70s and looks well. His skin is almost without a wrinkle, but his hair is greyer than before. Although they did not look alike when they were younger, the resemblance between my father and Tej is increasing over time. Tej has more of Tula, something of his physique and facial shape. Dad has his mother's nose and brows.

Chancham called dad, "the prodigal one". The brothers have had very different lives. She used to joke that one of her sons was an Ambassador of the Kingdom of Thailand and the other Ambassador of the Lord Buddha.

It feels somewhat strange to share family intimacy with my uncle. My experience of Tula and Chancham is so coloured by my father that it is hard to see the relationship outside of this framework. I know dad's anecdotes and where he was at a given time, but I know far less of Tej. I have a memory of Tej coming round to visit Chancham, while I was staying with her, but I can't say if it's in the last year of her life or earlier. They are together in the library, talking and laughing, sharing jokes. There is such unique tenderness and complicity; I am a spectator.

Tej began by giving me Chancham's translation of the Thai classic *Prisna* by Princess Vibhavadi Rangsit, that had recently been republished. He also handed me a short book he helped produce on Thai-Burmese diplomatic relations, "this might interest you, it gives an idea of how they used to do things at the Foreign Ministry."

To my surprise, I have been in almost daily contact with Tej for months. When I wrote to him, saying that I wanted to put together an anecdotal history of the family, he didn't hesitate. I have been curious for many years about how the larger historical picture relates to the personal. As I expressed my gratitude, he insisted that it had been a pleasure, it refreshed his memory and caused him to look back at his papers to check things. That morning he had stumbled on a note that great-grandfather Tom was attacked in Parliament in 1934 for something to do with a government rubber purchase.

Tej's career bears similarities with that of his grandfather Tom. Educated at Malvern College, then King's Cambridge followed by the Ministry of Foreign Affairs, they both held Ambassadorships in the United States and China, both became Foreign Minister. There is much more besides that is less symmetrical.

• • •

The restaurant is an atmospheric place, with a few older French expatriates sitting at the bar, an ideal setting for talk about the past. Tej introduces me to the owner, "c'est mon neveu," who asks if I speak French, "like the rest of the family?"

Tej and my dad had the same education, English boarding school and then Cambridge, with compulsory Latin and French up to the first year of University – and equally fraught relations with their father.

As with so much else in life's patterning, the experience of one brother from the next is different and distinct. Inconsequential details represent rotations around time like a narrative trick in fiction, a Rashomon effect.

Tej read History at King's where he was an Exhibitioner, which gave him a grant of 80 pounds a year, and better rooms, with central heating. The hierarchy was Scholar, Exhibitioner, Commoner. He chuckled when he recounted that the Scholar's rooms were so unhealthy that Cambridge council had them condemned at some point. Water would seep down the walls, and freeze in the winter.

I had once asked his first wife, Jane, what he had been like as a young man. "I thought he was the smartest man in his college, the best dressed, and he always knew what was going on. Charming."

They met at Cambridge, before Tej began his D.Phil at St Antony's, Oxford. Initially he had been drawn to the history of Ayutthaya in the 17th century, focussing on Constantine Phaulkon and the later period of Narai's reign. Then, on closer examination, he decided that the period of reform under King Rama V was more interesting, and exciting. David Wyatt had already written his thesis on Education Reform, and Wyatt would be his advisor. Tej's thesis was to become a book, *The Provincial Administration of Siam 1892-1915*, and it is something of a classic.

Thai history, he warns me, is prone to factionalism; as in other spheres of life conversations quickly become quarrels, which lead to persecutions and prosecutions. In addition, he goes on, history, here and elsewhere, is on the decline. Students are more interested in light economic history, and marketing. The whole field is becoming unrecognisable. And yet, ironically, the Thai past, which is often glossed over, and crudely drawn, has become so topical.

In 1932, which was 150 years after the founding of Bangkok, and in rhyme with the prediction, the system of Absolute Monarchy in Siam came to an end. Over the last couple of years there has been a small but vociferous conflict raging about the events of 1932, and the treatment of various monuments relating to this time. It is a subject that has raised the nation's blood pressure.

Currently 1932 is summarised as a battle between Reactionary and Progressive forces, in which the king's supreme power was curbed by a swift and bloodless coup by Western-educated reformists. Some historians hold the view that 1932 was not a real Revolution. Power was divided between conservative factions, and the military, thereby evoking the status quo before the reign of King Rama V.

As we depart from the restaurant, the owner hands me a name card and we make our way back down the alleyway, with its shuttered go-go bars, towards Surawong Road. Amazingly, given the pandemic, one of the titty bars is open. Three bored girls are sitting outside, they call to us as we pass, and I hear something obscene.

Standing on Surawong Road, which was built by its namesake, my great-great-grandfather, Tej tells me that when he was a boy the top of Surawong Road was an area for grazing cattle. Another relative had an enormous house around there and when Tej would pass with his step-grandmother, Lady Ruen, she would be very disapproving, saying that this man had too many wives. Tej of course was too young to know what she meant.

His kindergarten was nearby, along Rama IV Road which is now a multilane, and there was a canal, that connected to those of Silom and Sathorn. Across the road, from the top of Surawong, was another canal running alongside what is now Henri Dunant; the road was once called Newman's Mile, after a British Consul General, and it is still exactly one mile long.

I receive an email a few days later; Tej has discovered that the old snake farm building was opened in 1930, but torn down and rebuilt in 2008. The Thai Red Cross journal of October 1998 denied any linkage to the City Pillar story.

The Master Bedroom

An image is lodged in my mind. It's a black and white photograph of a room, in which a man is looking out of a window, while a shadowy form lingers in a doorway to one side. The two figures are slightly blurred, either artistically or by my own poor recollection. The scene sounds dull but the picture is eerily strong, in tone and composition, and in mystery. The photograph hangs just inside the entrance to my grandparents' bedroom, it was taken by Chancham, of Tula looking out at the Old Brompton Road in London. The image somehow recalls the contradictory aspects of a space that was both filled with propriety – being the master bedroom – and comforting – being a family refuge in a large house.

As tensions eased between my dad and his parents, I was sent to stay with them. It was an opportunity for us to grow closer, and Tula and Chancham did their best to make up for lost time. As a boy, I would often sleep in their room. Accordingly, the symbolic space of the main bedroom revolves around transmission – things said, imparted and intimated in the house's somnolent zone.

The room is a long rectangle, giving at one end onto a small dressing-room and the other a bathroom. After Chancham passed away, it is discovered that rats have eaten all of her clothes, the dressing-room cupboards are full of rags and scraps of fabric. The bathroom features some tiles depicting roosters, Chancham's zodiac sign, and a small bookshelf stuffed with detective novels by an author Tula favoured.

It is night and yellow lamp-light pools over Tula propped up in bed. Behind the bed is a ledge bristling with framed pictures, including one of the Crown Prince at the time, and small statues, Buddha amulets, and objects. An enlarged photo of my elder sister Tanya, as a baby, sits on the sideboard. It was taken in the English Fens after my parents moved back in 1975.

A radio hisses and wheezes. Tula, on his night bed, is tuning in to the BBC World Service with a small short-wave radio. The sound of the news-hour jingle, an imperial musical whirl, floats in the dense atmosphere.

Watching, and listening, are faces – portraits in pencil by Tula of Tej and dad, as boys, which hang low on the opposite wall. At the end far end of the room, is Lui, Chancham's father, in an oil painting by Chatchai Puipia (a nephew-in-law) done specifically for the funeral. Close by is an intricate drawing by Peter Bunnag, of cousin Jaru, as a little girl wearing a large hat – a note in his hand describes the happiness of an afternoon.

As well as the enigmatic image at the door, of the blurred figures – two more photos join this family gallery. Separate pictures in a matching pair, dad and Tej as boys standing in a London flat, in school uniform – shorts and v-neck sweaters. The boys are holding up trophies, Tej wears a delicate smile, dad looks reserved, his face a juvenile glower. I inquire and Chancham is beside me saying, "they both came home from school with prizes. Tej for a poetry recital, of Alfred Noyes' *The Highwayman*. Your father for boxing." She swings a punch in the air for emphasis. "I was so proud." It must be the mid 1950s, while Chancham was translating *Prisna* – a book Tej had brought over in his suitcase when they left Thailand.

The boys were initially sent to a school in South Kensington, where they lived. Dad insists that he is in a famous photograph by Henri Cartier-Bresson. The top of his cap is visible in a shot of English schoolboys being marched along a west London street. Dad came across it by chance in a magazine article about Bresson's series "The Europeans", and recognised the boys in the picture. In those days, dad had a psychopathic teacher with red hair, who hastened dad's grasp of English by hitting him every time he made a mistake.

Distant, in the dark of the room, in time – and in demeanour – are the tough-looking visages of Bunnag ancestors. These grace a large print from illustrations by Peter Bunnag. The first time I notice it, Tula stands with me, and explains the line of descent. Chuckling as he points out Mom Bunnag, Dit, Chuang, Won, " this is your great-great-great-great-great, are you following? It's five greats now..." Reaching his era, Tula shakes his head. "Look, Peter has drawn in himself. You know the line should go in our direction, because we have the last Chaophraya in the family." Peter's chart describes a shift from the fabled to the everyday. I take in the awkward permutation, from the ancient grandees in exotic garb, to the European dress of the 19th century, into the bespectacled and suited relatives of today.

The room is a swirling fuzz of small innocuous details and uncertainties: a small black-board, with wooden finials either side, which taper inwards and have beautifully turned ends where Chancham writes her weekly engagements, a Chinese cabinet, its top piled with papers, a view onto the small house and the bamboo grove, book titles, *May We Borrow Your Husband?* by Graham Greene, and *The Bridge of San Luis Rey*, and *The Magic Mountain*, which I borrow, and return. A postcard stuffed inside the latter, of a Persian miniature, invites a thought about the endlessly replicated world inside the painted reproduction.

Out of this radio crackle, this white noise of memory – Tula's voice. It is the afternoon and he is attempting to transmit our family story, which seems to flow into his dreams – anecdotes about political rivals, and an enormous chandelier, a gift of ancestor Chuang to the king, become blended with Tula's desire to spend his final years gazing out at the Mediterranean, cooled by the summer breeze. He has harsh words for many of our relatives, but also fondness, and wants me to understand our collective story. At one point Tula matches his little finger to mine, the top notches on our pinkies curve inwards slightly, it is the same on dad's hand – we all have similar ears. Tula laughs.

• • •

The first trip to stay with Tula and Chancham occurred suddenly. It was a scorching September, a few days before school term began – the end of a Greek summer. I was 12, playing in our garden when the phone rang, and the plan was hatched.

On the flight over with my sister Tanya, I woke up with a start, a foretelling of adulthood, when all of a sudden you find yourself autonomous – orphaned by liberty. We had a stopover in Singapore, where a group of very short and wizened elders approached me and began to ask me questions in Malay.

When we landed in Bangkok we were taken to an immigration office to meet Tula and Chancham, our papers were checked there and Tula told me off for making an error. It was late at night. We got back to the house, which was to step back in time, and were put to bed in my grandparents' room. I slept on the bed next to Tula, Tanya and Chancham slept on mattresses on the floor, surrounded by dogs.

A few nights later – a ghost stands by the bookshelves, as if browsing. The figure of a man distinctly indistinct, as seen in the half-light of an unfamiliar room. The figure is in profile to me. I lie with my heart in my mouth, as still as possible. Tula is asleep on the other side of the tubular "Dutch wife" pillow. I cannot see my sister or Chancham on the floor. My mind takes in the details obsessively. The man wears brocaded clothing, the lower part gathered together by a belt, a sash, or a loose cloth like a sarong. The patterned shirt is tucked into this sash. I cannot make out the face, but he wears something on his head. Everything speaks of gold leaf, gilded fragility.

It moves slightly, I shiver in fear.

"Last night there was a ghost in the room." I say over breakfast. Tula glances at me, says something inaudible in Thai, and my grandparents continue with their day.

Chuang's Eclipse City

Chuang shone brightly – he can be seen but he is hard to make out, like the sun. This ambiguity of motive and meaning will characterise Chuang's history. Sir John Bowring, locked in Treaty talks with Chuang, would heap great praise on him while remarking, "Either he is a consummate hypocrite or a true patriot".[1]

Chuang steered the Sun Chariot of the state for a time. His final title would be Somdet Chaophraya Borom Maha Sri Suriyawong, approximately "Lord of the Sacred Sun Lineage", with solar insignia inherited from his father and bequeathed to all of his lineal descendants. He would also be known as "Phra Prasart",[2] a Pali title meaning, "He who commands."

It is casually said that Chuang presumed too much, went too far; and thus invited the enmity of peers, the estrangement of family members, and the distrust of higher powers – such hindsight obscures Chuang's nature. It would suggest that Chuang ought to have been more cautious, or more calculating, when what comes across consistently in Chuang's story is his confidence, and zest.

Chuang was born in 1808, and would have been acutely aware of the threat and opportunity the Western powers presented as they began to appear in Siam. Chuang was 11 years old when the Portuguese arrived. As Dit's eldest son, he had a lot of exposure to the foreigners, he would have been a teen when his father commenced negotiations with the British, first under John

Crawfurd, then Henry Burney. Chuang appears in the records of foreign captains and envoys, often being the first Siamese to receive them as their ships entered Paknam, at the mouth of the Chaophraya, and accompanying them, as was the custom, upstream in Siamese barges to Bangkok.

An exchange of correspondence from 1850 between American envoy Balestier, and the U.S. Secretary of State, John Clayton, shows Chuang (who is identified as the son of the Phraklang, and commander of Siam's naval forces) far from obsequious as he exercises his power. Chuang has insulted Balestier by leaving him unattended upon arrival, while taking the opportunity to interrogate Balestier's Chinese waiter about the American party's prior activities in Vietnam.[3]

Presumably this contact with the Europeans and Americans was an education that charged his fascination with the outside world. Chuang's desire to learn speaks of the autodidact, evidenced by a request to Bowring for books on gunnery and naval architecture.[4]

• • •

Although later considered a figure of conservatism, Chuang was a moderniser. He took a delight in technology and architecture that exceeded his duties as an official in the War Ministry, which handled the building of fortifications, and ships. As a youth, Chuang built a number of the dragon-headed royal barges,[5] and, in 1835, the first western-rigged boat in Siam.[6] Before his time the fleet was made of modified "fish-faced" junks with oarsmen for river navigation and sails allowing for ocean travel. Chuang designed the first European steamers with sails, side and stern-wheelers and corvettes – which are small, fast-moving gunboats. Frederick Arthur Neale intimates Chuang's potential, encountering in 1840 the village and naval yards at "Paklat Boon," downstream from Bangkok. "The dockyards are kept in excellent order and the whole town is neat and cleanly, rather a marvellous fact in these parts and solely attributable to the place being under the immediate supervision of Prenawi Consitt… he is a perfect European in manners, speaks English fluently, and has adopted the manners and customs and tastes of our country."[7]

Chuang would later be responsible for the construction of the Phadung Krung Kasem Canal, and he built Charoen Krung Road, making it a thoroughfare that could be used to subdue rebellions. Built straight and wide, it allowed for artillery volleys, with a defensive curve at the north end.[8] On Bangkok's river he erected the star-shaped Pajjamitr Fort, and in the provinces he had the Damnoen Saduak Canal dug, while putting up numerous buildings throughout the western provinces,[9] which were under his control.

Less than a kilometre from his father's temple, Wat Prayurawong, was an ancient monastery called Wat Dok Mai, the temple of flowers. It had been built centuries before, and Chuang, along with his half-brother Kham, decided to renovate it, ostensibly in memory of Chuang's mother Lady Chan. The restored temple was to be called Wat Buppharam,[10] also meaning Temple of Flowers.

At the end of King Rama III's reign there was disquiet once again surrounding the impending succession. Prince Mongkut, the most likely heir, had been a monk for almost three decades. He was close to Chuang; they had grown up together and had a shared interest in western culture. While Prince Mongkut had been a monk he had founded a Buddhist sect, Thammayut Nikaya, which was felt to be a purer, more rational form of Buddhism, eschewing some of the superstition and corruption found in some of the other schools. When Chuang founded Wat Buppharam as a Thammayut monastery, it was thought to signal his support for Prince Mongkut.[11] They used to meet at this monastery, according to legend, and it was there that Dit and Chuang made it clear that they would back Mongkut in the succession struggle brewing at the end of King Rama III's reign.

Having appointed a relative as governor, at this point Dit and Chuang had control of Paknam, a fort at the mouth of the Chaophraya River. This meant father and son could cut Bangkok off from the outside world at will. The pair also had control of most of the military forces, large amounts of munitions and vast political clout through family and business connections. King Rama III might have preferred for the crown to go to one of his sons[12] but Dit and Chuang took steps to weaken the position of these claimants. The principal western arms dealers were forbidden to supply anyone but Chuang, whose troops guarded Prince Mongkut. Dit made a statement before the assembled nobles that he would see to it that Prince Mongkut would be the next king, and anyone who disagreed should be prepared to take up arms against his forces.[13]

It was noteworthy that Mongkut invited the abbot of Wat Buppharam to attend his coronation. After his accession to the throne, Mongkut, as King Rama IV, would reward Dit with a supreme position, as elder statesman of the land. He would make Chuang the new Minister of War.

Relations between Mongkut and Chuang were not always good. Chuang may have hoped that the new king would adopt political reforms to match the opening of trade with the British.[14] This was not to be. Early in the reign the two men had a falling out, apparently over disagreements about taxation, and the details of the Treaty Chuang had negotiated with the British in 1855. King Mongkut was upset that Japan had been granted more favourable terms. Chuang is reported to have said, "kings who claim their title by right of birth often forget they originated from the people, consider themselves as superior beings and don't lend an ear to the sufferings of their subjects – so there was often a change at the fourth generation of princes of the same dynasty."[15]

However, the rift was soon healed and by the late 1850s Chuang was considered Mongkut's Prime Minister and right-hand man.

• • •

In August 1868 the king, along with over 1,000 members of the royal court, favoured members of his family, the Heir Apparent, foreign dignitaries, expatriate merchants, foreign naval officers and crew, travelled to a remote, uninhabited stretch of coast.[16]

Two years previously the king had discerned that within his kingdom there would be an important solar eclipse. He had made his calculations using both eastern and western methods. A proclamation was issued publicising his projections. It was clear that the greatest duration of this rare event would be on the seaboard west of the gulf. Having made their calculations independently, a team of astronomers set out from France in the hope of capturing this phenomenon.

The king was concerned about the prospect of a French warship visiting and surveying his southern coast. But the French would not be dissuaded. They insisted that since this would be the best place to view the eclipse, they must be granted access and space to make their calculations. As a counter balance, the British, under Governor Ord of the Straits Settlements, were invited to join, bringing a number of gunboats. All in all, there were 18 Siamese and British warships in the vicinity before the French arrived.

The site was a stretch of shore called Wa-ko, south of Petchburi Province, where thick jungle rolls down from the mountains to the sea. A French botanist, who visited for the eclipse, was able to collect 200 unknown plant specimens from the immediate environs during his short stay.

Chuang held control of the Siamese coastline, stretching down to the Malay regions of the south. He built a vast pleasure ground for the event. In the words of Malcolm Smith (in his memoire *A Physician at the Court of Siam*), "Out of the barren sands, almost overnight, sprang a noisy encampment, a straggling line of huts and buildings, spreading along the shore for a couple of miles."[17]

The folly town was made of wood, with some buildings three storeys high. Many roofed with thatch, while some were covered in fabrics that had been painted to look like the glazed tiles of Bangkok's monuments. There was a palace, with its own forecourt and a large audience hall, featuring a temporary throne. A kitchen had been set up under the command of a French chef, with 40 European and Chinese cooks at his disposal. Steamboats had been running in luxuries and supplies to the new wharfs for weeks, including a vast quantity of "the best procurable"[18] wine. There were also stables for 50 elephants, and many more horses.

The Prime Minister, Chuang, turned over most of the rooms in his house for uninvited and unexpected Europeans and Americans and their wives, keeping just a single bedroom for his own use. His reception room was said to have become a club for the foreigners.

In spite of the underlying tensions, the atmosphere was congenial and relaxed, like a picnic party. The rigid protocol and social hierarchy of Bangkok was suspended temporarily, with foreigners allowed to converse with royal princesses and consorts. The king's eldest son took the visitors for an outing on which they rode elephants.

On the 15th of August they celebrated Napoleon's fête day and on the 18th the entire encampment prepared their telescopes to view the celestial event. The morning did not start well. The weather was overcast but at just the right moment the clouds lifted.

It was a success. The king's calculations proved to be accurate. People noted that the years seemed to fall away from the Prime Minister during the eclipse and that he ran about like a young man, calling out to his wives to trust in foreign science, and dashing from his viewing station to the king's. It was said that Chuang hugged the king and they both cheered, shouting "Hurrah! Hurrah!" in English.[19] In the immediate aftermath talk was informal and jokes were exchanged.

The next morning the party gathered for a photograph. The

king is surrounded by foreign officers, to one side Siamese nobles pay homage on the ground.

The French steamer was the first to leave, heading for Saigon, followed by the British. After the guests had departed the "Town of the Eclipse melted away like a snow heap in the sun."[20]

But by the time the king reached Bangkok it was clear that he had contracted malaria from the jungle. He died not long afterwards.

Exploring Khlong San

Walking around Khlong San, the most historically Bunnag district, is also a journey into books and learning, the pulp and print of written material. The ancestral houses are largely gone, turned from residences to schoolhouses, and from those portioned up again into the concreteness of Thailand's Everywhere. Those private lands have now become messy neighbourhoods that look eternal, but have in fact sprung up over-night like mushrooms after a storm.

I turn into a quiet neighbourhood, around Wat Thong Nopphakhun. I am looking for an old school called Ban Phraya Nana. It was one of the first institutions to offer English instruction, and was the alma mater of Phya Anuman Rajadhon (1888-1969), the first Thai folklorist. There is no sign of it.

I view some young monitor lizards sunning themselves on the concrete embankments of a small stream. It is only as I leave the backstreets, and once again hit the busier Somdet Chaophraya Road, that I realise this is a district I had been pointed to by Tej, in search of other family stories. This was the birthplace of Chancham's colourful grandfather, Lek Samitasiri, who had been the eminent publisher of Rama VI's day, in the first decades of the twentieth century.

We always made much of Lek. The dinner chat conjured a first generation immigrant rising through the epoch to rank and wealth in Siam, unfairly transformed by loose talk into an opium lord, or a tax farmer. Tej set the record straight.

Lek was born in 1875, the son of Sunheng and Li. His parents were Chinese and died within 14 months of his birth, after which he was brought up by his maternal grandmother. He married a woman called Yin, who owned a publishing house, which together they turned into the Sophon Press in 1900, located on Rajbophit Road from 1906. The Sophon Press published many of King Rama VI's books, and works by Prince Damrong, the father of Thai history. Some titles include Damrong's, *A Historical Account of the Abolition of the Chinese Lottery* and *Gambling Houses in Siam* (1919), *Accounts of Various Travels* (1920), and *Conversations with a Thief in 1903* (1925).

My ambulating mind treads to Chancham at her dining table, handing me some notes. The pages are hard to follow, and I do not recognise that this will be her last translation work, unfinished, of Prince Damrong's last work, unfinished.

Lek earned the title Khun Sophon Aksornkit in 1919 (Khun is a Siamese title, not the same as Khun, the modern Mr or Mrs). Sophon means beautiful while Aksornkit can be broken into words for lettered and business – hence "beautiful publisher". He was promoted to Luang Sophon Aksornkit the following year and Phra Sophon Aksornkit in 1924, this final Phra being similar to Sir in English.

He had a large family. Chancham's mother was his second eldest, and favourite. She was one of seven children, four girls and three boys by the main wife. Lek also owned a theatrical troupe, which performed musicals and provided him with mistresses, who in turn gave birth to 16 of his children.

Lek's things were both beautiful and brash – a grand house at the top of Silom Road, with a billiards room, and a beautiful housekeeper who married the neighbour's son, which became the talk of the town. Lek had seven cars, one for each day of the week, painted in the astrologically auspicious Siamese colours of the weekdays – Monday, yellow, Tuesday, pink, and so on through green, orange, blue, purple, and red.

The Silom house was for his wife; he stayed at the old house with his mistresses, until his death in 1948. Tej remembered visiting the grand mansion on Rajbobhit Road and enjoying running around there as a child. He loved the smell and the noise of the printing presses. However, due to diabetes, Lek's legs had been amputated and he sat on the floor when Tej visited, it was a sad sight.

In the mid 1950s, the Sophon Press was sold to the Teachers' Association, along with the beautiful mansion, which burnt down shortly after. A part of the property was cut off for the grandmother's house, which still stands in a dilapidated state.

• • •

Khlong San is also a voyage through essays by David Wyatt I read years ago and barely grasped at the time. Wyatt's particular expertise was late 19th century Siamese education. I never paid much attention to these works, since he also wrote about family politics and these pieces described my ancestors and bloated my young ego, blunting my sensitivity to context and other more nuanced topics.

Wyatt's essay on the lost Ban Phraya Nana school sets it within a lineage. The building had belonged to a nobleman, Phraya Nanaphitpasi, a Bunnag. After his death the property was inherited by the crown, and it was decided that an existing school, temporarily located at Wat Prayurawong (Dit's temple) could be relocated to this property. Ban Phraya Nana School was opened in 1894, only to be closed in 1903.

It is doubtful, given the dates, that Lek attended this local institution. However, the tale of Ban Phraya Nana resonates gently, as Lek's house on Silom Road also became a school at some point before being torn down and eventually replaced by the Robinsons shopping mall.

I skip around obstacles as I go. A walk is motion, both physically and intellectually, all those sedentary hours reading about places and things and then referring back to them during the stroll, the peripateia. A phrase from Thomas Aquinas turns about in my mind, "Nothing is in the intellect that is not first in the senses". It takes me back – I am arguing with dad about Buddhism after a dinner in London – I am 20 and think that westerners are drawn to Buddhism because it lacks figures like Aquinas. Buddhism is an escape from all that Christian scholasticism and intellectual baggage. I am ignorant and he is getting annoyed with me. The debate lasts for our entire walk home and is not concluded.

I soon reach the area of Khlong San where my direct family once lived. As I near Prajadhipok Road, I see a modern structure, looking like a miniature segment of a fortified wall. It is in the motorway island. I wonder if it might commemorate Chuang's walled residence, upon which it stands, but the theme-park wall is merely welcoming people to Thonburi.

I take an overpass to cross the road. This grants me a clear vantage point of where Chuang's house would have been. His compound was enormous but his actual residence would have been directly beneath what is now a six-lane road network.

After Chuang's death, his main heir went into debt to the crown. Chuang's mansion was taken, and some of the buildings became a school, the King's College. This boys' school then became the Suksa Nari girls' school under the patronage of one of Chuang's granddaughters, Chao Chom Manda Phae. She had been King Rama V's initial wife, and took up residence next to the school in her final years.[1]

Chao Chom Manda Phae had met Prince Chulalongkorn, who would be King Rama V, when they were teenagers. She caught his eye performing in a palace play. She bore him three daughters, who were unable to marry anyone less than a king, and subsequently remained single. Phae and her daughters lived out their lives in a floating universe, far away from reality; she had a pleasure boat, and her own theatrical troupe and would travel each year to a private island in the gulf of Siam for long vacations. In a late life photograph, Phae is pictured holding a box which is decorated with her daughter's portraits; she outlived all of them.

The school is still running but her home is gone. I am allowed to enter the school since it is the weekend. It is during the Covid plague, so I have my temperature taken at the gates, and they note down my phone number. The school is made up of cube-like buildings from the 1990s that surround a covered central yard, with basketball and volleyball markings on the ground. Over looking this playground is a monument to Chuang. There is a plinth, statue, a plaque with some writing, and places for offering incense and flowers. The statue itself is cast bronze, in the style of the famous photograph of Chuang by John Thomson. He is seated beside a side-table, and looks out at an angle, his impatience dulled by the years.

School scribbles. Books and schoolhouses. Children reciting, bored tones, then shrill voices at play, chanting lessons, the repository of memory, the repurposing of palace into school, the erasing of the past. The chase and capture of the past, with its feelings of remorse and futility.

ARCHIVES

Siamese Souvenirs

Photography arrives in Siam with a priest, Abbé Larnaudie. In 1856, he makes daguerreotypes of King Rama IV, and Dit's brother, Tat, who is mistaken for the King of Siam by the British press.[1] These things are of the antique world, they resemble bronze rubbings, impressions taken from nature that have been embellished. The king's miniature portrait presented to Queen Victoria had been touched up with gold flecks.[2]

By the 1860s foreign photographers, and one Siamese, are using wet collodion on glass plates. This technology can evoke war, it brought the battlefield directly to the public eye – the modernity of Roger Fenton's cannon balls in the Crimean Valley of the Shadow of Death, or of Alexander Gardner's carnage at Antietam years later. Photographs present bodies, breath held still, stilled by breathlessness. They make crowds into clouds of wraiths and freeze over tropical water. They turn the past into negatives and positives that flicker between dualities of recognition and otherness.

Chuang is a subject of these endeavours, moving through history. A Prussian, Fedor Jagor, jots in his notebook on the 16th of March 1861, "waited a long time, done nothing." Chuang has not shown up for his photograph. The day before Jagor captured Chuang's second wife, Lady Phan, surrounded by slave girls on the steps of a pavilion.[3]

A year later, Chuang is seated in a group portrait by Carl Bismark.[4] The picture commemorates the signing of a treaty between Siam and Prussia. At 54 years old Chuang looks young, fit, and well composed. His half-brother Kham stands to the side behind him, thick set, scowling myopically.[5]

The most famous portrait of Chuang is by John Thomson. He has cropped hair, a style known as the Mahatthai, a ministerial coiffure. He looks sullen, ready to leave, with his eyes elsewhere, his mind on other matters. Thomson's fabric backdrop has been draped crudely over a chair, to provide visual depth. The chair legs peep out uneasily from beneath this curtain. It suggests last minute adjustments, a lack of space, difficulties from the subject. Thomson was using natural light, he would have prepared the setting in advance, carefully framing the props before the arrival of Chuang. It can be surmised that Chuang arrived late, the light had changed and subsequently the photograph came off in haste, imperfectly.

A handwritten string of words trail down the right hand side of the original plate: The Prime Minister in 1865. The late Kalahom, Bangkok, Siam. The note has been added after 1868, when Chuang was elevated to Regent, he is no longer Kalahom, Minister of War. There is a long scratch running across the plate, from the tip of Chuang's nose, a mockery by time and chance of this august figure.

He wears white stockings, and slippers decorated with acorn leaf embroidery. His feet rest on a piece of carpet with distinctive floral patterns. The carpet appears in a number of photographs: John Thomson's portrait of Lady Phan, Chuang's second wife, and in others which may not have been the work of Thomson[6] – a picture of Lady Run, Chuang's full sister, and one of Lady Nern, a half sister. It is tempting to read stories into the details. The carpet bringing to mind an episode in which British Merchant Robert Hunter attempted to sell the king a carpet that was too expensive and too small for the Throne Hall, and which finally Dit was allowed to buy.[7] The controversial carpet was to adorn Dit's sitting room for many years.

Thomson's portrait of Lady Phan is perfect. The carpet is aligned with a Chinese stone sculpture of a lion, which still exists. She stares at the camera, posed and attentive. All of the details in the composition are on point, precise, there is a bouquet of flowers on the table beside her that speak of her famous garden.

In 1863 a Siamese Catholic named Francis Chit opened a photographic studio on a floating house.[8] This studio boat was moored in front of the Santa Cruz Church, in the vicinity of Dit and Chuang's residences.

Advertisements he posted state that he had for sale "a great variety of photographs of Palaces, temples, buildings, scenery and public men of Siam," adding that "Parties can be waited on at their Residences."[9] Initially Chit reproduced and sold photographs by Abbé Larnaudie and Pierre Rossier, a Swiss. It is speculated that he learned his skills from these men, and was quick to grasp the market.

There is something awkward about Chit's work, which could be explained by the uneven nature of preservation, (it is not known how much of his work has been lost) and the process of editorial selection. As the first significant Siamese photographer it might have been hoped that he would reveal a distinctive vernacular and yet Chit was exoticising, framing a Siamese experience through a western eye. His vantage point is not local, nor is it foreign; it is a self-conscious gaze. However, the images were successful. They were sold abroad under other studio names and, at home, he was to be the longest serving court photographer, active from 1868 until 1891 when he died of cholera.

Could there have been another way to view Siam, beyond court and temple, elephant and monk?

In contrast, when leafing through Jagor's early photographs[10] it seems as though he is trying to understand Siam visually. He lowers himself to the ground in a portrait of a prince, to the vantage point of the men paying homage. Or in a series on Siamese dance, he includes the mess and chaos at the edges of the frames. Views of streets and canals and temples seem intentionally jumbled and disorderly; it is Siam.

Photography was, and will be, a bourgeois art form. It brings the thrill of distant lands, nudity, news, war, glimpses of the high-born and the most squalid, the exaggerated and foreign, yet it should also capture the mundane. People do not play a leading role, not in Siam. There are personages, and stereotypes: monks, and artists and criminals. If people appear they are accidental or thronging in the wake of some stately event. A lilliputian face might be caught staring up through the frame, but the masses are a collective detail not the subject. There are of course some exceptions, photographs by the Macao Portuguese photographer Joachim Antonio, and by Englishman William Kennett Loftus.

Photographers were craftsmen. They took commissions, or they made things they thought might sell. The technology was cumbersome, it needed a room, or a level street, a subject willing to sit still. The heavy stand and camera, with the stultifying back blanket required time and effort; it was not made to be carried in the heat and rain, along a muddy embankment. It is hard and inconvenient to capture the small chance moments in life with this equipment.

Chit took many photographs of Dit's family. The most memorable are not the portraits of Chuang, with his sword and his medals, but the groups of sons and grandsons of Dit, a crowd of boys with strong eyes and faces; the pictures of wives and sisters, and others that narrow down the selection of offspring to just the grandchildren of a particular wife. These are Siamese facts, small observations about polygamy.

And then there are the tantalising clues about the houses, the secrets of the residences. There are no photographs of the family homes. Only small details on the edges of portraits, and confusing scraps from post-diluvian photographs of schools and students. A private theatre can be made out behind the subjects, flag-stones catch the eye in another, there is a row of plaster, or stone, balusters in a shot of a woman and her three sons.

The houses are lost to time. Their remains exist only in sentences, scattered here and there in old books.

NATIONAL ARCHIVES OF

The Drawing Room

The childhood impression was persistent – the drawing room was the one with the sword and the portrait of Chuang, two things that I found fascinating. When I came on holiday I would traipse over to look at the pair. The sword was a scary looking thing, it had a thick blade, with disembowelment spikes along one side. It was no longer sharp, and the metal was dulled but it looked like it had seen action. Of course I couldn't help but connect it to the face of Chuang, hanging from the wall nearby – as if this weapon had carried out some of his more unsavoury work.

This room is directly opposite the workshop and rain-drum pavilion. The building looks out on the garden and is aligned with the canal. It has a large veranda; to the left side of its entrance is a shrine room. I have never known the drawing room to be used. In my explorations I would unlatch the front doors, and step gingerly into the dark chamber – it was warmly inviting, in contrast to the menace felt in other spaces. I would then cross the room and begin to open the shutters to let in light, after which it was brighter than the bedrooms, since there was no mosquito netting on the windows, and because it gave out onto the open garden.

It is filled with antiques, and laid out in readiness for people to settle down after a meal and talk over a digestif. The seating is Thai style on the ground, with triangular pillows, upon mats, all grouped around a low, ornate table, such as nobility once reclined on.

On the floor is that sword, with ivory hilt and jagged blade. In cabinets are various Buddha images, and artefacts. A wall displays a framed advert from Thai Airways, featuring Tula in this room holding a mother-of-pearl inlay box, one of his creations. The caption reads, "Thai, Smooth as Silk." Further along that wall is a print of Ok-Khun Siwisan Wacha, a Thai envoy to the court of Louis XIV, and an image of the Thai embassy to Napoleon III, in which an ancestor, Won, was second ambassador. The historic figures are matched by a photograph of Tula sitting at the feet of King Rama IX, and another of the royal court: Tula now standing next to Princess Vibhavadi Rangsit.

The centre of the room is dominated by Chuang. He is wearing a dinner jacket, and looks very distinguished. The photo is an old copy of the original, in an oval frame. Tej had found it in a storage room at the Silom house in the 1960s, while the property was undergoing building works. It was on the ground and had been eaten by cats or dogs. Tej had it repaired and framed at a shop in Asoke.

This portrait captivates me. I wrote a short story about it when I was 13 that was selected for the school magazine, a stream-of-consciousness writing; it brings a feeling of the crepuscular via T.S. Eliot's *Preludes*, with which I began my school-boy piece.

"The showers beat, on broken blinds and chimney pots, and at the corner of the street, a lonely cab horse steams and stamps, and now the lighting of the lamps."

I open the large cabinet beneath the portrait, and discover a photo album from Tom's time as Ambassador in Rome. The photographs are small, attached to black paper, and include a series capturing an excursion to Pompeii. Lady Ruen is being carried around the site in what looks like a palanquin, with two bearers clutching the poles. It must be 1929-1930.

The shrine room, to the left of the drawing room entrance, has a framed painting of a temple scene on its outer wall, and a large glazed jar by its door.

It is a small square room, perhaps four by four metres, dominated by a three-tiered altar. The tiers are made up of various small wooden ornamental tables, used to support Buddha images, of which there are many, in various poses, holding their classic mudras. The altar includes some bone ash vessels, of recent ancestors.

My grandparents are not devout but they show me the correct way to pray, how to bow, where to place the flowers, which images are of the Buddha, and which are of disciples.

1994. I wake up, after a late night on the town with cousins; having received my A-Level results the day before. A gaudy table greets me by the spirit house, on which sits a pig's head, fruit, desserts, and piles of flowers, incense, and garlands. Chancham has arranged an enormous ritual offering to make merit for my completion of school. I run around the house offering flower garlands to all of the Buddha images in every room. It takes me some time; I am full of joy, and bleary eyed.

As I stumble and prostrate myself, Chancham tells me that she did the same for Tej in the 1960s, before his results came in.

He joked that perhaps it was not a good idea, the house spirit might get fickle and mess up his grades.

Back outside the drawing room is a covered seating area, looking out across the upper terrace. I have some snapshots in mind when thinking of this space, photos of Shakespeare productions that were staged here the late 1960s. The photos are in colour, people are sitting on the step of this area smiling, in summery clothing. Ing K tells me that there had also been a production of "Romeo and Juliet", as well as "A Midsummer Night's Dream". Ing was about eight years old, so it must have been the late 1960s. Her mother, Noonie, played Juliet and her stepfather was Romeo, but Ing was not allowed to attend because it was for grown-ups, and Noonie's costume was exquisite.

I am there on the day that people arrive for the Bunnag family lineage book – a gargantuan tome on the main family blood-lines. We are seated on the Chinese furniture outside; it is daytime, and bright, but we are in the deep shade of memory. There is at least one man and one woman, who are strangers to me. He is a distant relative, he shows us his chest hair, "look I have some of the Persian blood." My dad says, "Oh, you should see how hairy my son is." The man shakes his head, "that's because he's a farang (westerner)."

THE BARD AT THE BUNNAGS

Scenes from Shakespeare

Produced by Nona Hartley
Directed by Perry Stieglitz
Music directed by M. L. Usni Promoj
Lighting by Desmond Lynch and Sally Anderson

Musicians : M. L. Usni Promoj
Veerapan Vawkalang
Suthin Srinarong
Solo tenor: Hanmer Webb Peploe
Scenes introduced by Anthony Hartley

PRESENTED BY KIND PERMISSION AT THE HOME OF CHAM-CHAM AND TULA BUNNAG.

The Palace Play

Chuang captured the imagination of many foreign visitors to Siam. He was noteworthy, and easy to write of, fulfilling diverse, useful roles within the traveller's account – native gentleman, student, soldier, dignitary, and scheming courtier. Typical of these textual remnants is the following by Eliza Hillier, wife of the British consul in Bangkok, who wrote in the mid 1850s, "he really behaved as if he had been accustomed to dine in the English fashion all his life, and I was fairly taken by surprise when he asked me to take wine with him in the most finished style possible. The effect of having to dinner a gentleman who wore no jacket or upper garment of any sort was in some degree peculiar."[1]

Anna Leonowens would meet him on her arrival in Bangkok. He boards her boat, shirtless and intimidating. It would be through her fanciful, but colourful testimony that Chuang would be reproduced in a musical. He is there in "The King and I", somewhere in the shadows around Rama IV, as he sings and dances alongside schoolmistress Anna. It is hard for Chuang to escape from this parody. But there is something of the performer within Chuang. He was self-aware, intentional about his comportment and effect on foreigners – a construct.

If he is found acting a role, his palace then is a stage for theatre.

The drama begins with arrival by boat to a private pier. The steps are slippery, a gateway leads through high crenellated walls. Guards stand to attention by this entrance; beyond is a large forecourt, with a covered stage for theatrical and musical entertainments on one side; on the other side are buildings, for soldiers and servants. Ahead is, in Bowring's words, "a beautiful building."[2] Anna Leonowens, who is not reliable, describes the façade as a semi-circle, like a rising sun. Inside is a spacious hall, and upstairs a room dominated by a large table, big enough to seat a party of dignitaries and their entourage.

Not far away, on Bang Luang Canal, is the naval-yard he has brought back to life, in which steamboats are built and fitted with Armstrong guns, and other artillery pieces. The residence is essentially moated, with an armoury and forge, like a bastion. Farther inside the compound, there are several residential houses, pavilions, ponds and pleasure gardens. His property sits at the centre of family land, his father is nearby, as are brothers and cousins.

The palace play exists in fragments.

Act One

Chuang is a young man, correctly known as Luang Sitti Nai Wen. His house is simpler, not yet a centre of power. It is full of European furnishings with a sign over the entrance reading in English, "This is Luang Nai Sit's home. Welcome."[3]

Chuang has returned from campaigning against the Vietnamese; he had led an invasion by land and sea, and is at this time the Head of the Royal Bodyguard.

Chuang is wooing a daughter of one of the chief ministers. He already has one wife, Lady Klin, who is a cousin, and a son, Won, by her, who is almost ten. Chuang knows this new marriage will be helpful, and is expected of him. He has never met the girl but sends her a snow-white pigeon and a rose. He knows that if she accepts him, she will put the rose on her breast and release the pigeon. Chuang waits in his garden with his friends. They see the pigeon flutter back, white against the darkening sky.[4]

He will build a house for this second wife, Lady Phan, where she will tend to a celebrated garden. Chuang will also marry her younger sister, Yaad.

He is sent to quell an insurrection in the eastern town of Chachoengsao. A Chinese secret society group has taken over the town and killed the governor. After he returns, victorious, blood-stained,[5] he begins to plan out his stately home.

Act Two

The British envoy, John Bowring,[6] is sitting across from him at the upstairs table. They have been working together for days. Bowring distrusts him, he must convince Bowring that they have similar interests. Chuang is frustrated, his father and uncle, Dit and Tat, are slowing down the proceedings. Chuang has been studying the British for years. He has watched them take Burma, a far more powerful nation than Siam. By his calculation the British might be appeased with trade.

Chuang's father is ailing, the great man seems addled, with a painful sore on his leg, "which gave him trouble."[7] Before long Chuang will be the king's closest adviser.

The house is only a few years old. It is not yet fully complete, and Chuang is still only acting Minister of War. His compound will expand, according to design. The construction and scale suggest confidence.[8]

Act Three

Anna Leonowens[9] is obliged to stay in the house. She has been hired by the king to teach English. Anna is afraid of Chuang, referring to him as Prime Minister. It is 1862. Chuang is 54 years old. His residence is filled with all of the *objets* and trappings requisite to his rank and standing. Members of his household play tricks on Anna, the serving boys do acrobatic leaps, and girls peep out from behind curtains to spy on the foreigners.

Chuang was on an observation tour in Singapore the year before. He is subsequently engaged in public works across Bangkok, building roads and canals. His energies are increasingly turning to the western provinces of the country. Chuang, as Minister of War, has control over the coasts, and family in commanding positions in these provinces, from where he gains a steady flow of manpower.

He has returned from Wa-ko, where the court has witnessed King Rama IV's successful calculation of the solar eclipse. The king is dying of malaria. Chuang's son, Won, is now an adult, and is with the king.

Chuang receives the message that the king has passed away. He crosses the river, and doubles the guard at the Grand Palace. The designated successor, Prince Chulalongkorn, will be the next king. Chulalongkorn is a teenager, himself very sick with malaria, and may die. But he recovers, and Chuang will be his Regent.

After some debate, Chuang pushes through a candidate for the Front Palace king, or Second King. It is argued by some, that only the king had the power to make this decision.[10]

There is a letter read aloud by King Chulalongkorn to one of his sons: *"At that time I was fifteen years and ten days old, without a mother. None of my relatives on my maternal side were particularly able. As for the paternal relatives, namely the high princes, they were all under the influence of the Somdet Chaophraya* (Chuang) *and to look after their personal safety and well being rather than support me… I was propped up merely to serve as a figurehead."*[11]

Chuang gets word that the revered monk, Somdet Toh, has arrived at his compound. Somdet Toh is 80 years old. He carries a large lit candle and has a sacred text wedged under his elbow. Chuang sits at the monk's feet. He reassures the monk he will not seize the throne and he will not "*allow his deliberations to be overcome with the darkness of defilement, and he would hold to the Dhamma as a rudder while steering the ship of state."*[12]

Act Four

It is 1872, Chuang is at the end of his regency, and the young king is abroad at present on a study trip to British India. Chuang receives foreign visitors aboard his steam-yacht, the "Rising Sun", moored on the river not far from his palace. Chuang smokes a small Chinese pipe, his attendants are "good-looking girls", who creep about silently. As the men converse, Chuang walks the deck in a "nervous, fidgety manner", making jokes in his English.[13]

By 1873 Chuang is spending less time at the residence. He is officially in retirement, and has moved to the town of Rajburi. Nevertheless he is still the most powerful political figure in the land.

Two years later, King Rama V and the Front Palace king, or Second King, are in conflict. The Front Palace king has been drilling troops. He has a small well-equipped army, trained by a Scotsman called Knox, who has been in Siam for decades. It is suspected that his soldiers are from the western provinces, Chuang's domain. Tensions have been rising, and fighting has almost broken out.

King Rama V reluctantly sends for Chuang, stating that now he has no choice but to visit the crocodile.[14]

The crisis has multiple focal points, which orbit and impact Chuang. At one point he receives a petition complaining of "demoncy", as well as the young monarch's circle of advisors, and the wearing of shoes and stockings inside temples.

In an audience with the king, Chuang states that the Front Palace king has served his purpose, which was to ensure the stability of the crown years earlier, Chuang agrees that the office of the Front Palace should be curtailed.

Factions who are against the ex-Regent are incensed at his re-emergence, a bill is posted up taunting Chuang, "Old man who vaunts his fidelity to the state… Don't stir up troubles, old man, or we shall come to blows, have no doubt."[15] The authors are discovered to be sons of Phraya Kasap, who is leading an investigation of Chuang's family for financial misconduct.[16]

Chuang attempts to mediate, but the Front Palace king is convinced he will be killed. Matters go from bad to worse, the Front Palace king flees to the British Consulate, and British warships are circling, ready to enter the fray. A compromise is found, with British assurances, and an unsteady peace holds.

Act Five

Some years pass, it is now 1878. Knox, the old drillmaster of the Front Palace king, is now the British Consul-General. He is acting in an abrasive and dictatorial manner. Knox has married his daughter Fanny, to a son of Phraya Kasap, called Preecha. Chuang has Preecha, who is in charge of a Royal gold mine, tried and executed for abuse of power and corruption. Fanny flees the country, while Knox attempts to convince the British government to intervene.[17]

Ulysses S. Grant, former U.S. President, is on his world tour.[18] He stops in Bangkok and is taken to visit Chuang at his residence.

"As our boat pulled up to the foot of the palace the ex Regent, his breast bearing many orders, was waiting to receive the General. He was accompanied by Mr. Chandler, an American gentleman who has spent many years in Siam, and knows the language perfectly. The ex-Regent is a small, spare man, with a clean cut, well-shaped head, and a face reminding you, in its outlines and the general set of the countenance, of the late M. Thiers.[19]

Chuang delivers a deliberate and cryptic speech about always trying to do what is best for his nation.

Grant's party notes that there is danger of an imminent British invasion. They could "be in for some fun."

There has been a row about the connection of telegraph lines between Siam and British Burma. Chuang would like to subcontract to a British firm, but the king has other plans and Chuang is accused of attempting to gain kickbacks from the British. Chuang adamantly refuses to allow the telegraph to run through the western provinces into Burma.[20]

The house is empty. Chuang is in the province of Kanchanaburi on a pleasure trip. He goes out to pick tamarind and spends a long time in the sun. It is a hot day, even though this time of the year is cool. His family asks him to rest but he is insistent. No, he would stay out and collect tamarind and enjoy the day.

He falls sick that evening. It is clear that it is very serious. His son, Won, is there, and takes him to their steamboat to make the journey to Bangkok. The water levels are low in the canal, it did not rain enough the previous monsoon, making navigation slow and difficult. Chuang dies on the boat enroute to Bangkok. He is thought to have suffered a stroke.[21]

The day after his death, the king signs an order to erect telegraph poles throughout the western provinces.[22]

The White Monkey

The ceiling fan spins unevenly above my bed. It seems a precarious aid against the heat, but I have done nothing to have it mended. The wobbling blades of the fan underscore a feeling of disquiet.

Lying there at night, I have a recurring waking dream that a creature is perched in the branches of the pikul tree, which reaches beyond my window. It is caught in the dim and varied lights reaching through the night from the street, passing vehicles, and neighbouring houses. I am already a grown-up when I start to have this vision. The effect is like stepping back into childhood, when a bedroom feature becomes uncanny and frightening. The wavering image watches me. A white monkey looking in; impassive, curious, mocking.

This house building, on the street-side, mirrors the master bedroom across the upper terrace. Both are rectangles, accessed by small centrally placed antechambers. This one has two beds, at either end of the room. I prefer to sleep beside a window giving on to the watchful tree. Between this bed and the wall is a low table, covered in LPs with weathered sleeves. Perhaps to stave off the ghostliness of the space, I set up a cheap CD player during one of my summer holidays. Music weaves into the sonic texture of the space. I can hear lyrics from Tribe Called Quest's *Low End Theory*, "You could find the Abstract listening to Hip Hop, my pops said it reminded him of be-bop". In my abstracted memory, I see a split screen: one half featuring my dad taken by Tula to see Louis Armstrong when he was a boy; the other half, a boyish me sitting next to my dad, looking up at Miles Davis on his last tour.

Next to the bed, on the other side, now looking into the long room, is a bedside table, with a blue Chinese lamp, and carved box. Above it on the wall, are some framed photographs of the Thai diplomatic mission to the People's Republic of China. Tej is seen assisting Prime Minister Kukrit Pramoj as he signs the normalisation agreement between the two countries in 1975. A group photo captures the entire team: Deng Xiao-Ping, Kukrit, and many others. Tej mentioned that the elderly Chou Enlai was still very charming and handsome. This would be Chou Enlai's last formal signing ceremony before his death the following year.

Further along the wall is a vertical calligraphy scroll from Taiwan, said to be by a modern master. It reads, "I do not know whether to tuck my long beard into my trousers or wear it loose." Filmmaker, Tom Reichman gave it to Chancham. Dad had befriended Reichman when they were learning Mandarin together at Taipei Normal University, where dad spent a year before going up to Cambridge. I caught Reichman's voice in a verité documentary he made about Charles Mingus – a thin voice, somehow adding documentary credence to a mishmash of family stories. The last time dad saw Reichman was on a cross-Channel ferry in the early 1970s; dad was nervous about getting through British immigration on his Thai passport. Reichman lent him some cash to show the officials.

The scroll hangs above a wooden Ottoman. In front of which is a low table, resting on a thick carpet. At least two opium pillows lie next to it on the floor.

The far end of the room feels even more haunted than the other. This part of the building looks out at the garden, and is occupied by a bed, in front of a dressing room, and a writing desk, with a glass-hooded lamp.

On walls are more framed prints, and an antique map of Java, which is Tej's from his time at the embassy there.

The bathroom features a tiny toilet, a shower, without hot water, an urn for washing Thai style with a ladle, a small sink, and mirror, and, at the entrance, a Chinese print of a child, and another of a gold-fish.

Over the years that second bedroom was where I stayed – it's joined in memory with hours of reading in bed. The room will always recall paradoxes and fabrications, and circular pathways, the edges of epiphany, or comprehension, that eluded me.

The room is dark, its features falling off into the tropical night. It resounds, startled by the raging weather, which claws behind the thin wood walls, to be followed by the hypnotic polyphonic undulations of the bull-frogs.

During the day, the room collects bird song, the koel birds with their passionate, desperate peals, the rolling cries of the plaintive cuckoo, the greater coucal issuing its rounded-out hooting, and, of course, those ugly roosters crowing at all hours.

Even in the day, the room is an eerie space – a place where one's back tingled as if being watched.

While Chancham's mother was pregnant with her – perhaps the night before Chancham was born – she had a dream that she was about to give birth to a white monkey. This was a highly auspicious sign, heralding Hanuman, the cunning and brilliant monkey general of the *Ramayana*. Chancham always thought of herself as that white monkey, naughty, intelligent and charismatic. The latter being an attribute prized by elephant-handlers. Elephants, according to lore, can be mollified by the charismatic. Incidentally, an apocryphal tale featured Chancham taming a raging elephant. It was in musth, its mating madness, and was running wild in the district near her school, Rajinee. She is said to have approached the maddened animal by the school-gate, away from the cowering children and staff. Reaching through the bars of the gate, Chancham touched the elephant, and calmed it down.

She wrote a poem about her teachers, which circulated about the school. Chancham's friends were still giggling about how she was caned during morning assembly, after the teachers found her out. Chancham didn't seem too traumatised, even if the teasing was still alive some six decades later.

This house segment is nearest the road, and the bridge over the canal. During the late 80s it started to shake. Bangkok was undergoing a building boom. A limit had been placed on construction trucks entering the city during the day, so instead, lorries laden with building materials would come in at night. As they crossed the bridge, the land would reverberate.

Chancham said that in those years, and throughout the 90s until the Tom Yum Gung Crisis, Bangkok's emblem should have been the construction crane, because that was the most familiar sight.

The city shot up and spread out, engulfing the house. By the year 2000, the motorcycle taxi had become the favoured means of transport between the main road of Sukhumvit and the apartments and houses further "inland". From 7.00 am the street was a buzzing sea of bikes carrying people back and forth.

Dust from the city comes through the open windows, with their greying mosquito netting, and settles on everything, coating the books, the record sleeves, the curios and historic photographs.

Tigers, Cobras, Crocodiles and Whales

"As regards the French, they are distinguished for their vainglorious disposition. Their Emperor, famed for his descent from a line of tigers and cobras, would, after his ascent to the Throne, seek colonies that are rich and vast. . . . These lands between Annam and Burma must appear to him to be ownerless and therefore desirable... Since we are now being constantly abused by the French because we will not allow ourselves to be placed under their domination like the Cambodians... it is for us to decide what we are going to do; whether to swim up-river to make friends with the crocodile or to swim out to sea and hang on to the whale..."[1]

It was 1867 and King Mongkut was writing to his envoy, Won, who had been sent to France to negotiate.[2] Mongkut's letter provides a glimpse of Siam's precarious position between Britain and France, the whale and the crocodile. In the wake of Cambodia submitting to French protection a rebellion had broken out. The French were accusing Siam of supplying arms to the rebels. At the same time, to Siam's south, north and west the British were quietly poised. The Siamese had to be careful not to offend French and British representatives, providing justification for conflict. The imperial march was not only about battleships- it was also executed by the gradual overtures and manoeuvres of colonial officers, men like Frenchman Gabriel Aubaret and British John Knox.[3]

Sir John Bowring, who had opened up trade with Siam in the 1850s, had ambitions to be appointed Minister Plenipotentiary of Siam, in charge of negotiating treaties between Siam and other European powers. Bowring's appointment would have placed Siam securely within the British sphere of influence.

Won had been dispatched to signal that Siam would speak for herself, presumably because he was deemed strong enough for the task, and, as Chuang's son, powerful in his own right. Beyond the letter, with its metaphors and expansiveness, there is scant information about the 1867 mission to France. On this trip Won would also visit Germany and the United Kingdom, but not much is known about these episodes except that they involved munitions factories and armaments.

Won had been to France already in 1861. On this occasion Won was known to the French as "Phra Navai", a transmutation of his title as king's Sword-bearer. He had been appointed Second Ambassador bearing gifts to the court of Napoleon III, in the embassy led by his cousin, Pae. It was a showy event. Here the Siamese in their finery were photographed and painted, at court, at the Paris Opera. During the westward voyage, Won sent his attendant engineer and mechanic to help, and observe, in the French ship's engine room.[4] Upon arrival, he would visit the shipyards and foundries at Le Havre, with an eye to purchasing a steam engine for Chuang. There and elsewhere, the French were intrigued by the appearance, with juvenile top-knot, of his eldest son, Chai, a 12-year-old who had been brought along for the journey.

The French depiction of the encounter focused on the exotic, archaic character of the Siamese. A painting[5] of their reception at Fontainebleau depicts a great Oriental undulation, bodies prostrated, like Magi before their saviour. The image speaks of hierarchy, with a distinct illustration of the contrast in civilisation between the two powers.

Nadar, who was the most celebrated French photographer of the time, and a famous caricaturist, photographed the diplomats in their Siamese court robes. His portrait of Won is of a stern, wiry man, with an almost defiant expression. The frivolity of his costume cut short by the look in his eyes. Beside him is Chai,[6] who will appear in the illustrated French journals greeting the son of Napoleon III.

In the dichotomy posed by the meeting of east and west, the Siamese envoys were in fact figures of modernity, part of a deliberate program of opening up, with considerable experience of Europeans. The Siamese might have enlivened the pages of the French press, but at least one observer, author Prosper Mérimée, would write perceptively of Won and his companions, "the Asians are taken for more naïve than they are."[7]

There had been a few diplomatic missions to France in King Narai's era during the 17th century. One was lost at sea. Another was shipwrecked off the coast of Africa. The envoys had made their way overland, enduring great hardship, to a Dutch settlement near the Cape. The most successful encounter occurred at the court of Louis XIV, and was led by a man called Kosa Pan. It is a captivating story but did not have a lasting impact. Part of the original diary of Kosa Pan was discovered by chance at the Archives of the Foreign Missions in Paris in the early 20th century. It had been lost to dust, and fell off a shelf as a researcher reached for another book.[8]

After the efforts undertaken in the 17th century, Siam had little interaction with the west until the 1820s. By the late 1850s Britain was in Burma, the Malay peninsular and China, while France was moving into Vietnam and Cambodia. It was deemed essential by the Siamese to send emissaries to France and Britain. Chuang's younger brother Chum, Phraya Montri Suriyawong, headed an embassy to Queen Victoria in 1857.

Chuang had grasped the need to learn from the west early on. He had wanted to send some members of the family to receive naval instruction under the British in Hong Kong.[9] This did not occur, but he had Won educated by foreign missionaries from the age of seven.[10]

As a young man, Won would impress John Bowring. In 1855 Won boards H.M.S. Rattler, where Bowring describes him drinking wine with the British, dressed in gold ornamented clothing, "very desirous of instruction and... quite popular with our officers."[11] Won was appropriately modern and well mannered – befitting a member of the family described by the French as "L'élément civilisateur dans l'extrême orient."[12]

Won, as Chuang's only son, was fated to be compared to his radiant father. Won would die in 1888, just five years after Chuang. There are many parallels between father and son. As a page he commanded one of the Royal Barges; later he built ships, replaced his father as Minister of War when Chuang became Regent, battled pirates and Chinese secret society groups. He oversaw the construction of canals and infrastructure projects. Close to King Rama IV, he had an ambiguous, contentious relationship with King Rama V. Even his title, Chaophraya Surawong Wayawat, chimed with Chuang's, Chaophraya Sri Suriyawong.

In 1868, on his return from Europe, he was to be found at the sick bed of King Rama IV, as the monarch succumbed to jungle fever. Mongkut asks Won if he has a sword. Hearing that he does not, the king calls out that someone must fetch him one from the armoury. King Mongkut would send Chuang a precious ring and rosary that had belonged to King Rama I, these were to be kept for the next king.[13] Some rumours suggest the sword and heirlooms were bribes to ensure the crown went to Mongkut's heir,[14] other whispers have Won keeping the items, although it was also said that King Rama V exonerated Won, and the objects were returned.

Won would be referred to as "Chao Khun Taharn," Lord of the Army. He was the last Minister of War, or Kalahom, of the old system, and the last family member to wield great power. As observed by Jules Harmand, French Consul in the 1880s, the family would be replaced by other factions, "une race de sangsues qui éliminent, petit à petit la lignée de vampires du Régent."* [15]

* "a race of leeches that sap, little by little, the Regent's lineage of vampires…"

Sanatoria

I had discovered that Won spent his last years in a property that sprawled along the Somdet Chaophraya canal. It was private park with a house designed for Won by a celebrated Italian architect called Joachim Grassi.

I found a map to the area in an antique guidebook, and a simple architectural plan of the house.[1] Won's villa was easy to locate on the map, close to "the Residence of the Ex-Regent".[2] With Won's death this botanical garden went to his uncle Tuam, Chaophraya Phanuwong, who added to it a zoo, with an albino monkey and other rarities. Eventually the land was sold, becoming the Somdet Chaophraya Psychiatric Hospital, whose non-descript buildings take up most of the original plot, leaving just the old villa and a small remnant of the garden.

Won had been suffering from a long illness, believed to have been lung cancer; he built the retreat for his convalescence. Built around 1878, Won's villa was one of Grassi's first works in Bangkok.[3] By this time, King Rama V was in the process of enacting reforms that would circumvent and restrict Chuang and Won's influence.[4] Won's family was fracturing under the strain. Pon, another uncle of Won's, had aligned himself with the king's reform movement, while Tuam wavered ambiguously between the rival camps. Won was said to have moved to the villa in 1885, the year he resigned as Minister of War. He stayed there until his death in 1888.

Won's house would have been reached by boat, with a pier flanked by large stone lions.[5] The journey along the canal, between Won's original home at his father's palatial residence and the villa, was direct and short. In contrast to Chuang's fortress-like complex, which housed the families of Won's 23 wives,[6] the villa was relatively modest, with little room for family and retainers; as such it was a sanctuary set apart from ancestral complications, and the politics of the bedchamber.

The Somdet Chaophraya canal like most of Bangkok's smaller waterways, now resembles a runoff sewer by the side of a busy road. At the property, trees overlook the canal's black water; they are miraculous, sickly, survivors from the early days. Behind this withered avenue, denser tropical foliage shields the house from the hospital and main road.

I had an idea of the house; I knew it was a two-storey building with three bedrooms, a small dining room, drawing room that looked onto the gardens, and a shrine-room at the top of the house. Before setting foot there I was already charmed – this being the only remaining family house in Bangkok, and a rare vernacular site from the epoch.

As I approached the old villa, a little girl ran ahead of me, evidently at home in the hospital compound. She played among the Chinese stone lions that I saw scattered about the garden. A row of these lions led to the main entrance of the house, where a young man was sitting on the steps, absorbed in his phone. I saw above him a plaque reading, "Somdet Chaophraya Museum". I was hopeful about finding the place open, anticipating a typically random display of artefacts for me to patronise, but the place was shut. If there had ever been a museum it was now extinct. I climbed the outdoor steps to a small terrace.

My hands cupped to a first floor window, I peered into the dusty space. The elegant proportions and high ceiling of the chamber benefitting nothing more than a wooden dresser, a large bronze bell, and a jumble of Thai traditional instruments. I stared hard into the room, hoping to catch something of a bygone era. Behind my curiosity stood loose notions regarding Won's travels to France, Germany and Britain in the 1860s. I would have liked to know if the place represented the attainment of a long held dream; if the impulse to build this neo-classical edifice, set within a romantic landscape, arose during one of those voyages.

My way blocked, I descended and began to circle the house. Soon standing in a courtyard of ancient flag-stones, I took in the back of the building with its shuttered rooms and open staircase. On the lower veranda were stacks of fake flowers, cheap decorative items and boxes, leftovers from tacky functions that were strangely matched by bright yellow petals and glassy spirit offerings at the foot of a grand old tree.

At the centre of the garden was the statue of a seated doctor, a plump 20th century form, presumably the founder of the modern hospital. He seemed to preside in Won's stead – or like a morsel waiting to be devoured by Won's petrified lions.

I had visited the house in the hope of discovering some kind of presence, but the sensorial effect of the place, compounded by the dry brightness of the day, and the cicadas, brought me back to myself. Sprinklers were at work in the front garden, casting up a faint earthy scent along with memories of my childhood – memories of sneaking with friends into the forsaken grounds of decaying houses, the 19th century summer homes of a vanishing Attica.

The villa, resonating so strongly with my own experiences – even its insensitive renovation reminded me of Greece – produced an inversion of context and location. By this process, a grove of luxurious ruffled-fan-palms, and other exotic plants, were no-longer features of a tropical garden but seemed transplanted wondrously to the Mediterranean.

The endless siesta hour of the place spoke also of dusk and drinks and family mirth. I imagined Tula waking to a late-day game of tennis with his cousin Terd; spectral on the property's neglected tennis court, its surface now uneven, the place succumbing to weeds and creepers. The young men, through Won and Tuam, two separate potential heirs to the property.

• • •

A few weeks later I visited another building by Grassi not far distant from there. I was with Tatiya on one of our strolls through the district. Beyond a weathered gate I made out the crumbling back wall of a house. The decaying building had once been part of a pair built in the 1870s, houses set in a large garden giving onto Bangkok Yai canal. They were erected for sons of Tuam: Tui and his brother Sudhjai. The houses would have been mirror images, two rectangular villas in parallel, with matching external stairways leading up to a covered terrace that ran the length of the building.

Only one house stands today, completely hemmed in by shacks and larger buildings. Having decided to venture in, we found ourselves pinned down by savage-looking dogs. Amidst barking and shouting a woman came to rescue us. We were forced to scamper unceremoniously up the Grassi steps to be scolded by the current owner. She was an elderly woman, busy making a cake, and not impressed with our excuses and pleas. The house was piled high with odds and ends, charming but dismal. On the steps as we were expelled, my attention was caught by two wicker trays of chillies brilliantly red in the sun.

While the house, and its phantom twin, seemed beyond repair, a tentative fictional version persists. Kukrit Pramoj, in his *Four Reigns,* describes an archetype of Bangkok, and its vanishing 19th century world. He writes of families disintegrating, values shifting, the world turning into memory. Phloi, a member of the

"Clan Across the River",[7] which is a nickname for the Bunnag family, will see a son ordain at the temple, referred to as, "our small Wat down the khlong."[8] Phloi's home in the novel seems to share much with the Grassi house – the location at Bang Luang, its proximity to the temple that must be Wat Buppharam, the period and style of architecture, and the layout of the house.

"Their home in Khlong Bang Luang had a brick and iron fence running the length of the grounds on the khlong side. There was a pavilion at the landing, then a spacious courtyard to cross to the big house where Phloi's father, His Excellency the Chao Khun, resided. The brick mansion was considered highly stylish by Bangkok's citizens during these years in the mid 1880s and 90s… From the courtyard one climbed either of the twin staircases that merged into a platform."[9]

After Won's villa, Grassi would go on to design and construct many significant buildings: the Customs House on the river, various palaces and the elegant Sala Daeng House, which stood at the top of Silom Road, and was built for Chaophraya Surasakmontri, an uncle of Tula.[10]

In spite of Grassi's popularity, his career in Siam was ended abruptly. Grassi had become a French Citizen and was forced to leave the country in 1893, in the wake of a naval skirmish. The French had sent gunboats up the Chaophraya River, blockading Bangkok and threatening to bombard the Grand Palace. Subsequently, Siam lost control of the east bank of the Mekong, and therefore most of Laos, which had been under Siamese patronage, as well as the ports of Chantaburi and Trat. Grassi returned to his native Capodistria near Trieste, and died in 1904.[11]

The Little House

In 2005 I was still living in Athens. I had a dream about my grandmother. A team of builders were at her house, fixing things, and ruining the place. She didn't have the energy to argue with them, and when I objected they grew angry with me. Gradually the old teak house was transformed into a modern dwelling made of concrete, with plain white walls.

The little house, in my grandparent's compound, was built for Tej, who was living in Thailand at that time. I don't think he used the house for very long. My subset of the family often used this building, and these were my dad's quarters for the long stretches he spent in Bangkok between 2000 and 2005, looking after his mother, and working in the Klongtoey slum with a Catholic priest called Father Joe Maier.

Architectural drawings of these building had been hung on the wall of the workshop. I always thought they were done by Tula, but they looked professionally executed, and in fact had been drawn by the architect Mitrarun Kasemsri, Tula's friend from the palace.

The house is situated along the canal. It stands to the right of the downstairs breakfast area, beyond a stone figure of a Chinese horseman that is attractive but not particularly old, and a small yard, covered by irregular flag-stones. The single-storey wooden house is built over brick foundations, the crawl space hidden behind some porcelain latticework. A large portal, with big wooden doors gives into a small courtyard with its own pavilion.

Once upon a time the house straddled water, and there was an inlet extending beneath and beyond to the back of the house, where boats were moored. The pavilion would have looked at the sleeping paddle-boats. In later years there was a bamboo grove here and the pavilion was used to house a washing machine and clothes rack. The courtyard is covered in glazed tiles, a step leads into the house, whose front can be opened up via a series of folding wooden doors. The front area inside consists of two levels, one at the entrance which terminates in a laterite stone feature that has flown from memory; the higher level has Thai floor cushions, book-cases, photographs, and leads to the bedroom, the doors of which are decorated with two female deities, painted by Tula. This is the first part of the house I can recall, being carried in as a six-year-old, and put to bed, the night we arrived.

The bedroom is comfortable, with one double-bed, and mosquito netting. Beyond the bed is the door to the bathroom, with steps leading down to the shower and sink. This would be the other side of the laterite wall of the entrance.

Dad is in the bathroom, having a shower, the door is open. He pops his head round the corner as he washes. He is in his thirties, looking a lot like his mother, animated with smiling eyes. Mum is telling me that when she first came to Thailand, dad's nanny Nark would still go into the bathroom while dad was washing and scrub his back. He agrees, and tells us how much he loved his nanny.

Some years later. Dad is in the pantry giving mum a swig of traditional Thai medicine for some forgotten ailment. All of the unknown ingredients are in the sediment, which she has just imbibed. Mum exclaims that she had been poisoned. It is right before one of Chancham's noodle parties. Mum deliriously takes herself to the small house where she sleeps off the concoction. She misses the lunch, which she had been dreading. I come in to find her and dad listening to Bob Dylan on a small cassette deck.

Being of the sixties generation, and out of the mainstream, my parents were often called Hippies, a term they abhorred. They liked the Beats, and Mods, and were connected to the music and cultural moment that sprang out of 1960s Cambridge,[1] mum's hometown. My parents had many shared passions, Martial Arts was one. They practiced Karate, and more seriously, T'ai Chi and Yoga to an obsessive, and professional, degree. My mum liked to spar, she fought an enormous man while she was six months pregnant with my sister. When he accidentally knocked her stomach, she grabbed hold of his beard and shouted, "don't you know I'm pregnant?!" ready to floor him.

That little-house-courtyard was straight out of a kung fu film, and it was private, so I trained there at times, even kicking a bamboo sapling to toughen up my shins one year, but I was never serious about Martial Arts.

As a student, I asked the gardener to cut a length of bamboo, to practice my Aikido form (I stuck to it for about a term), which I did every day in the courtyard. Chancham, finding me eccentric, remarked to me that she was, "surprised at this kind of behaviour in one so young," – the tone iterating a fear that I might follow my parents with their manic kicks and punches.

As presaged in my dream, the bedroom is whitewashed all of a sudden for no good reason. Inside it is brighter but sadder.

From Wat Buppharam to Ton Son Mosque

A walk through Thonburi, with Tatiya as guide. This exploration takes us from Wat Buppharam towards the Bangkok Yai canal. We set off at 8.00 and get back at 13.30, a round trip from the temple. We do not drift. It is a journey through the urban forest, punctuated by clearings and landmarks along the way: The district around the temple, the Somdet Chaophraya Rajabhat University, Wat Lao, Wat Mon, Bang Luang Mosque, Ton Son Mosque, back to Wat Buppharam. Sweaty, with leaden feet.

Thonburi is the ancestor city; it was there before Bangkok. It should be addressed in familial terms, as father, eccentric uncle, forgotten twin. And twin-like, Thonburi is that nurturing mass, turned after-birth.

I cannot define Thonburi's boundaries, but neither can I define the limits of Bangkok. Broadly speaking it sprawls out of an historic quarter, which is across the river from Bangkok's palaces. An old fort at the entrance to Bangkok Yai canal looks out at the downstream river, guarding the stately monuments of Thonburi. Here is King Taksin's Palace, properties belonging to the defunct institution of the Second Kings, and various temples: Wat Rakhang, haunted Wat Suwanaram, and the Temple of Dawn. Across Bangkok Yai canal is a patchwork of former villages – Cham, Lao, Mon, Chinese, Malay, Siamese, European, thrown together over time under different circumstances. It is no longer bucolic. The modern city has brought incoherence, mergings and dismemberments.

Our walk is about monuments, The Somdet Chaophraya University is located on land donated by one of Chuang's wives. His martial statue stands in front of a University building, his bone ash in the pediment. From there to the temple of the Lao war captives, the golden Sheldrake of the Mon community temple, Muslim graveyards and ancient mosques. The places melt into each other.

Instead of buildings, my recollections of the day are taken up with fleeting impressions of people on the street. A speculative form of history arises as we go, in which the individual becomes the monument. I attempt to discern human agency in its relationship to the character of the city, because sites and stories have no meaning devoid of people.

I want desperately to capture the consequences of past events on the present moment, but this is futile. There is no way of knowing what experiences constitute another person, or how they might have been affected by events and times and places.

I stop and ask a monk how to drive into the temple, where the guard asks me my business. He kindly gives me a parking space, as the temple car-park is full. I wander around – a woman in nun-white is glaring at me, I have neglected to wear my pandemic mask.

A man sits in his shop house, his face filled with despair at the opening day. There is nothing old nearby except for the scent of old rot, rising irrepressibly through the years. What is not under concrete is worshipped. I see the broken past – spirit shrines, deities with severed limbs, drying garlands – piled under dusky trees.

We cross a road, via a bridge, floating over the scruffy side of Isaraphap road into an alleyway. A "Win", motorcycle taxi driver, sits on his bike topless. A man jokes, "the police will arrest you for being shirtless." He's flabby, about 60 years old, with some tattoos on his pasty torso.

We walk to a small pavilion in honour of Chuang. It houses a couple of busts, one of which was donated by Vilat Bunnag or his father, Wong.[1] It is an "original", made in England of porcelain. There are many papier-mâché roosters adorning the shrine, spirit votives. Two children are playing, they both bow to Chuang, as to a protector spirit.

Turning down a tight alleyway, Tatiya asks a passerby for directions; his tone distinctly military, the stranger seems to jump to attention. The alley is lush and verdant, with plants growing from well-tended wall gardens; Muslim names on the gates, Arabic calligraphic flourishes, and southern Thai architectural features.

Crossing a small bridge, following canals and winding pathways, we share the way with motorbikes and veiled women. It looks like a slum, resembling parts of Klongtoey. Soon we reach Bang Luang Mosque, where six old men, with strong faces, and stocky builds are just finishing prayers. The imam welcomes us and allows us to enter. It is a building from the late 18th century, early Rattanakosin, in the shape of a Thai temple, with an exquisite carved pulpit. The Muslim men speak a kind of patois. There are old Persian plates embedded in the walls. It is a Sunni mosque, and has a large graveyard nearby. On the cemetery wall, and in containers hanging from trees, are chunks of banana, to feed the noisy ravens, who swoop around like lost souls. We take an easier way out of the labyrinth.

Finally, Ton Son Mosque. In the courtyard, a mother and son, with smirks and striking features, are putting rolls of raw meat onto wicker drying trays to cure. I head up into the graveyard. Some of the graves are sprinkled with red and yellow petals, they look fresh. The earth has been raised in mounds, and is cracking from the heat. Before long we find the patch where the Chularajamontris are buried, all those Ahmadchulas and Aghayees, Muslim relatives of the Bunnag family.

Funeral Books

Thai Buddhist funeral traditions display various contradictions. Doctrinally, all that is born must suffer sickness, pain and death. Non-attachment should be cultivated regarding the body, which will fail and lose its beauty, and wealth and name, which are equally transient. The corpse is cremated, turned to ash, returned to dust. Death is the great leveller.

And yet funeral rites are not made equal. Certain chants are reserved for the elite, during which monks hold prayer fans before their faces, to obscure the view of the temple patrons, fans often decorated with noble insignia. The bone ash of the rich and powerful are kept in jewelled urns, made of gold, and placed in the stupas of fabulous temples erected by members of the family, so that they might be commemorated each year, that their memory will not fade. At funerals, books are distributed, often funded by donations, that will include biographies of the deceased, old photographs, and perhaps recipes, alongside dharma texts.

These books, associated with the ritual of accepting loss, display a huge wealth of information, and are a mainstay of the Thai historical practice. It is through funeral books that family lineages are kept alive, anecdotes recorded, artefacts inventoried.

The tradition started in 1880 after King Rama V's favourite queen, Sunanda Kumariratana, died in a boating accident. She was pregnant at the time, staying at Bang Pa-In Palace near ancient Ayutthaya. It is said that when her boat capsized the male attendants were forbidden from touching her, since she was a royal lady, and she drowned before their eyes.

The commemorative volume produced for the royal funeral was composed by Prince Damrong, a half-brother of the king. This would have been one of his first publications. At the time he was a royal page, and his next published text would be five years later. This was an article in the Wachirayan Journal about the functions of organs in the body. It also included digressions on the meaning of physical pain in the Buddhist context.[1]

It was under the reign of King Rama V, 1868-1910, that a truly national conscience was born. The lands that would become Thailand were pulled together, the system of the *Ancien Régime* was reformed, a national story was created. Prince Damrong was largely responsible for the creation of a Thai historical identity. He wrote dozens of works on the Thai past, notably editing Kham Bunnag's histories of the first four reigns, and compiling and writing a series of studies that would be known as *Our Wars with the Burmese*. Damrong would also have a brilliant career as Minister of Education and Minister of the Interior, helping to create the nation's modern civil service. After leaving the Ministry of the Interior in 1915 he ran the National Library, where his mark was left on the National Archives, the practice of archaeology, Thai arts, crafts, dance, and the founding of museums. Damrong was a man of his time, and as such has been accused of censorship, and selective conservation, practices that were common throughout Europe during this era.

• • •

At the centre of the king's reforms was a distrust of the old family oriented power networks. On his accession to the throne the main ministries and provincial governorships were in the hands of a few old families. The Ministries of Trade and War had been dominated by the offspring of Dit and Tat since the 1820s. Rama V took steps that would shake up this system, replacing the old family networks with his own brothers, sons and close allies.

The noble families were pushed into the margins. They held onto important positions in the bureaucracy but would no longer exert the control they had enjoyed in Chuang's era. The sense of hereditary entitlement would be gone.

The new national narrative would have little time for anomalies. The past was straightened out: a Thai race fighting outsiders, orders top-down with vertical flow. The disquiet of the Thonburi Kingdom, or the trial of Prince Rakronnaret, who was accused of corruption, sedition, and immorality, could be expunged.

The funeral books were a space for remembrance that might rekindle something of the old family stories, and the receding atmosphere of the former system. They became fragments of a larger history in which the monarch was not always the focal point.

• • •

Funeral rites were to play a role in the fortune of Toh, Won's main heir. Toh's life spanned this period of reform. He was born in 1852, a year before King Rama V, and died a year before him, 1909.

Toh was a son of Won's first wife, and after his elder brother Chai died, he became the leading figure in Chuang's lineage.[2]

Toh was to die in Rajburi on the 8th of October 1909. The king had decided to take an excursion out of town to lift his spirits and Toh was part of the entourage. Toh began to feel unwell, and it seems that he died of a stroke. His cremation took place after a longish delay, as was the custom. Toh's corpse lay in honour at Wat Prayurawong for two years. By this time King Rama V had also passed away. Toh's cremation was presided over by the new king.

A book was made for the occasion along with a silver snuff bottle decorated with the Apollonian face of Chuang's sun crest.

Toh's ultimate title, Chaophraya Surawong Wattanasak,

matched that of his father, Surawong Wayawat, and echoed Chuang's, Suriyawong. He was the last in the lineage to achieve the rank of Chaophraya. Toh did not take over the Ministry of War, as had been the case for six generations, as far back as Jai, in the Ayutthaya period. He also lost Chuang's grand estate. The king had already called in large outstanding debts, that Chuang was seen to owe the crown in unpaid taxes. It is not known if Toh was involved in the repayment. The estate, which was the main collateral, stayed in the family for a few more years. By this time Toh was living in his own compound and Won had moved to his Italianate villa a few kilometres away.

After Won died, followed shortly by Chai, Toh was obliged to sponsor the joint funeral rites. His only option was to borrow from the king. Unable to repay the loan, Toh gave up Chuang's mansion along with the rest of the canal-ringed property.

Weapons

Oak is a distant relative. He is an expert on Siamese weapons and antique photographs, and is explaining the motifs and symbols that can be found on sword and spear blades. For example, in the Ayutthaya period, a blade might feature lotus designs; one would signify the rank of phraya, two for chaophraya and three for kings. By the time our family began to control the Ministry of War, the era of swords was largely over, and battles were fought with cannons and guns. Swords and pikes were increasingly ceremonial and part of the pageantry of power, a high-ranking official would be accompanied by his own sword bearer.

I was curious about the weapons and folklore relating to our martial ancestors. It was known that Siamese warriors would have been versed in magical practices, known as Wicha, which were meant to confer invulnerability, and were associated with weaponry as well as spiritual and physical protections. I had been asking various relatives about such matters to no avail.

The fate of their arms was also a mystery – some of the late 19th century swords were in family hands but mainly they were lost. The weapons could have disappeared for a number of reasons. The law in Thailand is strict and outdated about the ownership of guns; antique muskets and pistols are in the same category as functioning firearms. People deny ownership for fear of legal consequences, and swords, deemed unlucky to keep at home, were often given to temples, where the monks extracted the precious materials and sold the rest as scrap metal. In past times they were also melted to make cannons.

I had been told to contact Oak by several people. We had arranged to meet at his new gallery in River City. I arrive early and spend some time walking around, looking at some of the exhibitions and shop fronts. The place is deserted, almost ghostly. No tourist queues, no one shopping. The world in pandemic standstill.

I spot Oak from a distance. He leads me to his gallery. It has framed prints and paintings on the wall, and a back room, in which there is some antique Chinese furniture and a wine fridge.

Oak passes me his phone. He has an image of Toh he bought from a dealer in London. Toh was Won's second son by his first wife, and my great-great-grandfather. The print is set within a white frame of card, at the bottom of which is some text, A.J. Melhuish, 12 York Place, Portman Square, W.

Toh must be about 20 years old. He has his hair parted in the centre, is wearing a cravat and double-breasted jacket. One elbow rests on the edge of an armchair, he dangles the fingers of that hand into the other at his lap. His legs are crossed. He has a faint moustache and the familiar semi smirk, and confident gaze he wears in a number of other photographs.

The picture has been lost until now. The dealer had no idea, he thought it might have been a Siamese prince. I feel as if something has been retrieved; there is a small feeling of remorse, for lost things, mixed in with the pleasure of identifying the photograph.

It is the early 1870s and Toh is either at the end of his first stay in Britain, which started around 1867, or it is during his second trip roughly between 1871 and 1874.

Toh had been in the second group of Thais to be sent to study in the United Kingdom. There would have been four or five of them. He was sent to a school in Blackheath to learn English. The school no longer exists but it was the same place his uncle Pon, who had been in the first group, had attended a few years earlier.

After school, permission was granted for Toh to be placed within the British army, where he remained for 15 months. He was attached to the Royal Cheshires and stationed at Aldershot for a time, before being sent along with the regiment to Ireland.[1] Toh returned to Siam for a short while in 1871, and then went back to England, taking with him the young Prince Prisdang, who was to have such a curious career as diplomat and monk.

On his second stint, Toh was sent to Chatham with the Royal Engineers and then Woolwich Military Academy where he completed his training as an artillery officer.

It might have been expected, since Toh was the first western-trained Siamese army officer, that he would have been put to good use back home.

Toh's career had a promising start. He became a Major in the Siamese army in 1874, a short while after his return. By 1879 he can be found subduing a rebellion by Chinese secret society members in Tambon Donkrabuang Rajburi. However, the following year Toh was accused of Lèse Majesté for contradicting a royal edict, and handed over to the king for punishment. Toh could have been executed but the king decided to grant clemency.[2] Toh would go on to be the king's aide-de-camp, head of the first National Military Academy, a member of King Rama V's entourage and cherished companion but he would never attain the rank and power of his father Won, or Chuang, his grandfather.

In contrast is the life of Choem,[3] Toh's cousin, who was to rise to Field Marshal, and would become the most important military figure of the era. It might be said that Choem had the career that Toh never achieved.

Like Toh, he received a traditional military upbringing. He studied the classic *The Art of War*, practiced martial arts, horse-riding, marksmanship and the "dance of the tasselled lance." Although Choem was from the Xuto family, he was very much a Bunnag, the two families had intermarried thoroughly over the past century.[4] Choem was a great-grandson of Tat, through his mother, and a great-grandson of Dit through his father, Phraya Surasak (via his father's maternal line). He grew up at Tat's mansion, before moving to one of Dit's properties. Even so, Choem's father decided that he would join the cause and clique of King Rama V, in tacit opposition to his uncle Chuang.

During the Regency, the young King Rama V decided to

create a new bodyguard corps, that would owe its allegiance to him, and not to his guardian Chuang. Surasak asked Chuang if he could have permission to send his son Choem to this elite force. Chuang agreed but said at the time, "when you want to destroy someone else's house, you first take down your own roof." Chuang understood that this would be a first step in the unravelling of the ancient patronage networks.

When his father died, Choem felt lost and orphaned, with no clear patron.[5] He took it upon himself to protect his siblings, who included a half-brother called Yaem. The king took Choem under his wing. Choem was briefly ordained as a monk at the Temple of the Emerald Buddha, and was soon afterwards awarded the rank Chaomun Waiworanat, the Royal Sword Bearer, a title that Chuang and Won had both been given.

After the tragic boating accident that drowned Rama V's favourite queen, the head of the palace guard was dismissed. Choem was made joint commander of the unit. Soon he outshone his colleague, who was older and more conventional. The king could see that Choem was highly competent, aggressive and ambitious.

In 1885, Toh and Choem were sent to fight in Laos. This was a crucial arena, the Lao states were vassals of Siam, and were being ravaged by Chinese bandit armies, the Haw, who included remnants of the Tai Ping rebels. France was accusing Siam of mismanagement and weakness. It was clear that if the Siamese did not act swiftly the French would use the Haws as an excuse to send in soldiers and colonise the Lao principalities.

Toh and Choem's force sallied forth under a Standard into which a sacred lock of King Rama V's hair had been sewn. Toh was put in charge of the Front Army of Prince Prajak, to advance on Vientiane, and Choem commanded the First Foot, who would, in their advance on Luang Prabang, see most of the hard fighting. Luang Prabang had been sacked by the Haw, who left a trail of rape and pillage across the region.

The army Choem took north was a ragged thing; the troops were poorly drilled, undisciplined, and their foreign officer was removed on the march for quarrelling. Choem had limited equipment, out of date artillery, which they did not know how to use, and scarce supplies of food and munitions.

Choem had to train the soldiers as they marched north and improvise when they encountered their foe. Descriptions of the war bring to mind images of the 20th century Indochinese conflicts. They fought in the mud, and jungle, barbarities were perpetrated on the locals by the Haw, and, no doubt, to a lesser extent, by the Siamese. At times the Siamese were forced to fight off the French, who were only too happy to gain evidence of Siamese weakness and ineptitude. Choem was an able leader, he created improvised landmines and devastating "land torpedoes" adapted from the munitions at hand. Choem's successes on the battlefield were to earn him the rank of Chaophraya Surasakmontri.

On the way out, crossing Charoen Krung, Si Phraya, into Rama IV, I am travelling not far from Surawong and Dechochai roads. Streets that Toh constructed, and which were named after him. A succession of images arises, a 19th century life in stills.

It is circa 1860. Toh is a boy, with his mother and two brothers. His mother smiles, they are at home, either in Won's compound or that of Grandfather Chuang.

A few years later. A group of boys, some of Dit's sons and grandchildren. The only one wearing shoes is the eldest. He placed something, a beret, on top of the umbrella that leans against a wall next to him. The other boys' bare feet rest on uneven tiles. Perhaps it is the rainy season. Behind them a backcloth, with woven bamboo fencing to one side. A garden, or green climbing plants peer out from the edge of the frame on the other side. Toh, sitting next to his brother Chai, is wearing a shirt with a plaid pattern. Toh holds still, but several of the other boys' faces are blurred.

In middle age now, Toh is in Japan. He is part of Prince Bhanurangsi's mission. It is Toh's second time in Japan, having already been in 1887 with his uncle Pon. Toh is wearing a light-coloured top hat, and leans slightly on his umbrella. Prince Prisdang,[6] who will flee from the party when they reach Hong Kong, is a little to the right of him in the image.

Toh also pops up in the corners of Royal photos. He accompanies the king on the European tours of 1897 and 1907.

Toh is alone with King Rama V, photographed at the temple fair of Wat Benjamabophit. The king is seated, while Toh stands ingratiatingly to his left, the side of the heart. The staging was arranged by the king, part of a famous series of images made by him on that occasion.

Toh and the king look very similar. An aunt had told me that at times the king would use Toh as a stand-in, for functions he didn't want to attend. It is tenuous apocrypha, leading to thoughts about doppelgangers, and scapegoats.

Then come official portraits of Toh alongside his main wife, Lady Talap. He is in his full court and military finery. He has dozens of medals, a plumed hat and a sword, and an upturned moustache.

Finally, a picture of Toh with his sons, Tin and Tom. Judging by their clothes and the style of the photograph they are in England. It would be 1907, and the boys would be finishing at Cambridge. Toh has a slight paunch, his jacket is open, buttoned at the top, as must have been the style. He has a hand in his pocket, which seems an affectation. He has a gentle expression on his face, a certain paternal pride.

The Pantry

The pantry was for the telephone. If one were to call from abroad it could be excruciating. Someone might answer and wander off in a leisurely fashion to look for Chancham. Minutes would pass, with the sounds of the house echoing across continents, pennies turning into pounds on the bill before Chancham reached the phone.

Chancham refused to get a mobile phone when they started to appear in large numbers during the late 1990s. She said, "I am not going to join everyone else. They use it to call from their cars, *I'm in traffic, I will be late*. Since I already know that there is traffic, and that I will be late, I shall just be late, no need to call!"

But mobile phones, as we know, are much more than that. The tidal wave of smart telephony has carried away the sense of space relationship phone calls once had, along with much else.

The room – in its antediluvian manner – was therefore dedicated to conversation, news, the relaying of information, the setting up of engagements, the fulfilment of obligations, the strengthening of connections, giggles, quips, and those doodles executed with a free hand and a ready pen upon scraps of paper left beside the telephone.

The pantry was between the main kitchen and the library, next to a flight of stairs leading up to the workshop.

A fridge takes up the left side of the pantry entrance, with the sickly sweet scent of flower garlands, decay slowed by the cool. Between the fridge and the sink, which is next along this wall, is a photo of cousin Carla, twenty-something, looking radiant on a boat in Burma, a handwritten note thanks Chancham for the gift of the shawl she is wearing in the picture. Carla gazes from the surface of her delta river across the pantry towards a shot of her sister Inka, on her wedding day at the house, a girl in bridal-white beside her husband.

On the far wall is a large school photo from Malvern College in 1960. Dad is not at the boarding school yet, but Tej is beaming somewhere in the middle.

On shelves are chipped odds and ends of crockery, with dusty tea cups tilting on their hooks. Over the years nothing matches, as things have been lost and broken.

The right-hand side of the room features a wall-mounted drinks cabinet, some cupboards, and a counter, upon which are pictures in standing frames. There are other photos on the wall above. A rare image of the Silom house is here. It must be 1918, as Tom holds his infant son, Tula. An ancient automobile is parked in front of them beside well-tended hedges.

The assortment of family snaps range from the 1940s up until 2000. Dad and Tej as boys, Tanya and Jaru as teenagers, Uma dressed as a Thai dancer, a 10-year-old me under a fig tree in Greece. Tej playing football with colleagues at the Ministry.

Above these is a medium-sized photograph of Toh and his wives. Handwriting in the corner tells us that the king took this photograph.

They are at Toh's house in Khlong San. In the background the side of a building can be made out. It is a European-style house, whose gateway and lane is fringed with vegetation. Toh is wearing a white uniform and is sitting on a bench under a large pikul tree. Next to him is Lady Talap, his main wife; she looks unflinchingly at the camera. On the ground, sitting on carpets are his other wives: Taptim, Yai, Chua, Pard, Chaem, Chum, Kaap, Thongbai, Thongkham, Fiam, Bua.

My great-great-grandmother "Yai" is in front of Toh and like the other ladies averts her eyes from the royal presence behind the camera. A mischievous scratch makes it look like Toh has a cigarette between his fingers.

The king took more images in this series, but they are not displayed here on the wall. The second is very similar to this one but Toh is sitting on the ground with some of his children, presenting his profile and a jovial demeanour.

The third is from another angle, and further back. Toh is absent but some of the ladies and his children are still there. It has been taken from across a canal – some young men are in a boat at the bottom of the frame, above them, the house, the tree, and a large pavilion.

In 1997, during a summer holiday, I receive a call that my mother's cancer has returned, I must get back to England at the soonest.

The room, the characters in the pictures, the anonymous boys in the school photo, those half-drunk bottles of liquor – this setting and its props merge with my pain, the inanimate all invested with emotion – shining with feeling.

Lost in the Supermarket

I wander through the shabby neighbourhood behind Wat Buppharam in the direction of Toh's compound, noticing a large teddy bear and a mattress pulled up under a bodhi tree, by a canal. It's not clear if this is an offering, an accident, or a child's play area. The place has that black stench of stagnant water and effluence.

Toh's first house was within the large domain of his grandfather Chuang's compound before he moved across the canal to another piece of land – this was where Toh built his main house. I have printed out old photos which feature glimpses of the property, and intend to use them to make sense of the current state of affairs.

According to old maps, this area's streets and canals are largely as they once were. After a bend in the road, I see the bridge. A pretty street cleaner sits in the shade of a ficus with her friend; I had noticed them before, they seem eternally happy. The base of the tree is cluttered with offerings and strips of fabric. It is one of the only old things in the area, and I wonder if it is a child or grandchild of a tree that once grew at the edge of Toh's residential compound, upon which it stands.

A daughter called Liam had inherited the property. She was a child of Toh's first wife, Lady Talap, and had been married off to King Rama V when she was 16 years old, around 1900. "Chao Chom" Liam resided there until the 1950s before she moved to Wat Buppharam, where she spent her final years living a simple Buddhist existence. The property then went to a brother, whose son decided to rent the land in the 1960s and had the buildings demolished. The plot was eventually sold. It is now the site of a supermarket chain.

A new road cuts across the canal side of the property, with a row of shacks between the water and the vast shopping centre. The old landing pier would have been here, with steps leading up from the water, and various pavilions.

Tatiya and Tej visited Chao Chom Liam at the property when they were boys. Tej's memory was eclipsed by the more vivid trip to an American's private zoo nearby. Tatitya recalls a pavilion, the Thai-style house and a pond at the centre of the garden.

The plot is ringed by access roads for the shopping centre, a small alleyway threads up from the canal to the main road, frequented by motorcycle taxis. It's a harshly urban setting, with very few trees, or open spaces, everything is crammed together, jostling against the white sea-wall of the mall.

On the busy main road, the shopping centre sits generically – it could be anywhere in Thailand. A slab of concrete, plastic and glass. People wait for a bus outside by a small shrine to the spirit of the place, set just next to the mall's car entrance, which winds upwards to covered parking. It dawns on me that this soulless mall could one day also become a lost place of memory – I imagine a nostalgic adult passing in the hope of regaining a fleeting glimpse of a spectral friend, a deceased relative.

I stand staring at the blank whiteness of the shopping mall, trying to lay down the details that I have teased from my printed photographs. The objects and symbols of a jolly day, a white bench at the base of the tree, carpets on the ground, a stucco-fronted, western-style house, with a terrace, a gateway with a carriage grooved lane leading through a garden, a portico for carriages, a pavilion, with tiered roofs, supported by pillars made of cast iron or wood.

I have sketched what I can, attempting to plot out the known features. These I have matched to a partial map I came across, which seems to reveal a bird's-eye view of Toh's carriage portico.

It is a fruitless task. The buildings of Toh's residence that arise in my mind are flimsy, they cannot stand because they lack supporting walls. The tentative places I have made are buttressed by my desire to reclaim, and restore, and by this inconsistent mental activity alone. If I quit the exercise, the elegant mansion collapses back into the mud.

The game is reminiscent of Georges Perec. In my mind's hall of mirrors, I am re-reading his piece about Rue Vilin,[1] simultaneously while standing on the edge of Isaraphap Road in Thonburi. In the work, Perec returns to his former home in Belleville, he records developments on the street between 1969 and 1975, when it is all torn down for social housing and a park. In my desire for clarity about the past, I am stumbling in others' footsteps; they smirk at me, shake their heads. A line by Raymond Queneau returns to me, "That mindless mist where shadows swirl, how could I pierce it?"

Perhaps photographs will come to me, or a relative will offer recollections so that I can take conceptual walks through this family home, and explore the rambling garden with its decorative structures and delightful pond.

The photos and anecdotes I have are like those Chinese paintings, in which small details are favoured, scenes from lives, unfolding in a clouded landscape, behind veils of incomprehension and obscurity.

Georges Perec's literary games, and playful taxonomies, seem intellectual but touch the heart. Much of his work resounds with the loss of his parents. His father was in the French Army and was killed fighting the Germans when Georges was four. His mother was murdered in the Holocaust when he was six.

To write is to resurrect. In this mindset, I am presented with time, in its strange proportions. I am thinking about the past on the anniversary of my mother's death. I am 44 and she died when I was 22. I have been without her for half of my life. But what do the years represent? What does it mean to remark that Toh's house, in some form, stood between approximately 1880 and perhaps 1960? If only to say that Toh lived there between 1880 and 1909, 28 or 29 years at most.

A few moments have passed, as I gawp and reflect with my scraps of paper. I walk down Isaraphap, take pictures of dusty broken things along the way before reaching Prajadhipok Road, which I take back towards Wat Prayurawong. Up ahead a group of men stand staring towards me, they line the road menacingly. They are waiting for a bus.

The Kitchen

Memory should be bodily, made up of senses. The archaeology of a family past might feasibly include recipes, and notes about digestion. Lui, Chancham's father, told me not to eat certain sweets after a meal, they would give me wind he warned. The offending article was the small crêpe-like "khanom buang", with its dab of sugary goo and piled up "foi thong" – an eggy gold-thread of a dessert, introduced by the Portuguese in the 17th century. I had the impression that I would be wracked by terrible pain if I touched these mouthfuls of Siamese history, and have been cautious ever since. It is mysterious, since these dangerous things were served at his table. Was it a test?

The main kitchen is at the far end of the house, beneath the workshop. It is a large space that looks out at the unused back of the property. The kitchen can be entered via a side entrance, beside a sunken gutter covered by concrete slabs. The area is not for public viewing. It is functional. It is where the delicate and deliberate fabric of the family fizzles into the non-descript. I find the zone replicated, obliquely, by the back areas of food-stops on the motorway.

At a spot in Petchburi Province a sharp hill juts out of the flat landscape, it is called Khao Yoi, and features a shrine and a population of monkeys. Khao Yoi is also a popular place to eat on the journey south from Bangkok to Hua Hin. Its open air diner is generic: presenting vats of food, tables, magazine racks and snacks. The kitchens are behind, its woks and cutting-boards just visible, and beyond that can be seen flashing emeralds of vegetation, a promise of the abundant green of the nation – into which ultimately spill our leftover filth, waste-water, rats and bugs.

By chance, I came across a recipe in an old cookbook attributed to Chuang Bunnag, the Regent. The book was written in the 1950s by a lady called Jiip Bunnag.[1] She describes a dish called Khao Mao Khao Yoi, which, as the name suggests, is a snack from Khao Yoi made of rice.

> *Khao Mao Khao Yoi*[2]
> *(of Somdet Chaophraya Borom Maha Suriyawongse, Chuang Bunnag)*
> *Slice a hard piece of lard into long, thin pieces, and fry until crisp*
> *Put the lard oil aside for later*
> *Cut some pork into long strips, fry until crisp*
> *Fry some small freshwater dried shrimps, as above*
> *Cut some yellow tofu into rectangles, fry until crisp*
> *Pan-roast skinless peanuts*
> *Fry "flattened rice" (Khao Mao) until puffed but not yet golden*
> *This rice will be the main ingredient in the dish*
> *Sautee garlic until brown, which has been crushed and chopped*
> *Mix all of the ingredients in a pan, season with powdered sugar, salt and pepper, mix thoroughly, keeping the pan over the heat until the ingredients are hot*
> *Sprinkle with fresh coriander leaf and julienned kaffir lime leaf*
> *This is the way that Chuang liked his, others have their coriander and kaffir lime fried*

Jiip Bunnag explains that Chuang ate this often while he was in Petchburi Province. The ingredients are all cured, it seems likely that the snack is a traveller's repast. I can imagine Khao Yoi, then as now, a place to rest on the long journey – with Chuang's entourage appearing in the distance, a 19th century train of carriages, horses, and retainers. But this is a fantasy, since Chuang would have travelled fast and by water.

• • •

Culinary preferences are touching, because they instantaneously conjure a real person. Tula complained that Thai cuisine was being ruined, too much sugar and too much salt. According to Tula, in the old days poorer people associated such flavours with wealth and status. Now that salt and sugar were more readily available they were being used injudiciously, and the taste was not as it should be. Naturally, Chancham was easier to please than my grandfather – only she couldn't stand onion in her fried rice.

While Chancham could not cook, Tula reputedly made excellent *moules marinières, pommes frites*, and roast lamb.

But the house cook was called Khem. She came first, of the other people who lived at the house, arriving pregnant from Si Saket in the 1960s, with her husband, Wang. They would have three more children while living at the house before she left in the late 1990s. In time she was joined by a couple of brothers, one of whom, Umpai, stayed on even after Chancham passed away. He had a son called New. Then there was Duum, and her son Ding, and eventually his daughter, First. After Khem left, two of her sisters, Wilai, and Kamsri, turned up but didn't last long.

I do not have sensorial memories of the kitchen. It does not recall the food, the scent of cooking, the spices and curries of Thai life. My gastronomic memories take place elsewhere, at the table. The food magically appears, is eaten, the soiled plates then vanish into another world.

I spend no time in this space, seeing it only from outside; if I wander in I feel like an intruder. Here is where I feel most foreign. The kitchen is the most typically Thai space in the house.

Chao Chom Liam's Notebooks

One of my first memories of Tatiya is from the late 1990s. We are introduced by Chancham at a family gathering. He sits me down and writes out a list of ancestors starting with Mom Bunnag on a piece of paper, telling me, "If you ever want to know anything about the family please get in touch." It will be a long time before I take him up on this offer. I have seen the family lineage reproduced a number of times, lists of names, monosyllabic first names followed by long titles. None of it means much to me. I am only interested in the Regent at this point.

The family story seems like something to be received, a rote-learnt list, but it is as much about renewal as the factual recall of a distant past. The grand houses and the commanding positions of power, and many of the precious things had been lost by the time of Tula's childhood. So to search and find information and small details, that make sense of the remaining traces, is to make something new. Like memory, the past is a process, requiring exercise. And memory, like history, needs to be refreshed, revisited. There is no absolute history; it is always shifting. The artefacts are then made new, in the repurposing, resurrecting, re-seeing.

Tatiya has a book of genealogy made by Chao Chom Liam. He brings it along one day while I am in the dark of a library room marvelling at her portrait. I am trying to take a video, and some photos of this extraordinary thing.

The picture is housed in a box, metal-framed, with an antique electrical cord at the back, and dirty glass at the front. When switched on, its three old filament bulbs illuminate Liam's face, in stereo. She is an old lady, wearing a delicate lace and silk top, at her neck a miniature portrait of King Rama V. The technology is uncanny, making the details sharp and lifelike. Two or three photographs have been combined to animate her, so that the image wears a roving gaze. Tatitya tells me he saw it at her funeral in 1961.

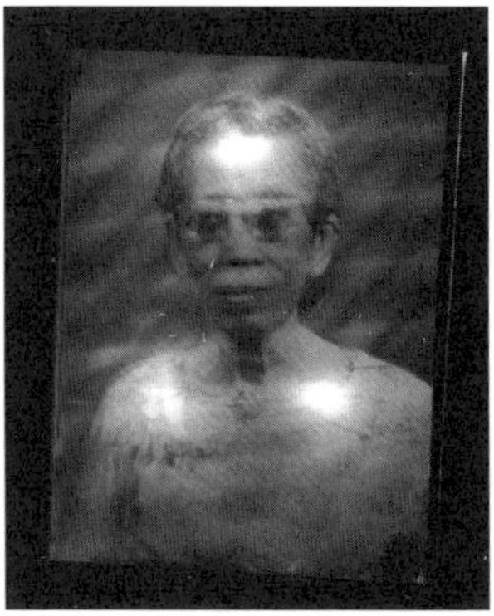

Liam was childless and when the king, her husband, died in 1910, she would have been in her late twenties. The future might have looked lonely. Her energies went into the family legacy, and as such she became a spiritual mother to Toh's many descendants. At Wat Prayurawong she commissioned buildings but her particular passion was Wat Buppharam. It had been bombed in the Second World War, losing a pavilion and two of its main halls. I believe the beautiful restoration of the temple complex was largely her work.

• • •

The book Tatiya has brought to show me is in her handwriting. It has a red cover, inscribed with one of the titles of Sheikh

Ahmad. Inside is a family tree, which Tatiya gently folds out, revealing the generations leading down to Toh, and that of Liam and her half-brother, Tom, who was my great-grandfather. The book includes biographical information, a hierarchy of births, and the ranks attained by Toh's children. It is something that is ongoing, individuals' titles are in flux, and additional births appear. One of the last entries states that Tom has married a lady called Son and they have a child called Tula. This would be 1918. Beyond this point the pages empty out, as if she became distracted or expected someone else to finish the work. It is the mother of genealogies.

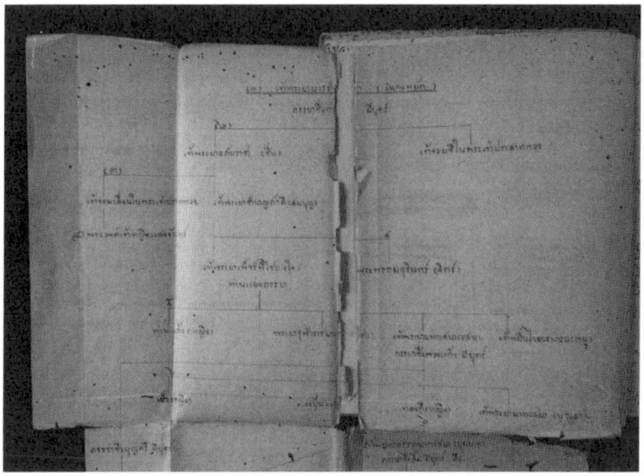

I look through some of her other books, which are disintegrating, literally turning to dust. One is a list of births and possible assignations at the Inner Palace, another is a small scrapbook featuring newspaper cut-outs. A child seems to have scrawled across many of the pages of these books, the pencil lines are faint and careless, the marks of an infant long-since old, long-since dead.

Mad Dogs and Englishmen

The Siam Society has a decidedly Anglo feel, with its signature punch, fruitcake, and auditorium, with the air of a school hall in the English countryside. But it is not the haunt of expatriates; The Siam Society is a venerable Thai institution, a capsule experience of a distinct tradition. It was established in 1904, towards the end of King Rama V's reign. The society and its journal, mainly in English with the occasional article in French, were to be a leading forum for Thai culture and history over the next century. It is a testament to the cultural trends of the era.

King Rama V's modernity bore many similarities to the colonial systems in place across the wider region. It was Bangkok-centric, which meant that the administration of the provinces was accompanied by the culture and language of central Siam. Concessions were awarded to companies for the extraction of commodities, like tin and timber, and foreign experts were often employed to manage and train the Siamese. Germans and Englishmen oversaw the railways, Danes organised branches of the military and constabulary, and Italians were commissioned to build palaces and public institutions. Meanwhile, from the late 19th century, increasing numbers of elite Thais were being sent abroad for their education. Kings Rama VI and VII both spent time in Britain. They both went to the Royal Military Academy at Woolwich (as it was then) and King Rama VI attended Oxford University.

By the reign of King Rama VI it no longer looked like Siam

would be invaded by a Western power. Not only was Siam not absorbed by British India, or French Indochina, but having contributed to the Allied effort, it was at the victor's table after the First World War. To a certain extent the country had survived colonisation by self-colonising. The royal form of Buddhism had been adapted to become more rational, more accessible to the western mind. Siam had reframed itself in a manner outsiders could comprehend and trust.

In the early 20th century, King Rama VI was staging Siamese productions of Shakespeare, and Gilbert and Sullivan. The reforms of his father had transformed, modernised and westernised at least a significant part of the Bangkok upper-crust.

• • •

Tom was born in 1885, the second son of Toh's third wife, Lady Yai.[1] She had three sons, Tin, Tom and Tao. Tin and Tom were quite the English gentlemen. In Tej's remembrance, "Tom drove a light-blue Morris Minor and played croquet on the front lawn of his house. He drank whisky in the evening with our step-grandmother and their friends who came to visit. He was not as English as his elder brother, who used to walk in the midday sun to visit, wearing crisp dark-blue long shorts, long socks, laced shoes, down Silom Road, with a black umbrella."[2]

The brothers had grown up at their father's compound in Khlong San. Tom would have been in his early teens, in the 1890s, when he was sent, along with his elder brother Tin, and a half-brother, Tiam-Surywong, to England for schooling. Tom and Tiam-Surywong went to Malvern College, and Tin was sent to Clifton – establishments selected by the Superintendant of Schools, an Englishman. After Public School, Tom and Tin both matriculated at King's College Cambridge and later trained in the Law.

The brothers, Tin and Tom, returning to Siam after their father's death, found themselves without an inheritance. Toh's land in Khlong San and the properties along Surawong Road had all gone to Lady Talap's children, their half siblings. They wrote to King Rama VI about the injustice of the situation, and the king exercised good judgement; only anecdotal fragments remain about the bad blood between the families. In spite of this, Tin and Tom's prospects in Siam were very good. Tin went to the Ministry of Finance and Tom found a position at the Ministry of Justice.

Tom was soon appointed judge at the international court in Phuket, an elegant posting where he would win a silver tankard at tennis. He then served at the Office of the Principal Secretary to King Rama VI before transferring to the Ministry of Foreign Affairs. These years would see Tom awarded the Siamese title Luang Nonthapanya, before being elevated to Phraya Sunthornchit. As a reward for his service, Tom received a property – a gift from King Rama VI, with a large house at the corner of Convent and Silom roads.

From 1913, with the king's introduction of surnames, Tom's family would now be known as the Bunnag Family. This moniker effectively threw a rough sheet over all sorts of knots, loose ends and mismatched strands – it was useful, and sometimes meaningful, and also misleading.

At some point, around the time of the First World War, Tom Bunnag married Son Saeng-Xuto,[3] a niece of Chaophraya Surasakmontri. In 1918 Tom and Son had Tula; but within two years Tom was a widower. Son, who was very beautiful, with melancholic eyes, had passed away, dying of tuberculosis in 1920.

These years heralded changes for Son's uncle, Choem, Chaophraya Surasakmontri. He had moved on from the military, becoming for a time Minister of Agriculture and Commerce. He founded a logging company with Son's father Yaem and other relatives, which did not do well.[4] At some point in the early 20th century he lost his Silom Road villa, Sala Daeng House, which went to another minister and was henceforth known as the home of Chaophraya Yommaraj, whose personal name was Sukhum. In 1921, Choem, the archetypal monarchist of the fifth reign, attempted to council King Rama VI to reform the Absolutist system, by reviving a royal advisory body. His proposal was dismissed as senility.[5]

After Son's tragic death, Tom remarried. His second wife was called Lady Ruen,[6] and they were wedded around the late 1920s, and would have a daughter named Didi.[7] For a time, Tom and Ruen lived in Rome, where Tom was the Siamese Minister at the Legation.

By 1932 Tom was back in Siam, soon becoming Permanent Secretary for Foreign Affairs after the Revolution. Before the system of Siamese ennoblement was ended, Tom would gain his final title Phraya Abhibal Rajamaitri.

285, Silom Road

Tom's house was an elegant colonial-style building. It stood two storeys high, was cream coloured, and fronted with extending shuttered verandas. The building faced Silom Road, with a garden that reached into Convent Road.

Stories about number 285, the Silom Road house, have an eccentric character. They spring from an era when the tram was still running, and the canals were flowing. The lady of the house, Tom's second wife – Ruen – called Tej "Puddles," and dad "Tittipoos." Ruen bred Siamese cats at the house. In the garden her tomcat could be found lying amidst his harem pawing gently at butterflies. A diplomat's child, Ruen spoke English and Japanese fluently, and brought to the house Japanese cuisine, her authentic Sukiyaki and *unagi* rice. She was always accompanied by a cocker-spaniel, and was fond of talking to animals, including her goldfish. They had a gardener who was skilled with snakes; he would catch them and gently present them to my dad. Yesterday, for the privileged few, was gracefully Chekhovian.

Tej remembered Chao Chom Liam visiting. He would be called to greet her whenever she came by, arriving in a chauffeured black car – still very beautiful, with kind eyes, wearing fragrant Thai perfume.

Today a high-rise building occupies the site of the original plot. A parking lot can be accessed from Convent Road and a generic office entrance takes up the Silom side.

I have never felt pangs at the loss of this place. The old house

had been torn down in the 1960s. Other buildings went up over the following years until it was sold in the late 1980s. The existing edifice is fitting for this busy street. The few old residences that remain in these districts must be shielded by high walls, else they float away on the tide of people, noise, dust and moving metal.

By the 1960s Silom Road had become very busy. Chancham called it Wall Street, and it was so loud from the traffic outside that the family had to shout to hear each other in the living room.

• • •

I am on Silom Road to buy photographic film; I can usually get it at the Thaniya building, the front of which is undergoing renovation. As I turn to look at Tom's former residence, it seems as if the entire street is a large building site. The place across on Convent Road has been torn down. This is where we used to park on nights out in the 1990s. The city was a mystery to me then. I would be bundled in and out of cars, without knowing where exactly I was heading, the city a dark blur. It was not helped that every time I came back to Bangkok the city had changed, there was so much construction going on. If I thought I knew something it was gone a year or two later – new highways, new high rises, new places to eat and drink – only the gang of cousin-friends remained the same.

My era has seen the Silom district become a backwater. It is no longer a Bangkok "Wall Street", not the most desirable residential area, and the old nightlife spots have become dusty and unfashionable – wedged between wide and busy Sathorn and Rama IV roads, and the river, it is a liminal zone of sorts.

I noticed on the way over to Silom, that Rama IV Road is also undergoing huge building works. The Lumpini park side of the road is being turned into an enormous complex called One Bangkok. The site of Choem's Sala Daeng mansion, which became the Dusit Thani hotel, is boarded off. The hotel is gone. Tej told me the old Sala Daeng House was beautiful, even in its dilapidated state, and stood well into the 1960s. On the opposite side of the road the old Robinson's shopping centre is shrouded for construction. This had been the Rose Villa of Phra Sophon Aksornkit, Chancham's grandfather.

The city, during the pandemic, is changing, getting ready for a bright new future, everything is still under-wraps but one day it will be unveiled. We are in mid leap, but towards what?

I take some photos of the corner of Silom and Convent. There is very little traffic on Silom Road, due to the pandemic. I am able to get some clear photographs from where I stand. It is not a pretty view, even without the cars. I know that it would not be improved by getting closer or further back; it's a monolith of glass and concrete, flat and non-descript.

The spectre of the house recalls great-grandmother Son. I picture Tula's face as a boy, something terribly sad in his eyes. I imagine Son died at the house. Tej tells me that when she was dying, Tula, who was two years old was allowed to kiss the soles of her feet.

The tragic anecdote brings to mind the ancient Greek belief that a family trauma, or curse, might take five generations to play out – the generations it takes for a Thai to go from noble to common. Growing up, Tula was spoiled by his great-aunt and nanny Nark, who looked after him. He was a difficult man, and could be hurtful. It is tempting to play hypothetical games.

Dad was born down the road at the Bangkok Nursing Home like my sister. He used to tell me about Tom's house where he grew up, describing it as a "plantation", where he loved to play in the grounds, would run into the kitchen and servants quarters and spend his time there.

He remembered the balcony where he heard his first row, between his parents about a venison his mother had been given.

Dad claims, like me, to have a memory from his cot, when only three or four months old – he is waiting for someone to come and get him. He remembers, as a three-year-old, playing at being a tiger with a rug in the downstairs living room and falling and breaking a glass ashtray that splintered and cut his forehead, almost reaching his eye.

It would have been at this house that dad was fitted out for cold weather clothes. He was six. They told him he would be going to England, and he asked if his best friend could come too.

The Workshop

Tula is smiling down from the window of the workshop above. If the house is a reflection of his personality and taste, the workshop is the inner-sanctum – it is his psyche. I'm standing in the driveway, near the pikul tree, about to go out. From on high, he is relating something amusing to Chancham, who stands beside me. He calls her "mom", which has nothing to do with the Siamese honorific – it's a shared joke from their time in 1950s England. But I am not listening to them. Tula has a look of contentment on his face, with that slight sardonic edge. His chin almost rests on the ornate window frame. I know he is sitting on his day-bed in the room above, which is next to that window. I wave to him and turn to go out. I will see him later.

After I leave, he leans back, laying his head on a pillow, he rests a foot on a drawn up knee. The loose fisherman trousers he wears at home reveal thin calves, almost hairless, silken skin, fine and taut at the end of life. Tula the dreamer reclines, lost in some kind of impenetrable reverie.

Above the bed on the wall is a photo of Tula as a boy. He stands next to Prince Damrong, an old man. Tom is nearby, as is one of the Vudhijai princes, and some European men. They are in Italy, during Tom's diplomatic tenure. Tula must be newly arrived, he has not gone to France for schooling yet. He wears a suit and holds a small case, flat against his legs, the small handle grasped with both hands. He might be 11 or 12 years old, has his mother's fine features, and stares confidently forward.

The floor of the workshop is made of thick, irregular planks, recalling its initial use as a floating house in Ayutthaya. It belonged to Chancham's family, who moored it in front of their property, near their shop on Koh Loy. Chancham and Tula used it during the War for a while, with Tej, who was a baby, while they sheltered from the Allied bombing raids on Japanese-occupied Bangkok.

A photo of the house, floating on Ayutthaya's Pasak River, hangs inside the current room. Close to it is another photograph featuring a group of King Rama VI's pages. Chancham's father, Lui, is here, sitting cross-legged in front, he wears a hat and shorts and a somewhat quizzical expression.

Beside Lui's picture is another of Toh's sons; they are lined up formally and their names are written on the print in English, all beginning with T: Tiam, Tom, Tin, Tao and so on.

The middle of the room is taken up by Tula's wood-working table, with its vice, brushes for glue and lacquer, and small electrical appliances. By the table is a swivel chair, covered in faux grey leather; on the floor a foot massage machine, to aid Tula's poor circulation and cold feet.

The workshop was Tula's escape from official responsibilities. Tula had joined the Foreign Ministry in 1942 but was seconded from there to be Secretary-General to Prime Minister Khuang Abhaiwong in the late 1940s. In 1954, he was back at the Foreign Ministry, with a posting to London. From 1960 Tula was in the Palace, where he was Lord Steward (Krom Wang Phu Yai).

Over these years he became very skilled at mother-of-pearl inlay, making delicate and humorous pieces: scenes from the *Ramakian*, curved boxes, a zippo lighter for Chancham, a paper knife. It was painstaking work, he drew the designs, traced them onto the wood, cut the myriad slivers of shell, which were glued to the work and then painted over with a thick coat of black lacquer. This was then sanded down to expose the glittering mother-of-pearl beneath.

The desk looks out of a glass-paned window. It has a view into the neighbouring property, but it is not possible to see their punch bags and Thai boxing training from this angle.

Behind Tula's desk, on the opposite side of the narrow room are cabinets, full of carved objects, unfinished works, projects he has delayed.

Next along from the work desk, is a small cabinet for collectable coins, and miniatures, and a built-in bench with leather-covered cushions. Above this is a long antique lithograph depicting a Siamese army marching to battle. It looks like a circus train, with its exotic beasts and elaborately dressed warriors.

The bench culminates in a low table topped by a lamp with a green glass shade. There are some books here. Leafing through Pitya Bunnag's history of the first Chularajamontris, about our Persian ancestors, Chancham comes to mind. She announces that the Persians stayed in Thailand because they were fond of dogs and pork. I ask her how Thais knew who was who before the advent of surnames. She tells me that they would have said that so and so was the child of such and such.

The wall facing Tula's day-bed is taken up by VHS cassettes, a mixture of black and white classics, and entertainments from the 1980s. Of these, their favourite is *Brideshead Revisited*, watched over and over again. In Chancham's final phase, becoming attached to a specific scene, she would call out, "Come quickly, Lord Marchmain is dying!"

The television is here, behind which is a large Chinese painting of a rabbit, a framed envelope addressed to Chancham and Tula, and an ink drawing.

This work of pen and ink depicts a doorway giving onto a flight of stairs. It was done by dad in Essaouira in the late 1960s. Those were the years when he was travelling with my mother, doing odd jobs – "on the road", as he called it. When they got to the Moroccan port town, he tried his hand at selling drawings, and worked as a waiter in a shicha house, fetching tea and replenishing pipes with fresh coals.

Completing the room tour is the small stretch of wall with bookshelves. These are taken up with more recent family photo albums. Here also is Tula's tennis trophy, 1936 winner of the schools doubles with Oleg. The trophy is inscribed to Tula Rajamaitri; recording the confusion between Tom's title, Phraya Abhibal Rajamaitri, and surname, which was Bunnag.

Just after the doorway is an armchair and a small desk, upon which is a framed photograph of Yajai, Tej's second daughter. She is a little girl, wearing a fur hat and smiling in a snowy garden in Beijing.

At this part of the room, near the television, is a round wooden table, that seats five or six comfortably. When we eat here, a large clay rice-pot is placed on the writing desk nearby – exuding an extraordinary scent.

Tula is known to hide out in this room, working on his carvings. When he is in a bad mood he might not leave the room to greet guests, who are not welcomed into his space. He tells me to fetch him sugary drinks from the kitchen. As a child, I marvel at the bubbles and the bright colours of the drinks.

Spatially the workshop is at the end of the upper terrace, beyond the rain-drum pavilion. From the terrace it is partly obscured by the top of a tree. Its doorway can be made out, along with a second entrance; this leads to an adjoining room used for storage – a handsome portrait of King Rama VIII hangs on the wall of this neglected space.

The Bridge

The Memorial Bridge was opened on the 6th of April 1932. It was the 150th anniversary of the House of Chakri. There were crowds of people and a certain tension in the air. Many had come to see the show – the courtly procession, the boats, the general pomp; others were there to see what would happen. There had been speculation for weeks that an uprising or a coup might occur.

This would be the first road bridge[1] to join the two banks of the river. Work began in 1929, from a design by the British firm that was responsible for the Sydney Harbour Bridge, with engineering supervised by an Italian company with expertise in such structures. It was to be monumental, load-bearing, with lifting bascule sections to allow river traffic. An aerial view, taking in the roads and gardens either end, would reveal the shape of a giant arrow, the symbol of King Rama VII, flying out from a statue of Rama I.

1932 had an apocalyptic air. In the 150-year-long timepiece, of the Bangkok prophecy, this was the moment when the sand would run out.

The divination of this fate was captured at the founding of the city. It spoke of a number of threats and endings, and was part of a folkloric tradition stretching back to King Narai of Ayutthaya, and even further back – into the Thai psyche. Ceremonies had been conducted to alter destiny. Rama IV had the city pillar moved slightly, to render a new birth date, with a fresh astrological chart. Some say that the site of the real pillar was kept secret, to prevent black magic being cast at the city.

The bridge, with its symbolism, iconography, and inauguration date, was intended to realign fate once again. The court astrologers advised that this would protect the institution of the Monarchy, and ward off the evil luck that was brewing for the 150th anniversary.

Meanwhile dissident factions, which had been growing in strength and popularity over the preceding years, made much of the prophecy. They publicised it in their manner – with whispers and gossip working without sleep in Bangkok. This, they said, would be divine justice – the system must fail, it was written into its very being.

King Rama VII had in fact planned to introduce a Constitution on this day, delegating his executive powers to a Prime Minister, supported by a semi-appointed Assembly. A team, that included Phraya Srivisarnvaja,[2] had worked out a draft proposal. Srivisarnvaja was an Oxford-educated lawyer, and had been involved in the post-First World War negotiations to revise and undo various treaties accepted by Siam during the 19th century. He was also Tom's close friend and colleague.

I picture Tom there, on that day of April in 1932, somewhere among the courtiers and the bureaucrats, perhaps recently back from Rome. Tom had been involved with the creation of the statue of King Rama I that would sit in the new park at one end of the Memorial Bridge. The statue had been designed in Bangkok by an Italian called Corrado Feroci, and cast in Italy while Tom was Ambassador. There is a photo of Tom at the foundry in Italy with the statue. In this bronze form, King Rama I is upon his throne, a warrior with his sword resting across his lap.

The new bridge was not just a crossing. It held particular significance for certain people there that day. Since Tom had been away for some years, he might not have seen the construction. I imagine him as he takes a moment to look about at the western riverbank and inland towards Toh's house, where he grew up.

To stand on the completed structure was to be raised above Dit's former mansion. The bridge piling sprung directly from his property. The new road feeding into the bridge ran over a filled-in canal and through the vanished house of Chuang; this newness described a long line of fire, smashing its way through a family's history.

The day went ahead without a hitch. There was no popular uprising, and no irregular military activity.

The film footage of the day records the routines and prescriptions of state ritual. It looks terribly hot, and the low-ranked officials and guardsmen appear scruffy and relaxed, bemused and even bored. But the film reel is frayed, the fatigued strip breaks apart; in retrospect it seems to capture pending hysteria – the crowd charges, desperate to get a view, a vantage point. That sea of unknown lives rush at the thin stream of functionaries.

A few months later, on the 24th of June, a group of military officers seized power. The king agreed to co-operate, accepting the new constitution, with his authority curtailed beneath the new regime. Phraya Srivisarnvaja was made Minister of Foreign Affairs in this initial government.

The first government was a weak coalition and fell after a bloodless coup in June of 1933. Tom was appointed Minister of Foreign Affairs for a short time. Later that year the government was threatened by a royalist counter-coup, led by Prince Boworadet. There was heavy fighting for a few days to the north of Bangkok before the royalists were broken. Tom was sent to see King Rama VII at Klai Kangwon Palace in Hua Hin, where he told the Court that the government meant business.

The king left the country the following year, and abdicated in 1935.

Although Tom was dismissed from government after this rebellion, and considered a royalist thereafter,[3] he was made Minister at the Siamese Legation in Washington D.C. from 1936 until 1940. He was Vice President of the Senate in 1946, before a final brief posting as Ambassador at the Embassy in Nanking in 1949, where his surname was transformed from Bunnag into the Chinese "Wen Na", meaning "cultured". He would be back in Thailand that same year, and rejoined the Senate, until its dissolution with the military coup of 1951.

"When our grandfather came back from Nanking in 1949, he went back to being a Senator, so he had work to do. Our mother would ask him what was going on during those difficult days and he would reply: muddling through, muddling through."[4]

Telegrams

Tej has been depositing documents from the Ministry of Foreign Affairs at the National Archives for years. I meet a woman who works for the ministry; she confirms that Tej has tried to instil some good habits regarding preserving documentation.

Some months after my lunch with Tej, I feel the impulse to browse the book he gave me. It is a hardback edition in A5, very official looking with a blue and white cover, at the top reading "Commemorative book on the occasion of the 70th anniversary of diplomatic relations between Thailand and Myanmar".[1]

I soon find myself following a story snippet, quaint with mentions of the British Overseas Airways Company, told in the punchy telegraphic voice of a cinematic insert. The episode features great-grandfather Tom and his son Tula, representing Thailand at the State inauguration of independent Burma in 1947.

To: Foreign Office, Bangkok.
Yesterday afternoon I met U Ba San… He said that the Foreign Office seems to be silent as regards the time of the opening of diplomatic relations with us. In the course of the conversation I have been given to understand that Burma is waiting for the lead of the great powers. I think it is better not to open the subject unless approached. However, he hinted that it may be a good opportunity while Phya Abhibal (Tom) is here to discuss the matter fully with the Foreign Minister.

(M.L Peekdip Malakul, Chief of Protocol Division, Ministry of Foreign Affairs of Siam)

To: His Excellency Tin Tut, Foreign Minister, Rangoon.
... I beg to inform you that Siamese Delegation headed by Phya Abhibal Rajmaitri, former Minister of Foreign Affairs and Vice President of the Senate and Nai Tula Bunnag, Secretary of Chief Delegate is leaving Bangkok... to attend the Independence Celebration.
(Phya Srivisar Vacha, Minister of Foreign Affairs of Siam)

To: Minister of Foreign Affairs of Siam.
Arrived safely...present at state luncheon given by Premier in farewell to Governor Hubert Rance.
(Phya Abhibal Rajmaitri, Tom)

To: The Prime Minister of Burma, Rangoon.
...I am happy to assure Your Excellency that Siam looks forward to a period not only of cordial friendship but of mutually beneficial collaboration with Burma in the interests of cultural and economic development of our two countries. It is therefore my fervent hope that under your enlightened guidance and endeavour Burma will from now on be blessed with an era of peace and prosperity...
(President of the Council of Ministers of Siam)

To: Minister of Foreign Affairs of Siam.
I have found a suitable house and grounds for our Embassy. Area of grounds about six rais with tennis court... the house is about four hundred yards from the American Embassy... I strongly recommend you to give me the necessary authority to close the deal with the owner before 10th January. If decision is given too late I'm afraid the Chinese government will take the property away from us.
(Phya Abhibal Rajmaitri, Tom)

To: Phya Abhibal Rajmaitri.
His Majesty's Government has decided to buy the house according to condition as reported. You are fully authorized to deal with the owner accordingly.
(Phya Srivisar Vacha, Minister of Foreign Affairs of Siam)

To: Foreign Office, Bangkok.
Arrive 10th BOAC.
(Phya Abhibal Rajmaitri, Tom)

A more lengthy report by Tom concludes with some words of gratitude to M.L Peekdip Malakul and Tula, who fulfilled their duties in a "most pleasing way."

Snapshots

The house is a large photo album. Each room has its pictures, on walls or framed on shelves and tabletops – over a century of pictorial stories. And my experience of Thailand – in refuge from the heat, the rain, the otherness – is photography and film, visual media: things shot, watched, edited.

This propensity started early, in schoolboy days, when I brought along my mum's camera. It was automatic, held in the palm, like a small video recorder. The mosaic background of my holiday snaps capturing the Cold War in its endgame. The camera being half frame it doubles a roll of film; photos come back from the lab paginated in shiny plastic folders, a flick-book of images. My photos are lost but the memories remain, bound to consumer technology – memory made by the machine.

In the 20th century technology and subject will describe similar trajectories, getting simpler, lighter, and more accessible. And memory becomes replicable: in posted artefacts, prints, books, photos, films – reproductions of copies.

Form is structure: the snapshots that fit the booklet. The film that exists in phrasings, with syntactical bursts lasting 24 or 36 images. Three-minute moving picture cartridges. Video-tapes that run to 90, or 120 minutes. The hierarchies of A and B sided vinyl albums. Computer memory that exists in the scrolling.

The medium is also emotion – defunct Polaroid squares and Super 8 strips of banal beauty, insulated against sonic realities. VHS, a nostalgic terrain of flat graininess, and Mini DV, rising from skate films and music videos, both bringing democratic poetry to broadcast media.

Those things belonging to the past, the 21st century will be different, but how? The smart phone, the instant every moment, the popular soliloquies for everything; all waiting for the digital apocalypse.

Our times seems lazier – not memorious, there is no need for memory, there is no codex, there is codec.

The struggle to resurrect lost memories shall be no more, because all will be eternally in the Cloud. The termites will not come to this utopia. It is not better, it is not worse, it just is.

And still, the lack of physical records and artefacts in our digital future raises an ancient spectre – the destruction of the past.

History will be more vulnerable to airbrushing because it will lack physical substance.

History will be more resilient because it will lack physical substance.

History will be more total because it will be everywhere and everyone's, but will anyone care by then?

The Library

The library, like the workshop for Tula, was Chancham's retreat. It was an escape from the atmospheric, and the quaintness of the Thai house. Chancham slept in this room in her final stretch of life. It was easier to care for her there when she could no longer make it up the stairs.

In a corner is a small desk that looks out at the muddy back garden, with its palms and bamboo grove. I picture Chancham sitting there, writing postcards in her fluid cursive, in green or red ink. She mentions trivial events, the dogs, or someone she'd met at the Oriental Hotel, or a dinner with relatives; she asks for news, a few lines, and tells me to come back at the soonest. She seems lonely, but always in a crowd of people.

One wall of the library is taken up by Tej's books, which are almost entirely mildewed histories. In between, is a glass-faced cabinet full of old Thai works.

Across the room are Chancham's books, although I remember pulling out a hardback edition of *Les Fleurs du Mal*, with an inscription to Tej and Jane, his first wife, as "a most Baudelairean couple". There are several copies of Scott Montcrieff's Proust, in single volumes, and in the larger combined editions, which came in three hefty tomes. Chancham loved Proust, and biographies, detective novels, poetry, short story collections, compilations of witticisms and quotes, and wonderful works like the Hobson Jobson dictionary of Anglo-Indian words and expressions.

The shelves by the entrance are filled with books on Thailand: Prince Bira's *Blue Wings to Bangkok*, *Lords of Life* by Prince Chula Chakrabongse, and titles like *Fanny and the Regent of Siam*, about the Knox Affair. All of the books in the little library have yellowing pages, spines that cracked, if they were paperback, and that scent, the essence of the old house.

While she sits at her desk, or stands in her busy manner, I read on the bamboo couch at the centre of the room. Inside a book I'm looking at is a letter, which causes me to chuckle. The letter is from Michael Smithies to Chancham, and is wedged between the pages of Smithies' book on the first Siamese embassy to Europe during the 17th century. He is unhappy with Kukrit's translation of his book, which has excluded large sections of the original. Would Chancham please contact "the Daddy of Thai Letters", and see if anything can be done.

The library was ruined during a huge storm. The rain did not let up. It was night, I ran downstairs to find the waters rising, and the room already flooded. I tried to grab arm-fulls of the lower books but it was too late for many. The maid, Duum, was giggling while very slowly lifting sodden books out of the flood.

At the end, I would bring her wheelchair into the library to fetch her, and take her on tours of the garden, until she uttered, "khao hong," I want to go to the room. Her English was almost gone, used up. One day she looked at me and then at my dad and asked in Thai, who is this Greek?

And so a library must represent the acquisition of knowledge and its loss. A snippet of conversation plays out:

Tew (my dad) to his mother, Chancham. "It's my birthday. I was born 54 years ago."

Chancham, earnestly. "Was I there?"

Tew. "Yes, definitely."

Chancham. "I don't remember."

Tew. "That's probably just as well."

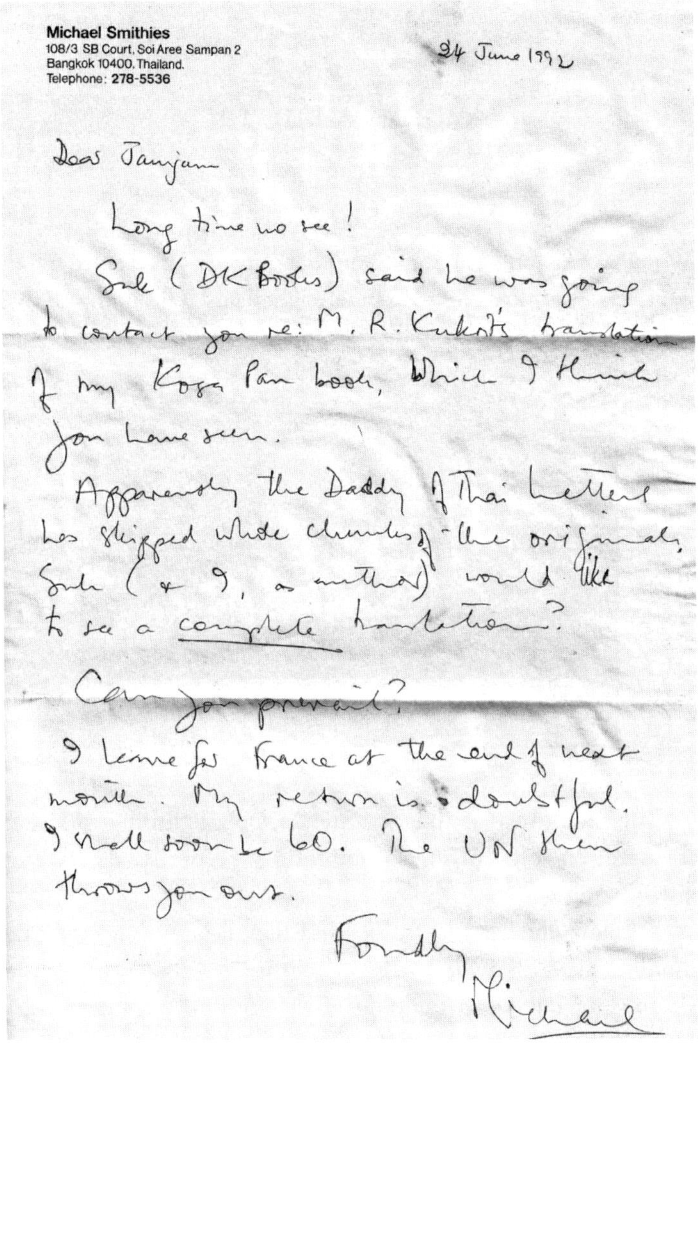

Michael Smithies
108/3 SB Court, Soi Aree Sampan 2
Bangkok 10400, Thailand.
Telephone: 278-5536

24 June 1992

Dear Janjam

Long time no see!

Suk (DK Books) said he was going to contact you re: M. R. Kukrit's translation of my Kosa Pan book, which I think you have seen.

Apparently the Daddy of Thai Letters has skipped whole chunks of the original. Suk (& I, as author) would like to see a complete translation?

Can you prevail?

I leave for France at the end of next month. My return is doubtful. I shall soon be 60. The UN then throws you out.

Fondly
Michael

Wong Wian Yai

Wong Wian Yai is a huge roundabout. At the centre is an equestrian statue of King Taksin, designed and built in the 1930s.

The monument is like an antenna, or a lightning rod, and the traffic circle a centrifuge – spinning out repressed desires and latent narratives.

I follow the circular footpaths, that lead me around the monument, cross wide roads on footbridges, and walk in the shadow of a tall empty building.

Down a side alley there is a second-hand stall: Thai soft porn from decades ago, paperback ghost and detective stories, clothes, and stacks of junk.

The place is tired, worn out, surrendered.

There is no tourism anymore. The pandemic has left us to our own devices. Months ago it felt like everything was the same. Still crowded, and hectic. In the rolling waves of disease, something emerges now – the city's idiosyncrasy, its submerged uniqueness – crabby faced, with lined visage and rotten mouth.

Bangkok's portrait is made of vending stalls, with mangrove density, choking fatigued streets, concrete oozing fetid water or split through with greenery, creepers on empty billboards, the rotting interiors behind the faded fronts.

But life in the city can be softened by conceptual games: imagine it's merely a fantasy about dystopian modernity. And this is easy. At some point in the 1980s, Bangkok became confused with various futuristic films. People would come back from holidays talking of the exotic city, with its showers of metal sparks flying off buildings at night, heavy rain, neon and bustle. The fairy-lights of Love and Death in the sinful dark.

But it wasn't the future they were seeing, it was the past.

In Japan they made up monsters after the War. But that's too far away. Our monsters were next door.

This is a capital of voyeurism. It's where people watched as Saigon and Phnom Penh fell. And gradually Thailand became a film set for depictions of those wars, the play-acting version of disaster and collapse – cinema scapegoating, producing celluloid votives.

After the Vietnam War, when the young soldiers left, Bangkok was alone with itself. But the lights at the go-go bars stayed on, although the girls got bored, since the feeling of death was less in the air.

The Vietnam War underscores part of the urban tale, those relic neighbourhoods with 1960s architecture. But beyond the drunken kaleidoscope of nocturnal experience, the war also played its role in historiography. Tej, who gives the Domino-Theory short shrift, told me about an unexpected by-product of American soft power. During this epoch, a large amount of funding was made available for scholarship in Thailand – a key front in the battle against Communism. Many Americans were able to spend long periods living in Thailand while they engaged in fieldwork and research. Bangkok was filled with writers and scholars.

It was during this period that David Wyatt published his study on the educational reforms under King Rama V, with his students Alfred Noel Battye, Craig Reynolds, and Tej, each working toward their respective theses on Rama V's military, monastic reforms, and administrative modernisation. In this hey-day, the period of Absolutism was comprehensively charted and made accessible to both the general public and other scholars.

• • •

I have completed the ambulation of the immense circle. I want to get into the big, empty building I have spied. Stepping up to an opening, I see an altar in the vast darkened foyer, made up of King Taksin's pointed hat upon a table bearing offerings. A man catches me peering in and hurries over. He won't let me approach. The escalators rise up to nowhere, everything is grey with city dust.

I leave Wong Wian Yai, imagining that large roundabout spinning us further into disease and isolation, mindful of one of Chancham's favourite quotes, "Cheer up, the worst is yet to come." (Mark Twain)

Deaths

Tom began to suffer from rheumatoid arthritis during the early 1950s. It would eventually cripple him. His hands became twisted and clenched, he was in pain and so incapacitated that he could not even swat away flies and mosquitoes.

When Tula moved back from London in 1960, he noticed Tom beginning to suffer from dementia. Tej and dad would also come back that year on holiday; it had been the first time they had seen Tom in six years.

Tom died of a stroke in 1961. By this point my dad had joined Tej at Malvern. Tej broke the news to him one morning before chapel. To his horror, dad broke into inexplicable fits of laughter. Tej looked at him and said, "Why are you laughing? Grandfather just died." Inexplicably, the painful laughter just came.

By the end of Tula's life he had emphysema. When we last saw each other his gait was stooped and he stopped often to catch his breath. A lifelong smoker, he went from two packs a day to a pipe, and then quit suddenly.

Tula and Chancham had planned to spend some months in Europe in early 1990. Tula was unwell on the flight to London. They stayed at a small hotel they liked in Kensington. The night they arrived he sat on the floor, Chancham held him and massaged his head. He died of a stroke in her arms.

In Athens at the time, I found out the next morning, just before school. I remember looking out of the car numbly as we drove down through Ekali, the pine trees, the dusty road riven by water channels, the brightness of the Attic spring, the day filled with something poignant and indescribable.

That night dad, standing by the mantelpiece over our hearth, cries. We try to console him but it feels futile. Choked words issue from him.

He went to England for the funeral without us. It was a small affair: Chancham, the two sons, people from the Embassy. On the way back, after the cremation, dad and Tej saw a car pull out in front; impossibly, it had the same number plate as Tula's car in the 1950s, which was OYY 5.

In his last years, Tula used to go to the Oriental Hotel several times a week while Chancham worked in the PR office. The staff knew Tula well, after he passed away they would see his ghost sitting in the Writer's Lounge at his favourite place, quietly listening.

After Tula died, Chancham had a building erected at Wat Prayurawong. She named it after Tom, using his title, Phraya Abibhal Rajamaitri. The building was used as a temple school for a while, and then as a place to house visiting monks, but nowadays it resembles a large storage space. Framed portraits of Tom and Chancham grace its entrance wall, they look into a space of neglect.

• • •

She always said that she wanted to die at home without any fuss. Chancham had seen her friends being kept alive on machines, and it could go on for years. She was terrified of the same thing happening to her.

Chancham had been ailing for some time before she was taken to Chulalongkorn Hospital. While she underwent surgery, I sat waiting with Tej, hoping dad would make it back to Thailand in time to see her. When I visited her alone, after the operation, I had a hard time convincing the ICU nurses to let me see her, they thought I was too foreign to be a relative. As she lay before me, I recited some lines from Eliot's Prufrock, before stopping. I was suddenly shy of the finality of this act. She gazed at me, I perceived recognition and gratitude.

She was taken up to another room, out of the ICU. Dad was there by then, as was Tej, and a few other people. I passed time reading Scott Moncrieff's Proust, while dad was struggling through some Henry James. Tej walked over, glanced at my book and said, "unreadable", then at dad's, "also unreadable."

A male nurse arrived to wheel Chancham off to see a cardiologist. As they were waiting for a lift, dad saw her sit up a little, then utter, "Sanuk," fun. The nurse was surprised. A few moments later she said again, "Sanuk," fun. This caused the nurse to titter then ask, "Grandmother, what is sanuk?"

Chancham seemed to look beyond my dad and the nurse, saying with deliberation, "Sanuk kap kwaam rak." Those were her last words, "Have fun with love."

Dad's last communication was later back in the room. He said to her, "Mae (mother) you had a great life." She looked at him and nodded.

I was in the room the night she passed away.

The funeral was at Wat That Thong, with the rites held in the pavilion named after her grandfather Phra Sophon. At the funeral, one of the officiants told me to prepare some low denomination coins. When I get home – I was no longer living at Chancham's – I was to throw the coins behind my back and not look.

Her body would rest there in the funeral Sala for months. Finally, after the right amount of time had passed, her corpse was burned. They made her ashes into the shape of a body that was peppered with coins. We were told to take some of these coins, sacred things to keep.

We dropped her ashes into the sea from a small navy boat at Sattahip; I wondered about all of the other urns sitting on the seabed.

Demolition

Not long ago, during the 2010 political violence in Bangkok, my dad received an anonymous email written in English. It told him that his time was up. They would hang him and the rest of our degenerate kin from the lamp-posts of the city. He called me up to ask if I had received one. I was not on the mailing list,

and it seems he was the only one in the extended family to get the email, which amused me, as did the colourful language of the work. If anything, it was flattering, our family sun had set a long time ago. As an act of revolution, or provocation, it was ill conceived and misdirected.

The authors sought a redress of historic injustices. It was our blood not our actions that was at fault; our ancestors would be punished through our living flesh. There was no follow up to this violent message. The stars of conflict swung away, and they have cycled through several times since then.

It is now 2021, mass protests continue and abstractions about the colour of one's blood, monuments, the past itself, have become Standards for the warring factions to rally around.

History haunts the nation. It is not events that still torment but the articulations about those moments that sow dissension. The mainstream is conservative but forbids analysis of the past it defends. The counter would be progressive and wants to set yesterday in structures that translate into cheapened words like feudalism, and absolutism.

My grandparents' house was crumbling, subsiding and rotting by 2005. The stairs were treacherous in the rainy season, becoming slippery, and worn down. The banisters could give way at any moment. Water leaked through from the upper terrace, and everything was mildewed.

Some of the walls to the master bedroom were paper thin, eaten through by termites. In my quarters, there was a green creeper bursting through the dressing room floor.

The house had been engulfed by the city, its noise and dust. It was not private, or comfortable, it stank of canal and sewage. So much needed to be restored. The rooms upstairs were barely used or visited. There were so many small objects that needed cleaning and looking after, the whole place was in need of love.

I am sitting with a friend in the workshop, feeling damp with rain pouring outside. Dad looks in and says with a laugh, "Sorry about the state of the house, it's how we are."

I overhear another friend describe it to an acquaintance, "He lives in a crumbling mansion that's out of a novel by Gabriel Garcia Marquez."

After Chancham's death I never go back.

The last story I heard about the house was to do with a team of workmen who had been hired to fix something. After an incident, which was never explained, they were so spooked by the house that they left all their tools and refused to return.

The family gatherings ended there. Without the house a disintegration was quickened; it was not simply because of the state of the house, distance and fragmentation had already set in. Dad came to Thailand less, the family rituals dried out.

The house was donated to a temple, to be restored and erected at a monastic complex in Ayutthaya. It was dismantled and transported there just in time for the great flood of 2011. The timber was washed away by the waters.

The Family Tree

I had been thinking about things that flourish in this soil, therefore about the nature of the earth in the region of Bangkok, what comes out of it, what goes into it. This is a theme in my life.

There are still orchards in the suburbs of Bangkok, in Nonthaburi, the northwest of the metropolitan region. These urban farms boast famous durians – that putrid delicacy. There are no better durians in the whole of Thailand. They flourish in the silty, saline ground here. And to the west of Bangkok, Nakhon Pathom is still proud of its "sweet pomelo, delicious rice and beautiful girls," as the provincial slogan runs.

It is not quite land, and not yet sea. Flat and featureless terrain. A whale carcass was dug up north of Bangkok, and large shells are to be found from time to time in the mud of the capital.

It is my son's first birthday today, and almost a year since I started thinking about this project.

We saved the placenta. It has been in our freezer all year. We never got a look at it. At the hospital they handed us a red biohazard bag. Last night I defrosted it, and this morning I poured it out onto a plate. Dark red blood, a large mass, like an ox's heart, veined and membranous.

We bought a tree to plant for the birthday, at a plant nursery in urban Nonthaburi. It is a three-metre high rose apple, that we hope will give us fruit around this time of the year, and red blossoms.

We were advised to plant the tree at 9.09 am, auspicious

numbers but we decided to wait until later, our son's actual birth time.

I had the city pillar in mind as we did our little impromptu ceremony. Dropping the beautiful placenta into the pit, then laying the tree, he touches the tree trunk but by now is tired and ready for a morning nap. Bags of nurturing soil are emptied around the tree and we drip the last of the blood at its base. There is no mishap. We are granted cloud for the ritual. As we finish, bright sunlight floods the scene.

Bangkok, January-April 2021

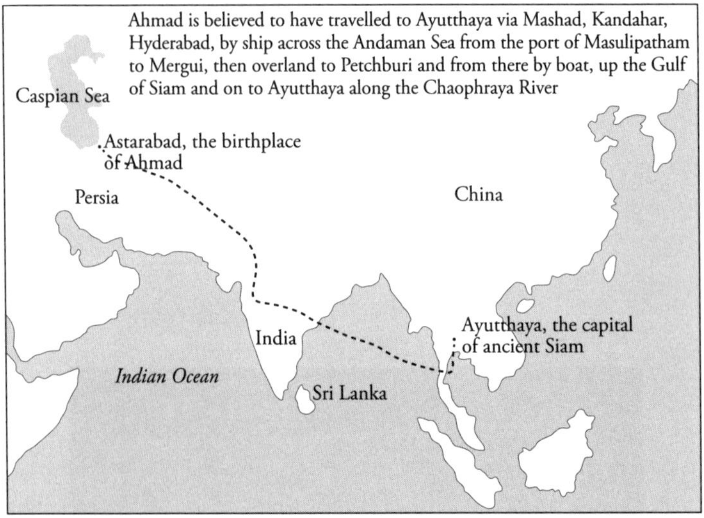
Ahmad is believed to have travelled to Ayutthaya via Mashad, Kandahar, Hyderabad, by ship across the Andaman Sea from the port of Masulipatham to Mergui, then overland to Petchburi and from there by boat, up the Gulf of Siam and on to Ayutthaya along the Chaophraya River
Caspian Sea
Astarabad, the birthplace of Ahmad
Persia
China
India
Ayutthaya, the capital of ancient Siam
Indian Ocean
Sri Lanka

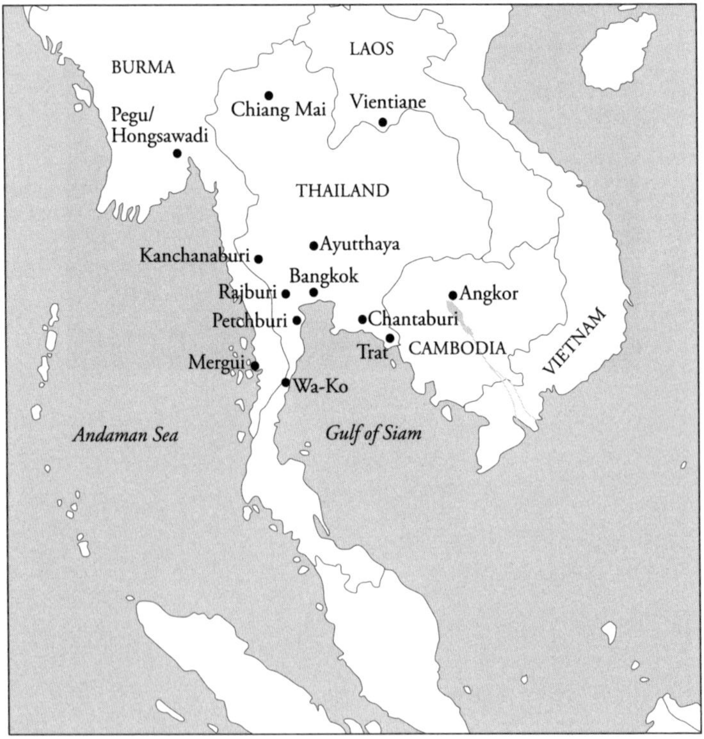
LAOS
BURMA
Chiang Mai
Vientiane
Pegu/
Hongsawadi
THAILAND
Ayutthaya
Kanchanaburi
Bangkok
Rajburi
Angkor
Petchburi
Chantaburi
Trat
CAMBODIA
VIETNAM
Mergui
Wa-Ko
Andaman Sea
Gulf of Siam

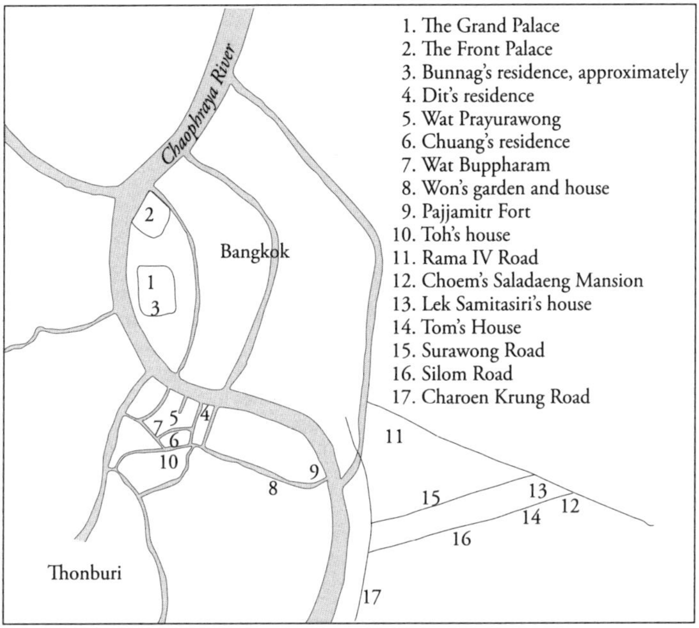
1. The Grand Palace
2. The Front Palace
3. Bunnag's residence, approximately
4. Dit's residence
5. Wat Prayurawong
6. Chuang's residence
7. Wat Buppharam
8. Won's garden and house
9. Pajjamitr Fort
10. Toh's house
11. Rama IV Road
12. Choem's Saladaeng Mansion
13. Lek Samitasiri's house
14. Tom's House
15. Surawong Road
16. Silom Road
17. Charoen Krung Road
Chaophraya River
Bangkok
Thonburi

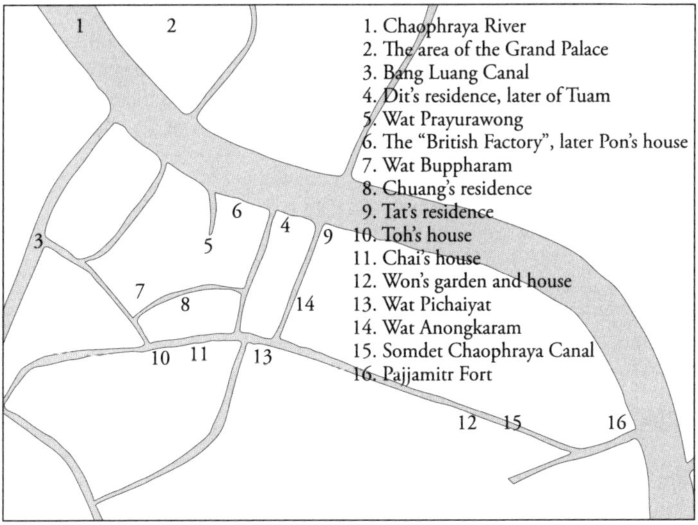
1. Chaophraya River
2. The area of the Grand Palace
3. Bang Luang Canal
4. Dit's residence, later of Tuam
5. Wat Prayurawong
6. The "British Factory", later Pon's house
7. Wat Buppharam
8. Chuang's residence
9. Tat's residence
10. Toh's house
11. Chai's house
12. Won's garden and house
13. Wat Pichaiyat
14. Wat Anongkaram
15. Somdet Chaophraya Canal
16. Pajjamitr Fort

Photo Credits and Captions

Front cover
Design by River Books from photograph by John Thomson (View of the Chaophraya River. 1864. Wellcome Collection) and detail from monk's fan (Wat Buppharam. Shane Bunnag. 2022)

Back cover
"B" initial on handkerchief that belonged to Tom or Tula Bunnag. Shane Bunnag. 2017

Opening section
Decaying book, belonging to Chao Chom Liam. Shane Bunnag. 2021

The Great Flood of 2011
Page from Chao Chom Liam's notebook. A list of Royal consorts. Shane Bunnag. 2021

Bunnags
Tula Bunnag and "Nark" (Bunnag Rattanakul). 1920s. Courtesy of Tew Bunnag

Tew Bunnag as a baby, held by "Nark" (Bunnag Rattanakul). 1940s. Courtesy of Tew Bunnag

Patsri Bunnag by Prince Kraisingh Vudhijaya. 1976. Courtesy of Eric Booth

The City of Memory
Chaophraya Thiphakorawong, Kham Bunnag. Mid 19th century. Photographer unknown. Wikimedia Commons

The Construction
Photographs of the construction of Tula Bunnag's family home. 1960s. All courtesy of Tew Bunnag

Nicknames
Lopburi early 20th century. Courtesy of the Prince Damrong Rajanubhab Library

Somboon's Eclipse
Engraving. King Narai and the Jesuits. Wikimedia Commons

The Fork and the Spoon
Snap-shot 1982, at the house of Tula and Chancham. From right: Chancham, Shane, Tanya Bunnag. Courtesy of Tew Bunnag

Tew Bunnag at 285, Silom Road. 1960s. Courtesy of Tew Bunnag

Four Reigns
Old Jacket. Shane Bunnag. 2017

Bangkok. Early 20th century. Courtesy of the Prince Damrong Rajanubhab Library

Buddha's Foot Print
A pagoda at the temple of the Buddha's Foot Print. Saraburi. Francis Chit 19th century. Courtesy of the National Archive of Thailand

The War
Tula and Chancham, newly wedded. 1942. Courtesy of Tew Bunnag

The Pikul Tree
Garden of Tula's house. Super 8 still. Shane Bunnag. 2000

Khlong Bang Nang Cham
Chancham reading, at home. Super 8 stills. Shane Bunnag. 2000

Water and Time
Ayutthaya river. Super 8 still. Shane Bunnag. 2000

Photograph of figure in landscape. Shane Bunnag. 2018

The Marble Dining Table
Photograph of guests at house. 1960s. Courtesy of Tew Bunnag

Photograph of the downstairs pond and setting, at Tula's house, by Alan Gilbert. Date unknown. The following page features the back of the photo, a letter from Chancham to Tej, she mentions correcting her translation of Red Badge of Courage

Mom Bunnag's House
Photo of Mom Bunnag's bronze bust, at Wat Prayurawong. Courtesy of Tatiya Bunnag

The Southern Wall
The southern wall of the Grand Palace, site of Mom Bunnag's residence. Shane Bunnag. 2021

Mnemonics
Untitled. Early 20th century. Courtesy of the Prince Damrong Rajanubhab Library

A Tour of Thonburi
Buddha image, disguised statue of Chaophraya Prayurawong, Dit Bunnag. Photo, Shane Bunnag. 2021

The Stupa of Wat Prayurawong, late 19th century. courtesy of Tatiya Bunnag

Exercise machines in front of the Pajjamitr fortifications. Shane. Bunnag 2021

Dit's Life and Times
View across Chaophraya River, with Wat Prayurawong in the background. 19th century. National Archive of Thailand

Empty lot near Wat Prayurawong. The location of Dit's coffee plantation. Shane Bunnag. 2021

The Upper Terrace
Super 8 stills of the upper terrace of Tula's house. Shane Bunnag. 2000

Dit's Folly
View of Dit's Khao Moh, Wat Prayurawong. Shane Bunnag. 2021

Lunch with Tej
Tej in his office at the Thai Red Cross. Shane Bunnag. 2021

Tej and Tew as boys. 285, Silom road. 1950s. Tej holds a chicken. Courtesy of Tew Bunnag

The Master bedroom
Bunnag forefathers. Illustration by Peter Bunnag. Photo by Shane Bunnag. 2021

Interior of the master bedroom. Video Still. Shane Bunnag. 2005

Chuang's Eclipse City
King Rama IV at Wa-Ko. Wikimedia Commons

Exploring Khlong San
Road networks running through the former site of Chuang's palace. Shane Bunnag. 2021

Chao Chom Manda Phae, one of Chuang Bunnag's granddaughters, and King Rama V's first consort. National Archives of Thailand

This is not a school photo, it is the first Bunnag Family Reunion at Wat Prayurawong. This was a gathering of the offspring of Dit and That Bunnag, therefore the "Rajinikul" ennobled lines of the family, but not the entire family. Late 19th century. The building in the background was destroyed in the War, and was once used as a schoolhouse. Courtesy of Tatiya Bunnag

Siamese Souvenirs

Chaophraya River. Unknown photographer. Mid 19th century. National Archive of Thailand

The Prussian Treaty Mission. Chuang is seated in the centre. Kham is top left. Carl Bismark. Courtesy of Tatiya Bunnag

Chuang Bunnag. John Thomson. Wellcome Trust

Lady Phan (of the Purananda family, an offshoot of the Bunnag clan). John Thomson. Wellcome Trust

Male offspring of Dit. mid 19th century. Francis Chit. National Archive of Thailand

The Drawing Room

Chuang Bunnag, late 19th century. Courtesy of Tatiya Bunnag

Super 8 still. Shane Bunnag. 2000

"Theatre" Programme. Collection of Shane Bunnag

The Palace Play

Chuang Bunnag. Francis Chit. National Archive of Thailand

The White Monkey

Photograph of the signing of the Normalisation Agreement between Thailand and the PRC. 1975. The note reads "For Tej, beloved grandson, grandfather Kukrit". Courtesy of Tej Bunnag

The second bedroom. Water colour and ink. Shane Bunnag. 1998

Tigers, Cobras, Crocodiles and Whales

Painting of the Siamese envoys at Fontainebleau by Jean-Leon Gerome. Wikimedia Commons

Won and Chai by Nadar. Courtesy of Tej Bunnag

Sanatoria

Won Bunnag in later years. Photographer unknown. Collection of Tatiya Bunnag

Won's house, designed by Grassi. Shane Bunnag. 2021

Grassi designed house in Khlong San. Shane Bunnag. 2021

The Little House

Video Still of the little house. Shane Bunnag. 2005

The wooden bedroom doors, painted by Tula. Family snapshot. Courtesy of Tew Bunnag.

Interior of the little house. Courtesy of Tew Bunnag

From Wat Bupparam to Ton Son Mosque

Graveyard at Ton Son Mosque. Shane Bunnag. 2021

Funeral Books

Engraving from photograph, depicting the joint funeral rites of Won and Chai. Courtesy of Tatiya Bunnag

Weapons

Toh in London early 1870s. Courtesy of Athada Khoman

Choem Saeng-Xuto. National Archives of Thailand

Toh and family, Toh is at the far right. Chai is far left, Lek and mother inbetween. 1850s. National Archives of Thailand

Toh with sons Tin and Tom (full brothers). In England, early 20th century. Courtesy of Tatiya Bunnag

Toh standing beside King Rama V. Courtesy of Athada Khoman

The Pantry

Toh with wives, a photograph by King Rama V. At Toh's mansion in Khlong San. Courtesy of Tatiya Bunnag

Toh's wives, years earlier. Photographer unknown. Family collection

Lost in the Supermarket

Toh's family and residential compound. Courtesy of the Prince Damrong Rajanubhab Library

The location of Toh's house, now a Big C supermaket. Shane Bunnag. 2021

Chao Chom Liam's Notebooks

Chao Chom Liam light-box portrait. Shane Bunnag. 2021

Chao Chom Liam portrait. From Wat Buppharam. Shane Bunnag. 2022

Inner pages. Chao Chom Liam's genealogy of Sheik Ahmad's family. Shane Bunnag. 2021

Mad Dogs and Englishmen

Tom in uniform. Family collection.

Son Saeng-Xuto, Tom Bunnag's first wife, Tula's mother. Family collection

285, Silom Road

Family House, Silom Road. 1920s. Family collection

The site of the family house. Silom Road. Shane Bunnag. 2021

Son Saeng-Xuto. Courtesy of Tew Bunnag

From left: Tula, his half sister-Didi as a baby, his stepmother Lady Ruen, Tom. Courtesy of Ravibhandu Panich

The Workshop

Tula with Prince Damrong Rajanubhab. Italy, 1920s. Courtesy of M.L. Apichit Vudhijaya

Tula in France 1950s. Collection of Shane Bunnag

Tula in the workshop, late 1980s. Collection of Shane Bunnag

The Bridge

Film still of the opening of the Memorial Bridge 1932. Courtesy of the Prince Damrong Rajanubhab Library

The Library

Letter from Michael Smithies to Chancham. Collection of Shane Bunnag

Wong Wian Yai

Double exposure on film. Wong Wian Yai. Shane Bunnag. 2021

Deaths

Chancham, Silom road. 1953. Courtesy of Tew Bunnag

Demolition

Tew Bunnag in study. Shane Bunnag. 2017

The house. 1980s. Courtesy of Tew Bunnag

The Family Tree

Family of Shane Bunnag, Dean, Pring, Camille (the dog). by the author. 2021

The Sun Chariot, and the charioteers. Detail Wat Buppharam. Shane Bunnag. 2021

Family Trees

16th-18th Century

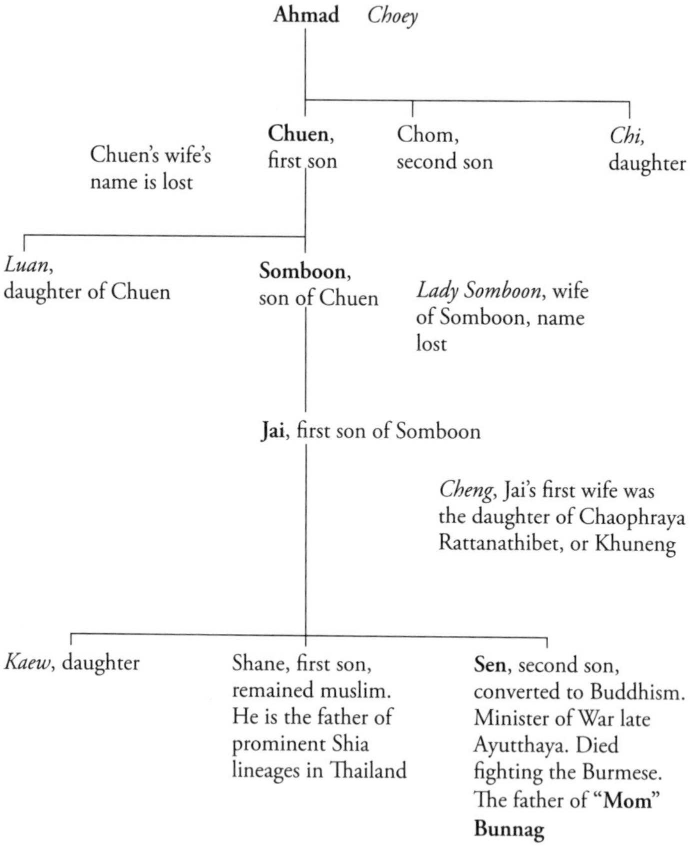

Family Trees

18th-19th Century

Sen

Mom Bunsri

"Mom" Bunnag,
son of Sen and Mom Bunsri

Lim, Bunnag's first wife. Killed during the chaos at the end of Ayutthaya

Nual, Bunnag's second wife

Thani, was the daughter of Bunnag and Lim. She became Consort of King Rama I, and the mother of Prince Surin

Nual was the younger sister of Nark, who would be Queen Amarindra of King Rama I. An elder brother, Xuto, is the ancestor of the Saeng-Xuto family, of whom Son Saeng-Xuto was Tula's mother, and Choem Saeng-Xuto, was Chaophraya Surasakmontri, Field Marshal of the Siamese Army

Dit, son of Nual and "Mom" Bunnag

Family Trees

18th-19th Century

"Mom" Bunnag

Nual of the Bang Chang family, Bunnag's principal wife

Dit, fourth son of Bunnag and Nual

Tat, sixth son of Bunnag and Nual

Chan, Dit's first wife

Tat's descendants are known as the Pichaiyat part of the Bunnag family

Chuang

Klin, Chuang's first wife

Won

Uam, Won's first wife, the daughter of a Chinese merchant

(Chai)

Toh

(Lek)

Talap, Toh's first wife, was the elder (half) sister of Yai

Yai, Toh's third wife

Tiam-Surawong

Chao Chom Liam

Tin, Phraya Suphansombat, first son of Toh and Yai

Tom, Toh and Yai's second son

Family Trees

19th-20th Century

Toh

Talap, Toh's first wife

Yai, Toh's third wife

(Saeng-Xuto Family)

(Tuam Bunnag's family)

Tiam-Surawong, the third son of Toh and Talap

Chao Chom Liam, Toh and Talap's second daughter. Consort of King Rama V

Tom, second son of Toh and Yai

Son, Tom's first wife

Ruen, Tom's second wife. Tom and Ruen were married about a decade after Son's death

Tiam, first son of Tiam-Surawong

Tula, Tom's only son

Chancham, daughter of Lui Indhusophon

Ramadi Teru, "Didi". Tom and Ruen's daughter

Tatiya, first son of Tiam

Tej, first son of Tula and Chancham

Tew, Tula and Chancham's second son, my father

Epilogue and Acknowledgements

I moved out of the house before Chancham died. My last experiences there were with a Greek friend, Alexander Seferiades, who has the honour of being our final houseguest. He took time out from his job as an economist, working in Eritrea, to finish editing a film we had co-directed in Athens in 2004. The first phase of the editing took place in the dusty and highly atmospheric basement of the ethnographic museum in Plaka, formerly the home of Alex's great-grandmother. The final cut was in Bangkok, where we occupied Tula's desk in the workshop, covering it in cables, bi-lingual notes, and Alex's overflowing ashtray and sticky beer-bottle tops (which did not belong to me, since I was abstemious, and rather weird, at the time). The film, *Ola Gia Tipota*, was an excuse to explore forgotten corners of Athens. We drifted through the modern city, picking up on the vanished town of the Ottomans, with its seven mosques and tea-house on the banks of the river Kifissos. Alex's family had been forced out of Asia Minor in the 1920s and they carried an infectious sense of nostalgia for old family lands and houses.

In completing the film, we took turns at the controls and the comfort of Tula's swivel chair. This would be the seat I used for most of *Chariot* – although now years later the chair is in a very bad shape, it's lopsided and very uncomfortable but it's one of the few things I still have from the old house.

Another Greek to aid in the creation of this work was Alexandros Georgiou, who kindly offered to read an early draft. After receiving his copy, he called to say, "Shane, I thought that your book would be filled with wistfully poetic photographs, but this thing has so many words. Do I really have to read all of them?" But he was a good sport, as well as a highly erudite and intelligent critic. He checked in after a few months to ask if my chariot had gone solar yet.

My father, Tew, is a fantastic storyteller, it is through his words that Thailand existed for me as a child, and it is thanks to him that my Thailand is so heavily associated with Greece. When I think of the Nang Nak Ghost story I instantly feel the hot southern wind of a night in Crete where he first terrified me with the tale, when I was seven years old.

Evidently *Chariot of the Sun* has a Greekness beyond its mythological title. The sun-like family emblem of Dit's descendents, evokes too the somewhat fraught symbol of Macedonia – it's an old joke with cousin Eric Booth, who helped me along the way with images and anecdotes, that the Bunnags being Persian must also be children of Alexander. The Hellenistic wish-fulfilment is only half in jest, we both grew up clutching works by Mary Renault, as we stumbled around Greek ruins.

I had been a little afraid of Eric's mother, Patsri, when I was younger. She had a fierce look about her, and I was always conscious of how poor my Thai was – so I often kept quiet in her company. I finally plucked up my nerve with Patsri towards the end of her life, aided by Patsri's fondness for my wife Pring (which had occurred before I had even met Pring). Patsri mocked me, "Why didn't you ever want to talk to me? You were always silent!" But Eric commiserated, "Oh, I know how it is, you're at a gathering with all of these people with the same name, and huge egos, best keep your mouth shut." It was a great joy to show Patsri one of my films, after which she said, "Puum jai laan" I'm proud of you.

After Patrsi passed away Pring was invited to curate a large-scale exhibition featuring Patsri's art collection and exquisite wardrobe. The exhibition was called *Mon Art du Style*, and was an inspiration, in the elegance in which it transmuted the memory of Patsri into a work of art.

Jean-Michel Beurdeley, Patsri's husband, is one of the finest raconteurs, and one of my favourite uncles. I would love to set down some of his experiences and recollections, in which he effortlessly combines a profound knowledge of Southeast Asian culture with humour, compassion, and sensory delight. He was the first person to tell me about the location of the home of Dit (and Chaophraya Phanuwong) beneath the Memorial Bridge, along with many other details – insisting that there is also a connection between the Bunnags and Cham royalty, which intrigues me but remains elusive. Jean Michel coined the "S.O.B. club" Spouse of Bunnag – of which my wife Pring is a member.

Lalana Panich is a close aunt, who supplied me with details about the life of her grandmother Lady Ruen, as well as photos; Ruen being another Bunnag who was somehow only marginally Thai. Aunt Salika Siddhisariputra, who is also Lalana's Mah Jong partner, shared some lovely anecdotes about displacement, that I was unable to use: her sister saying as a child that she would like to be reincarnated as a Thai; of their extremely Anglicised grandfather, Tin, and the fights he'd have with his wife over her predilection for spicy and very pungent Thai cuisine, which he couldn't abide. Salika was delighted that I was interested in the family, but less pleased when I bantered about her brother Decho– who had been arrested and sent to a camp in the mountains after the fall of the Kingdom of Laos. I knew him as a tough, rather debonair ex-Public Schoolboy, and had taken him at face value when he boomed, "Those days in the prison camp, they couldn't touch me, the prefects at my school were much worse." But of course his bravado was there to hide the full horror of that nightmare.

Salika's son, Sanya, her first child with Prince Panya Souvanna Phouma, is currently writing about the lives of his paternal ancestors, royalty of Luang Prabang. Our conversations about our parallel researches spurred me on, and gave me fresh perspectives. Sanya was also the cousin who got me interested in the court of Narai, as well as introducing me to Raymond

Queneau, Baudelaire, and Balzac; he handed me a copy of Lost Illusions just as I was leaving Thailand one year.

Sanya and I both feel the morbid quality of these endeavours. As I got started I felt an urgency to simply take record before the continuity is lost – with elder family members dwindling and increasingly unable to speak about the past. Most of the areas I was curious about appear in histories or are easy to find but the narrative thread is something that exists within the family, and is transferred via storytelling, accompanied by hoots of laughter. The book is about family stories and memory and mnemonics, but it is also a mnemonic device in itself. There is so much that could not be captured directly in these pages.

When I contacted Soraya Bunnag, who is of my generation and knows a great deal about the Bunnag family, she very humbly deferred to Tatiya, insisting that he was the best person to talk to, knowing "every little detail" about the family. I was a bit sceptical at first, but he exceeded Soraya's introduction.

It might be wondered why I stopped the story with my grandparents, and only touched on the experiences of Tej and my father. An answer comes via a conversation I had with Tatiya. I asked him if he thought there was such a thing as a Bunnag character, if the family displayed a distinctiveness. He shook his head and said, "If they did, it was all about the conditions of their upbringing. The later Bunnags could not be that way, it essentially ended with Tula's generation." As the nature of the family changed, the story became something else.

Tatiya has been an extraordinary guide through the family past. He was generous with his knowledge and wise in its delivery. In addition to the explorations I have described in the book, we exchanged vast numbers of messages; he fact-checked, and dug up photographs, and arranged things with family temples.

I was profoundly touched when Tatiya told me, after he read through the manuscript, that it was now my generation's turn, I was to continue the transmission of knowledge. I hope that I can do a good job, but I am not capable of doing this alone. It might be tenuous for others but this work is not an exclusion, it is more about the reclaiming of plurality, and I hope that the story and its music can be for everyone – not just the Bunnags.

A character who pops up in the book a few times is Pitya, or "auntie Pitya" as I was once told to call him. He is Tula's first cousin, so one of the last remaining members of that generation, the grandchildren of Toh Bunnag. I called him before this was published to ask if he minded the mention of his research on penis ornamentation. He gave me his blessing.

One of my interlocutors was Sueb Punyaratabandhu, who is not a relative, as I had believed for most of my life. He knew my grandparents from childhood, and was in the crowd of friends who saw off Chancham at Hualampong station in 1938, when she left for her studies abroad. I recall him at the house acting in a 1980s TV series, being shot there, in which he played a 19th century doctor; and officiating over the first Bunnag reunion I attended as a gangly 13 year old, when I fell down a flight of steps in front of half of the clan.

It is my fate to be called foreign, wherever I may be. In Thailand I am called either a farang or a khaek. I know very well that in a crowd I stand out; perhaps this is fitting for a member of a Siamese family with Persian, Tai, Mon, Lao, Hokkien, Teochiu, and Indian heritage; to which I add my mother's Hiberno-Norman and west-coast Irish blood. If any of this still matters I will take foreign, and be alive with open eyes.

One way the book is not just Bunnag is in its remembrance of Chancham. I am grateful for the input of her sister Netrachaleo Sanpitak. I wish I could have stretched out the digressions about the Samitasiris and Indhusophons; however, I am glad to record the familial warmth of Pinaree Sanpitak, Chatchai Puipia and Shone in these pages.

On the thorny issue of being Thai, I reproduce a recent line told to me by Ing K, "It's not about the way you look or speak, it's what's in your heart." She was an early reader of the book, who offered many insights and useful suggestions.

The book covers a great deal of territory but it leaps past many fascinating subjects, and is clearly not a comprehensive history of the Bunnag family, the narrative is confined to my direct ancestors and the members of the family I happen to be close to. Even with this restriction *Chariot of the Sun* tangentially features many descendents of Dit, through his sons: Chuang, Pon, Tuam, and Tet. The book's representative of Tat's "Pichaiyat" branch of the family is Athada Khoman. He is one of my generation's best in his grasp of Siamese history and specialised knowledge, and he very kindly allowed me to reproduce some photos from his collection.

My "elder brother" Art, M.L. Apichit Vudhijai, suggested I get in touch with Athada, but it was Paisarn Piemmettawat who actually connected us. Paisarn was enthusiastic about the project, and gave me good advice and some photos.

Art has been family to me since we met in England as children. He has always looked after me – providing me with an, often humorous, education on Thailand, as well as insights into its glories and mysteries. Art helped me get in touch with the Prince Damrong Rajanubhab Foundation, and many thanks go to its Chairman M.L. Panadda Diskul for the support and use of images.

The book caused some gushing and welling-up. I shared a bout of teary speechlessness with my dad after he first read the manuscript. Dad had helped me along the way with photos, and stories, but was unaware of the book's character. Having read it, he told me he was proud of me, to which I replied, "Well that's almost enough for me with the book", which felt true at the time. But had that been the case I would not have had the opportunity to see it through. This end-stage has been with M.R. Narisa Chakrabongse, my brilliant, and patient, publisher. We also had a moment of sympathetic light weeping, in our recollections of departed family members, and struggles to restore and resurrect.

I had Narisa in mind as I wrote *Chariot*, and it is a dream come true to have it at River Books. Narisa was also one of my inner critics, as I wrote I would channel her voice, "That's too florid Shane, what on earth are you trying to say here?" But ultimately she proved to be highly supportive, doing the line edit and pulling me up on facts, as much as my ramblings. It has been a great pleasure working with her.

My dad and Tej both wrote introductions to the book, but I decided that they were too good to be appendages and opted to absorb them into the main body of the text. The introductions were examples of how differently the two brothers approach the subject of the family story, and this came up time and time again, while putting together the book. *Chariot* is almost as much about siblings as parents, and this divergence in the act of storytelling is something that must arise. I have it with my own elder sister, Tanya, with whom I share some many of my earliest experiences. I thank her for imparting impressions of the old house and our grandparents. If this had been a different work I might have found space to include at least her first two children, Zahara, who played next to Chancham when she was an infant, and Skylar who was born in Bangkok, a year before Chancham passed away. I might also have found space for my stepmother Denys, and younger sister Uma. I would too have included Jaru, and her daughter Amber. But the story I chose ended with Tula and Chancham and the small details about Tej and Tew, myself, and other junior members of the family are incidental.

Tej is the only person who could tell the immediate family story, correctly, with all of the facts to hand, and in its context, but he is far too busy to do so. I'm happy if I have been able to act as his mouthpiece or scribe from time to time.

Until this book Tej had been an enigma to me, getting to know him better has been a pleasure and at times a complete revelation. He appears through out the book, so no need to dwell on what he has meant for the work, suffice it to say that he is one of the major sources. I also thank his assistant, Pacharadon Srinavarat, who did a lot of work on this book, chasing up and double-checking information. I must also thank Tej for the "programme" of the Shakespeare event at the house, which reads like a who's who of British Ambassadors, and for the beautiful photo of the house pond – both handed to me at the funeral of Peter Bunnag.

I recently noticed that Tej had donated various artefacts from my grandparents' collection to the Siam Society. These are things I recognised from their drawing room, and the Siam Society library is a wonderful home for them. I am truly indebted to the Society, in particular its journal, as must be apparent from a glance at my references. I would like to believe that my book belongs somewhere in the curious niche of Anglo-Thai letters of which the *JSS* is the torchbearer.

• • •

It goes without saying that this work could not have been done without the love, patience and support of my wife Pring. She had to put up with me, disappearing into the centuries, she read and offered advice and checked over the text. I also want to thank her father, Pichai Chindahporn, for his kindness and wisdom, and for putting us up, and putting up with us during this pandemic pause. Pring has always been there to motivate and nurture me, it is not an exaggeration to say that she brings out the best in me, as does our son Dean.

Endnotes

Hyrcania

1 Herodotus. Histories 7.62
2 Herodotus. Histories 3.117
3 www.iranicaonline.org/articles/gorgan-iv
4 Also www.iranicaonline.org/articles/gorgan
5 There are of course conflicting opinions about the chronology of Sheikh Ahmad. Bearing in mind various accepted facts, or stories, regarding Ahmad (the rough date of his arrival in Ayutthaya, details about his activities, and the approximate date of his death) I have followed the chronology put forward by Outhai Phanuwong, www.bunnag.in.th/english.
6 David Wyatt. Siam in Mind. Silkworm Books. Chiang Mai. 2002. p 40
7 Majid Daneshgar. The Study of Persian Shi/ism in the Malay-Indonesian World. Journal of Shi'a Islamic Studies. Volume 7. No.2 Spring 2014. ICAS Press. p196
8 www.nationthailand.com/life/30206285
9 Prince Chula Chakrabongse, Lords of Life. River Books. 2019. p 69
10 Majid Daneshgar. The Study of Persian Shi/ism in the Malay-Indonesian World. Journal of Shi'a Islamic Studies. Volume 7. No.2 Spring 2014. ICAS Press. p198
11 *ibid* p198.

Bunnags

1 Classic Thai. Periplus Editions. Hong Kong. 2002
2 The Thai word "laan", which means both grandson and nephew*
3 Things Thai: Antiques, Crafts, Collectibles. Tuttle. 2012

The City of Memory

1 Chris Baker. The Final Part of the Description of Ayutthaya with Remarks on Defense, Policing, Infrastructure and Sacred Sites. JSS 102. 2014 also- Chris Baker. Markets and Production in the City of Ayutthaya before 1767. JSS 99. 2011
2 Chris Baker. The Grand Palace in the Description of Ayutthaya. JSS 101. 2013. p96
3 Pitya Bunnag. Pathom Chularajamontri jak Persia thung Krung Sri Ayutthaya. Matichon. 2005
4 Mohammed Ismail Marcinowski. Persian Religious and Cultural influences in Siam/Thailand and Maritime South East Asia in historical perspective: a plea for a concerted interdisciplinary approach. JSS 88. 2000. p188

5 Pitya Bunnag. Pathom Chularajamontri jak Persia thung Krung Sri Ayutthaya. Matichon. 2005

6 Indo-Iranian Foreigners' Field*

7 For example, Chris Baker and Pasuk Phongpaichit. A History of Ayutthaya. Cambridge University Press. 2017. p125

8 Mohammed Ismail Marcinowski. Persian Religious and Cultural influences in Siam/Thailand and Maritime South East Asia in historical perspective: a plea for a concerted interdisciplinary approach. JSS 88. 2000. p90

9 Outhai Phanuwong, www.bunnag.in.th/english

10 "Siamese dignitary in court uniform; Oc-Chau Phraja Bovora Raja Najok (Xekamat) (Sheik Ahmad?) The Prime Minister of Siam and Commander-in-chief during the reign of Phra Chau Songdham King of Ayuthdhaja A.D 1603." Pitya Bunnag. Pathom Chularajamontri jak Persia thung Krung Sri Ayutthaya. Matichon. 2005*

11 Guy Tachard. Voyage To Siam. White Orchid Press. Bangkok 1981. p 266

12 David Wyatt. Family Politics in 17th and 18th century Siam. Studies in Thai History. Silkworm Books. Chiang Mai. 1994. p99

Calling Up The Past

1 Pitya Bunnag. Kep Wai Nai Kwarm Trong Jam. Self published. 2020

The Construction

1 Andrew Turton. Architectural and Political Space in Thailand. Natural Symbols in South East Asia. SOAS. 1990. p113-130.

2 Martin Stuart-Fox and Paul Reeve. Symbolism in City planning in Cambodia. JSS 99. 2011. pp120-124

Nicknames

1 according to Kulap, from David Wyatt. Family Politics in 17th and 18th century Siam. Studies in Thai History. Silkworm Books, Chiangmai. 1994. p99

2 Prince Damrong Rajanubhab. *Our Wars With the Burmese.* White Lotus Press. 2001. p209

3 Mohammed Rabi Ibn-Mohammed Ibrahim. The Ship of Sulaiman. Translated by John O'Kane. London. 1972

4 *ibid* p77

5 Mohammed Rabi Ibn-Mohammed Ibrahim. The Ship of Sulaiman. Translated by John O'Kane. London. 1972 p94

6 *ibid* pp95-96

7 David Wyatt. A Persian Mission to Siam in the Reign of King Narai. Studies in Thai History. Silkworm Books. 2004. pp93-94

8 *ibid* p94

9 Chris Baker and Pasuk Phongpaichit. History of Ayutthaya. Cambridge. 2017. p127

10 Outhai Phanuwong. www.bunnag.in.th/english

11 Mohammed Rabi Ibn-Mohammed Ibrahim. The Ship of Sulaiman. Translated by John O'Kane. London. 1972. p101

Somboon's Eclipse

1 Guy Tachard. Voyage to Siam. White Orchid Press. Bangkok. 1981. p235
2 Bunnag Lineage Book. Thai Wathana Phanit. 1999
3 Guy Tachard. Voyage to Siam. White Orchid Press. Bangkok. 1981. p232
4 *ibid* p231
5 *ibid* p230
6 *ibid* p203
7 *ibid* p230
8 Michael Smithies. Eclipses in Siam, 1685 and 1688. JSS 91. 2003
9 David Wyatt. Short History of Thailand. Silkworm Books. Chiang Mai. p103
10 Smithies. As above. p6
11 Baker and Phongpaichit. History of Ayutthaya. Cambridge. 2017. p168
12 Baker and Phongpaichit. History of Ayutthaya. Cambridge. 2017. p169
13 *ibid* p155
14 Julispong Chularatana. Indo-Persian Influence on Late Ayutthaya Art, Architecture and Design. JSS 105. 2017 p30
15 Richard D. Cushman. The Royal Chronicles of Ayutthaya. Siam Society. 2006. pp385-6
16 *ibid* p405

Four Reigns

1 Kukrit Pramoj. Four Reigns. Silkworm Books. Chiangmai 1998
2 *ibid*
3 Princess Vibhavadi Rangsit (aka V na Pramuanmark). Prisna. Penguin 2020
4 SEA Write Anthology of Thai short stories and poems. Silkworms Books. Chiang Mai. 1998

The Buddha's Footprint

1 The sacred properties of the footprint were evidenced by an injured deer Hunter Bun, "Hunter of Merit", had shot that ran in there and was healed of its wounds
2 Richard D. Cushman. The Royal Chronicles of Ayutthaya. Siam Society. 2006. p209
3 Richard D. Cushman. The Royal Chronicles of Ayutthaya. Siam Society. 2006. p218
4 *ibid* p308
5 *ibid* pp361-2
6 *ibid* p372
7 He would be given the title Chaophraya Chamnan Borirak. David Wyatt. Thailand a Short History. Silkworm Books. Chiang Mai. 2004. pp111-112 Chamnan Borirak was a descendant of an Indian Brahmin, Chaophraya Siri Wattana, who had arrived in Ayutthaya during the reign of King Prasat Thong. His family, like that of Ahmad, had risen over the past century, holding various powerful positions. Chamnan Borirak was to take over the Trade Ministry, and on his death was accorded the funeral rites of a royal. His great-granddaughter would be the mother of a prominent Bunnag ancestor, Chuang. David Wyatt. Family Politics in 19th Century Thailand. Studies in Thai History. Silkworm Books. Chiang Mai. 2004. pp114-115.

8 Richard D. Cushman. The Royal Chronicles of Ayutthaya. Siam Society. 2006. p419
9 in 1734, according to Baker and Phongpaichit. History of Ayutthaya. Cambridge. 2017. p214
10 Baker and Phongpaichit. History of Ayutthaya. Cambridge. 2017. p214
11 Richard D. Cushman. The Royal Chronicles of Ayutthaya. Siam Society. 2006. pp426-427
12 *ibid* p447
13 *ibid* p447
14 David Wyatt. Thailand a Short History. Silkworm Books. Chiang Mai. 2004. p114

The War

1 Ruen's father was Ambassador in Tokyo from 1910- 1928, he was Siam/Thailand's longest head of mission ever. Lady Ruen was educated at the Sacred Heart's School in Tokyo

The Pikul Tree

1 Branigan and Merrony. The Gardens at the Royal Palace of Ayutthaya. JSS 87. 1999
2 folklore.usc.edu/pikul-flower

The Ministry of War

1 Michael Smithies' introduction to The Diary of Kosa Pan. Silkworm Books. Chiang Mai. 2001. Smithies quotes David Wyatt p15
2 Ian Hodges. Time in Transition. JSS 87. 1999
3 He was also known as Prince Gung, gung means shrimp*
4 David Wyatt. Thailand a Short History. Silkworm Books. Chiang Mai. 2004. p113
5 *ibid.* p458
6 *ibid.* p469
7 Prince Damrong. Our Wars with the Burmese. White Lotus Press. 2001. p292
8 Richard D. Cushman. The Royal Chronicles of Ayutthaya. Siam Society. 2006. pp479-480
9 *ibid* p480
10 *ibid* p495
11 *ibid* p492
12 *ibid* p519
13 *ibid.* pp518-19
14 Yodyar Naing Mawgun. Translation by Soe Thuzar Myint. JSS 99. 2011. Stanza 33. p18

A Decade of War

1 David Wyatt. Family Politics. Studies in Thai History. Silkworm Books. Chiang Mai. 2004. p117
2 Chaophraya Thipakorawong. The Dynastic Chronicles. Bangkok Era, The First Reign. Translated by Thadeus and Chadin Flood. Tokyo. pp9-10
3 Prince Chula Chakrabongse. Lords of Life. River Books. 2019. p61
4 Edward Van Roy. Prominent Mon Lineages from Late Ayutthaya to Early Bangkok. JSS 98. 2010. p217
5 Richard D. Cushman. The Royal Chronicles of Ayutthaya. Siam Society. 2006. p495
6 Chaophraya Thipakorawong. The Dynastic Chronicles. Bangkok Era, The First Reign. Translated by Thadeus and Chadin Flood. Tokyo. p316
7 David Wyatt. Thailand a Short History. Silkworm Books. Chiang Mai. 2004. p126

8 Baker and Phongpaichit. History of Ayutthaya. Cambridge. 2017. p266
9 *ibid* p267
10 *ibid* p267

Mom Bunnag's House

1 Edmund Roberts. Embassy to the Eastern Courts of Cochin-China, Siam, and Muscat, In the U. S. Sloop-of-war Peacock. During the Years 1832-3-4. p281
2 Edward Van Roy. Bangkok's Bunnag Lineage from Feudalism to Constitutionalism. JSS 108, part 2. 2020
3 Chaophraya Thipakorawong. The Dynastic Chronicles. Bangkok Era, The First Reign. Translated by Thadeus and Chadin Flood. Tokyo. pp192-197
4 Sala Magazine Issue no.20 January- February 2020
5 Craig J. Reynolds. The Case of KSR Kulap. JSS 61. See second footnote on the first page of the article.
6 David Wyatt. Thailand, a Short History. Silkworm Books. Chiang Mai. 2004. p229

The Southern Wall

1 Joti Kalayanamtra. Six Hundred Years of Work by Thai Artists and Architects. 2003. p18

Mnemonics

1 The institution was altered over time, becoming a Second Kingship under King Rama IV, until its abolition under King Rama V
2 The story can be found in both Prince Chula Chakrabongse's Lords of Life. River Books. 2019. p93-4 and Sala Magazine, no18. p40
3 B.J. Terwiel. The Origin and Meaning of the Thai City Pillar. JSS 66. pp170-171

Dit's Life and Times

1 Embassy to the Eastern Courts. Edmund Roberts. p302
2 George Findlayson. The Mission to Siam and Hue. 1821-1822. Oxford. 1988. p119
3 W.S.W. Ruscenberger. Two Yankee Diplomats in 1830s Siam. Orchid Press. 2006. p172
4 Findlayson p129
5 Frederick Arthur Neale. Narrative of a Residence in Siam. London. 1852
6 *ibid.* Neale is possibly wrong, but this is what he wrote. Tej insists that Anu's cage was suspended to the left of the main entrance to the temple of the Emerald Buddha, and he may not have been tortured.
7 Edmund Roberts and W.S.W Ruschenberger. Two Yankee Diplomats in 1830s Siam. Orchid Press. 2006.
8 *ibid* p35
9 *ibid.* p43
10 *ibid* p46
11 Edmund Roberts. Embassy to The Eastern Courts. p277
12 Howard Malcolm. Travels in South-Eastern Asia. p135
13 Ruschenberger. Two Yankee Diplomats in 1830s Siam. Orchid Press. 2006. p185
14 Frederick Arthur Neale. Narrative of a Residence in Siam. London. 1852. p26

15 *ibid.* p28

16 Sir John Bowring. The Kingdom and People of Siam. 1855

Dit's Folly

1 David Wyatt. Thailand, a Short History. Silkworm Books. Chiang Mai. 2004. p151

2 Edward Van Roy. Bangkok's Bunnag Lineage. JSS 108 part 2. p24

3 A. Noel Battye. The Military, Government and Society in Siam, 1868-1910. Cornell. 1974. p95-96

4 also Edmund Roberts and W.S.W Ruschenberger. Two Yankee Diplomats in 1830s Siam. Orchid Press. 2006. p191

Chuang's Eclipse City

1 Sir John Bowring. The Kingdom of Siam. 1857. p282

2 Prasart can mean Castle/ Fortress. The word is also lodged within the name of a temple Chuang built in Rajburi.

3 Letter dated April 30th 1850. U.S. Congressional Records volume 1851-52

4 Bowring writing to Harry Parkes. May 8th. 1855.

5 Joti Kalyanamitra. 600 years of Work by Thai Artists and Architects. p45, note 11

6 *ibid.* p46, 50, and Adey Moore. Early British Merchant… JSS 11. p25

7 Frederick Arthur Neale. p23

8 Edward Van Roy. Siamese Melting Pot. Silkworm Books. Chiang Mai. 2017. p182 (not expressly attributed to Chuang, but presumably under his direction).

9 Rajburi, Samut Sakhon, Samut Songkram, Petchburi and Kanchanaburi

10 Prawat Wat Buppharam. Printed as a temple offering. 1992. pp1-4

11 *ibid*

12 A. Noel Battye. The Military, Government and Society in Siam, 1868-1910. Cornell. 1974. p 95-96 there is also an account written by Dan Beach Bradley for the Straits Times, which can be found in B.J. Terwiel. History of Modern Thailand 1767 - 1942.

13 A. Noel Battye. The Military, Government and Society in Siam, 1868-1910. Cornell. 1974. p96

14 This conjecture rests on a quote of Kham Bunnag (translated and perhaps embellished by Charles Bells and Robert Hunter Junior, two Englishmen in Siam in the 1850s). Kham at the time was working closely with Chuang during the "Bowring" trade negotiations. Kham and Chuang, who were half-brothers, were in agreement regarding the existential necessity of opening up to the British in trade, and reforming the taxation system. "Let us not have our ministers appointed for life, let them be elected for a term of years, and let their election depend on the voice of the people." Cited in Simon Landy. The King and the Consul. River Books. 2021. p37

15 A. Noel Battye. The Military, Government and Society in Siam, 1868-1910. Cornell. 1974. p99. There also are hints of this story in Simon Landy.

The King and the Consul. p52, pp80-81
16 David Aubin. Eclipse Politics in France and Thailand in 1868. 2007.
17 Malcolm Smith. A Physician at the Court of Siam. From Aubin p13
18 These details of the event from Henry Alabaster, quoted in Manich Jumsai History of Anglo-Thai relations. Bangkok. 1970. Pp79-88
19 Tamara Loos. Bones Around My Neck. Cornell. 2016. p175, note 17
20 Henry Alabaster quoted in Manich Jumsai History of Anglo-Thai relations. Bangkok. 1970. p87

Exploring Khlong San

1 A Chao Chom, now defunct, was the title of a consort who was not of royal blood, and therefore could not be Queen.

Siamese Souvenirs

1 Anake Nakigawune. Tale Telling Old Photos. Bangkok. 2020. pp83-85
2 Paisarn Piemmettawat. Siam through the lens of John Thomson. River Books. 2018. p13
3 Joachim k. Bautze. Unseen Siam. River Books. 2016. p38
4 *ibid* p75
5 Kham would eventually go blind, after paying a fortune to a Dutch oculist to surgically remove his cataracts. Lippincotts. 1873. p239
6 Bunnag lineage book. Thai Wathana Phanit. Bangkok. 1999.
7 R. Adey Moore. An Early British Merchant in Bangkok. JSS 11. 1914
8 Joachim k. Bautze. Unseen Siam. River Books. 2016. p83
9 *ibid* p83
10 *ibid* p31

The Palace Play

1 cited in Simon Landy. The King and the Consul. River Books. 2021. P116
2 John Bowring. The Kingdom of Siam. 1857. p275
3 William L. Bradley. Siam Then. Pasadena. 1981. p40
4 Frederick Arthur Neale. Narrative of a Residence at the Capital of Siam. London. 1852. p58-60
5 A. Noel Battye. Military, Government and Society of Siam, 1868- 1910. Cornell. 1974. p24
6 Sir John Bowring. The Kingdom and People of Siam. London. 1857.
7 Sir John Bowring. The Kingdom and People of Siam. London. 1857. Entry of April 9th.
8 The Palace, like Chuang himself, was perceived to carry a threat by some foreign observers. An example of this is the rather far-fetched, "(Chuang)… is to commence the erection of a new palace which will exceed that of the king in size and magnificence. There all the brothers are to take up their residence and bold must be the king who dare attack them." Harry Parkes

quoted in Simon Landy. The King and the Consul. River Books. 2021. p36
9 Anna Leonowens. The English Governess at the Siamese Court. 1870.
10 Prince Chula Chakrabongse. Lords of Life. River Books. 2019. p186
11 Kullada Kesboonchoo Mead. The Rise and Decline of Thai Absolutism. London. 2004. p 39
12 webpage- www.accesstoinsight.org/lib/authors/thanissaro/toh.
13 Frank Vincent. The Land of the White Elephant. 1874. pp153-157
14 Kullada Kesboonchoo Mead. The Rise and Decline of Thai Absolutism. London. 2004. p 61
15 for sources used in this loose rendition of the Crisis please see A Noel Battye. The Military, government and society of Siam. Cornell. 1974. pp194-196
16 Mead. As above. p59
17 Manich Jumsai History of Anglo-Thai relations. Bangkok. 1970. pp125-130
18 John Russell Young. Around the World with General Grant. 1879. M. Thiers is a mystery.
19 *ibid* p231
20 David Wyatt. Thailand, a Short History. Silkworm Books. Chiang Mai. 2004. p183
21 Anake Nawigamune. Tale-Telling Old Photos. Bangkok. 2020. p 89
22 David Wyatt. Thailand, a Short History. Silkworm Books. Chiang Mai. 2004. p183

Tigers, Cobras, Crocodiles and Whales

1 Kukrit and Seni Pramoj. A King of Siam Speaks. Bangkok. 1987
2 There is some confusion surrounding this date. It might be noted that the Pramojs date the letter 1864. But I have gone with 1867, as the letter is dated in Thai archives, and following most other authorities. 1867 was also the year in which a treaty was signed between France and Siam
3 John Knox was in Siam working for the institution of the Front Palace. King Mongkut was suspicious of his actions, which were to be apparent under the following reign, Knox seems to have attempted a British capture of Chiang Mai (see Manich Jumsai. History of Anglo-Thai Relations. pp125-126)]
4 Dominique Le Bas. La venue de l'ambassade siamoise en France en 1861. Aseanie 3. 1999.
5 Painted by Jean-Leon Gerome
6 Joined in this historic voyage to the west, Chai will eventually die within a year of his father.
7 cited in David Aubin. Eclipse Politics in France and Thailand, 1868.
8 Michael Smithies' introduction to The Diary of Kosa Pan. Silkworm Books. Chiang Mai. 2001. p 22
9 A. Noel Battye. The Military, Government and Society of Siam, 1868-1910. Cornell. 1974
10 According to Kulap, and Tatiya. This would have began when

Chuang invited American Missionaries to stay with him in Chantaburi, where Dit was building forifications, and Chuang was busy with ship construction.

11 *ibid.* p283

12 According at least to the French Governor of Cochin-China, A. Noel Battye. The Military, Government and Society of Siam, 1868-1910. Cornell. 1974. p 108

13 Abbot Low Moffatt. Mongkut, the King of Siam. Cornell. 1961. p177 Moffatt seems to have taken the story from Kukrit Pramoj.

14 Kullada Kesboonchoo Mead. The Rise and Decline of Thai Absolutism. London. 2004. p38

15 cited in: P. J. N. Tuck. The French wolf and the Siamese lamb, the French threat to Siamese independence, 1858-1907. White Lotus. Bangkok. 1995.

Sanatoria

1 Piriya Pittayawattanachai. The Architecture of Joachim Grassi in Siam. M.A Thesis. Silpakorn University. 2011

2 The map is of Bangkok in 1901. It displays the distinctive canal-cut rectangle of Won's property. The book is entitled Portrait of Bangkok.

3 Grassi's second commission after the Concordia Club, which has long since gone.

4 For example, through the introduction of the State and Privy Councils, the Supreme Court, the Royal Pages Body Guard and later the First Foot Guard

5 visible in an old photograph I believe is of the site. Mark Graham. Thai Wood. Amarin. Bangkok. 1996. p82

6 The first and second wives were daughters of a rich Chinese merchant, and named Lady Uam, and Lady Im– then came Sanphi, Li, Bua, In, Prik, Kaew, Pu, Tap, Klaam, Chun, Rum, Jap, Pring, Thet, Siangyom, Kliang, Chaeng, Won, Tua, Tawsrisunthornnat, and Yaem.

7 Kukrit Pramoj. Four Reigns. Translated by Tulachandra. Silkworm Books. Chiang Mai. 1998 edition. p23

8 *ibid* p635

9 *ibid* p4

10 Piriya Pittayawattanachai. The Architecture of Joachim Grassi in Siam. M.A Thesis. Silpakorn University. 2011

11 and in Cambodia, Battambang Province, and areas around Siem Reap were to be ceded in 1907

The Little House

1 pictorial traces of my mother's youth can be glimpsed within the early work of photographer Mick Rock, and somewhere in the pages of *Pigs Might Fly: the Inside story of Pink Floyd. Mark Black. 1st edition.*

From Wat Buppharam to Ton Son Mosque

1 Wong was Phraya Phrapakorawong, and my great-grandfather Tom's (full) first cousin.

Funeral Books

1 K. Breazeale. The Writings of Prince Damrong Rajanubhab. 2008. p15

2 In June 2021 (just after I finished the first draft of this book) Moolee, Peter Bunnag's daughter, died in New York City, where she was living. We gathered at Wat Prayurawong for a makeshift outdoors funeral, the temple was about to go into lockdown due to the worsening Covid situation. A month after her death, and the day after her cremation in New York, Peter passed away. His spirit wandered two nights before his water-rites, he was seen standing and smiling next to his coffin. For his funeral a small number of us gathered again at the family temple, five monks were allowed to chant, but the rest of the community was kept away from us on strict orders from the Abbot. I thought of the legacy of Chai and Toh, and of all of the family funerals in this space over the years, and looked about at my relatives, all offspring of these two brothers, Chai and Toh, and felt we were like the wreckage left after the passage of a great event.

Weapons

1 A. Noel Battye. The Military, Government and Society of Siam, 1868-1910. p278, as well as Toh's funeral book

2 *ibid* p 234 In 1880 the king was attempting to reform the military. A conflict had emerged involving the abolition of an antiquated and inefficient system of raising manpower. King Rama V wanted to create a standing army while Chuang's party didn't want to lose control of their grip in the western provinces.

3 I have relied on Battye again for this. From p217

4 Choem's paternal lineage can be traced to a nobleman called Xuto, who was the elder brother of King Rama I's main queen.

5 Yaninie Phaithaiyawat. The change from traditional nobleman to modern bureaucrat in Thailand: a case study of the Saeng-Xuto family. Waseda University. 2018.

6 The life of Prince Prisdang is the subject of Tamara Loos' Bones Around my Neck. Cornell. 2016. It might be noted that some of Prisdang's troubles stemmed from a love affair with a Bunnag lady (Si) who was the widow of Choem Saeng-Xuto's (full) brother (Jan/Chan), so in some respects his history winds loosely around the narrative of this book.

Lost in the Supermarket

1 Georges Perec. The Rue Vilin in Species of Spaces. Penguin Classics. 2008. p212

The Kitchen

1 who was a Xuto married to a grandson of Chaophraya Bhaskorawong. Nang Samaknantapol (Jiip Bunnag) aka Laan Mae Krua Hua Paa. Thamra aharn-wang kruang nam cha. Ban Phibulwet. Bangkok. 2498

2 *ibid* p67

Mad Dogs and Englishmen

1 "Mom" Yai had Lao Phuan ancestry, her family had been settled in Chachoengsao Province by King Rama I, after he defeated the Lao Kingdom of Vientiane. Yai's paternal family would eventually be known as the "Osathanonds".

2 As recounted by Tej. 2020

3 Son was the daughter of Yaem, a mineralogist trained in England and France – during the Paknam Crisis, when Siam and France were briefly at war. Yaem is known by his title Phraya Prachacheepboriban, and was a half brother of Choem, Chaophraya Surasakmontri – the hero of the Haw Wars.

4 Yaninie Phaithaiyawat. The change from traditional nobleman to modern bureaucrat in Thailand: a case study of the Saeng-Xuto family. Waseda University. 2018.

5 David Wyatt. Thailand, a Short History. Silkworm Books. Chiang Mai. 2004. p 220

6 Lady Ruen was a grandchild of Chaophraya Panuwong, Tuam. She was born in 1904, and moved to Japan with her father in 1910, Ruen would be a Lady-in-Waiting to Queen Rambhai, who was to preside over Ruen's funeral

7 Didi's formal name was Ramadi Teru, a combination of the "r" names of Lady Ruan's family, and the "t" (tor tao) names of Tom's. Teru is Japanese for Lotus blossom. Didi/Ramadi Teru would have a daughter named Lalana (Ravibhandu), my dad's (half) first-cousin.

The Bridge

1 The first bridge over the Chaophraya River was a railway bridge built in 1922 and named after King Rama VI. It was bombed in the war. When the restored bridge was reopened Prime Minister Khuang held a party and rode the train down to a coastal resort town. Tula and family were invited to join. This was Tej and my father's first trip to Hua Hin. Tej remembers that the Prime Minister's party occupied an entire carriage. "It was a family holiday and not a political gathering. I remember vividly we arrived at sunset and I went to bed soon after because it had been a long and hot journey. Funnily enough, I don't even remember going into the sea or the presence of your father." Tej 2021.

2 David Wyatt. Thailand, a Short History. Silkworm Books. Chiang Mai. 2004. p230

3 Told to me by Tej in 2020.

4 *ibid*

Telegrams

1 (English title) 70th Anniversary of Thailand-Myanmar Diplomatic Relations. East Asian Department of the Ministry of Foreign Affairs, Thailand. 2019.

Index

(Author's note: I have not included Tula, Chancham, Tej and Tew in the index since they appear frequently in the text.
The entries are by name as well as title, therefore, certain individuals appear more than once.)